# THE MYSTERY OF BEING

## I.  REFLECTION  &  MYSTERY

# THE MYSTERY
# OF BEING

BY

GABRIEL MARCEL

---

I.
REFLECTION
& MYSTERY

---

GATEWAY EDITION
HENRY REGNERY COMPANY
CHICAGO, ILLINOIS

REFLECTION AND MYSTERY contains
the first of the two series of GIFFORD
LECTURES given by Gabriel Marcel
in 1949 and 1950, at the University
of Aberdeen. The English translation
is by G. S. Fraser.

*all rights reserved*

*First published in Great Britain* 1950
*by* THE HARVILL PRESS LTD. This
Gateway Edition published 1960.
Manufactured in the U.S.A. 11.61.

# CONTENTS

*Research* has always seemed to me the word which most adequately designates the manner in which philosophic thought moves essentially towards its goal; I shall not therefore expound *my* system, but rather retrace the movement of my thought from its outset, but in renewed light, and, so to speak, map out its itinerary.

But how do we set about retracing a road where heretofore there have been nothing but broken trails? Is it not by setting out for a precisely situated goal, with the intention of reaching it? Does not this presuppose a result?

We must distinguish here between:

(1) Research of the type where *result* can be severed from the *means* by which it is obtained, e.g., a product discovered by a scientist can be purchased at the chemist's by *anyone*.

This type of research involves furthermore a *notion* or a *pre-notion* bearing on a certain *working* and the certainty that the operations (mental or material) entailed are within the capabilities of anyone.

(2) Research wherein the link with the result cannot be broken without loss of all reality to the result; the seeker who engages in such an investigation, starts, as it were, at random.

This leads to the question of:

How research without pre-notion is possible.

In reality, to exclude the *pre-notion* implied in techniques is not to exclude the origin of philosophic research; this origin is a certain *disquiet* —a certain exigence (a term which will be defined in Chapter III). The research is then the successive moves which enable me to pass from a situation *lived* as fundamentally discordant to a situation in which a certain expectation is fulfilled.

The 'ego' of the seeker, as well as the 'ego' of those he addresses, is here *neither* the individual at the mercy of his states (of being) *nor* thought in general.

In philosophical research a literal and simplistic conception of universality cannot be accepted, and a certain order of enquiry becomes established: there are, as well as questions which can be answered by 'yes' or 'no', other questions which the philosopher cannot elude, and which cannot be answered thus.

His research—philosophical research—will appear therefore as an effort to put *true* questions (cf. Chapter IV, on Truth), which implies that he is endowed with the *courage* of *thought* inseparable from *liberty*.

Enquiry into one of the conclusions of the foregoing chapter, which dissociates *truth* and *universal validity*.

Is not this dissociation dangerous?

If not, how, and from what point does it appear so?

Note that the objection implies a pre-notion or anticipated schematizing of the relation between the subject and the truth which he will have to recognize.

Truth is indeed conceived as something to be extracted; this extraction is referable on principle to a universal technique, with the result that truth should be transmissible to anyone.

But we are prone to forget that the more intelligence transcends technical activity, the less the reference to anyone as indeterminate is called upon to intervene.

This objection is on the other hand a product, as it were, of a world that ignores exigencies of reflection.

This world of ours is a *broken world,* which means that in striving after a certain type of unity, it has lost its real unity. (These types of unity in the *broken world* are:

(1) *Increased socialization of life:* we are one and all treated as agents, registered, enrolled, and we end by merging into our own identity cards. (2) *Extension of the powers of the State,* which is like a searching eye on all of us. (3) This world has lost its true unity probably because privacy, brotherhood, creativeness, reflection and imagination, are all increasingly discredited in it.

*Therefore*—it is of the very utmost urgency that we reflect, and reflect upon reflection, in order to bring to light that exigence which animates reflection (cf. Chapter III), and in order to show that this exigence when at work transcends any sort of process whatever, and sweeps beyond the opposition of the empiric ego and the universal ego.

## III. THE NEED FOR TRANSCENDENCE *page* 48

What is the nature of this exigence, lying at the origin of philosophic research (cf. Chapter 1), and in danger of being smothered by the *broken world* of techniques and socialization?

It is essentially an exigence of transcendence, this term being taken in its traditional meaning, as opposed to immanence; its implication is that to transcend is not merely to *go beyond, spatio-temporally* (in space or in time).

This exigence is existentially experienced as a non-satisfaction, but all non-satisfaction does not entail an aspiring towards transcendence, for there are non-satisfactions which crave the possession of a given power, and which disappear, once this power is attained.

Another non-satisfaction occurs, or can occur, within possession; another call comes from my innermost being, a call directed not outwards but inwards. (This may be a call to create, and to create means to create something higher than one's self.)

Transcendence is thus evoked as referring to man; but is not this negating it, absorbing it into experience?

This objection takes for granted the *figuration* of experience as being a sort of given element, more or less, without form; and it ignores the impossibility of a representation of experience.

*With the result that:* not only can 'transcendent' *not* mean 'transcendent of experience', but, if we are still to talk sense, we have to admit that there must be an experience of the transcendent; to experience . . . is not indeed to enfold into one's self, but to stretch out towards . . . , consciousness being always consciousness of someone else than one's self.

*So that* the exigence of transcendence is not the exigence to go beyond all experience whatsoever, but to substitute one mode of experience for another, or, more accurately still, to strive towards an increasingly pure mode of experience.

## IV. TRUTH AS A VALUE:
THE INTELLIGENCE BACKGROUND *page* 70

What do we mean when we state that we are guided by a love of truth, or that someone has sacrificed himself to 'the truth'? These assertions are void of meaning if truth be defined as *'veritas est adequatio rei et intellectus';* they make sense only if truth is *value,* for only in this aspect can truth become a stake to be striven for.

*Truth and Judgment.* Are we to exclude from the problem sensation and feeling, which seem indeed to be what they are on the hither side of all judgment?

Yet a sensation (a taste, for example) is immediately recognizable, which would seem to attest that it has a certain kernel of identity which makes possible a consonance between *me* and *someone else;* so the connoisseur does exist, in every domain, and the non-connoisseur, if he recognizes himself as such, is 'in the truth', because he does not shut himself to a certain light. What is this light? Whence does it come?

*Truth and Fact.* There is no meaning in imagining that this light emanates from facts taken in a grossly realistic sense, and that it comes to us from outside.

There is not, indeed, *exteriority of the fact* as regards the subject; the structure of the latter is an open structure, and the fact is, so to speak, an integral part of it; this is why the fact can become illuminant, on condition that the subject so place himself in relation to the fact that he receive the light radiated by it. So it is all between *me* and *me,* the me of desire and the me 'spirit of truth' (although there are not two me's) and it is only as referred to this source, to this living centre, that facts can be called illuminant.

It is therefore in the light of truth that we succeed in mastering within us the permanent temptation to conceive or represent reality as we would like it to be. Stimulating and purifying power of truth which enables the subject to recognize reality; active recognition, far distant, both from constraint and from pure spontaneity.

Truth cannot therefore be considered as a thing, or an object. A conversation may be taken as an example, in which truth is at one and the same time that towards which the speakers are conscious

of moving, and that which spurs them towards
this goal.

Idea of a sort of 'intercourse' which takes place
in an intelligible medium, to which man perhaps
belongs in one of his aspects (the Platonic reminiscence). An idea which demonstrates that it is
inadmissible to isolate a judgment and then look
for the truth in connection with this judgment.

## V. PRIMARY & SECONDARY REFLECTION: THE EXISTENTIAL FULCRUM          *page* 95

Once we have the definition of the intelligible
medium in which philosophic thought evolves
(unfolds itself), the question of the relation between reflection and life inevitably comes up. It
must be said that, contrary to a thesis common
amongst the romantic philosophers, this relation
is not an opposition. Reflection occurs when, life
coming up against a certain obstacle, or again,
being checked by a certain break in the continuity
of experience, it becomes necessary to pass from
one level to another, and to recover on this
higher plane the unity which had been lost on
the lower one. Reflection appears in this case as
a promoter of life, it is ascendant and recupera-
tory, in that it is secondary reflection as opposed
to a primary reflection which is still only decom-
posing or analytic.

It is on the question 'what am I?' that philosophic reflection is called upon to centre. None of
the answers that fit under headings (son of . . .
born at . . .) can be satisfactory here. Reflection
discovers that I am not, strictly speaking, someone in particular, but neither am I purely and
simply the negation of someone in particular. We
must find out how I can be both at once.

I am led to recognize that the me (ego) which
I am, and which is not someone, cannot be set
down as either existent or imaginary.

Passage from this ambiguous and undecided
situation to the fathoming of existence considered
in its aspect of immediacy, not as the predicate
of *I*, but as an undecomposable totality. The fact
of being linked to my body is constitutive of my
own existential quality.

Reflection is thus led to concentrate on my body
as mine. Whereas primary reflection, being purely

analytical, treated this body as pure object, linked
with or parallel to another thing, another reality
which would be called the soul, secondary reflection recognizes in my body a fundamental *act of
feeling* which cannot amount to mere objective
possession nor to an instrumental relation, nor to
something which could be treated purely and simply as identity of the subject with the object.

To recognize my body is to be led to question
myself upon the *act of feeling;* the *act of feeling*
is linked with the fact that this body is mine.
What is the meaning of *to feel?* How is it possible
*to feel? To feel* cannot be reduced to an instrumental function, to a function made possible by
a given apparatus.

Sensation cannot be interpreted as a message
emitted from X, picked up and translated by Y.
*To feel* is not a means by which two stations
can communicate with each other.

*In fact:* Any instrument presupposes my body.
Any message presupposes a basis of sensation;
it cannot therefore give an account of it. A non-
mediatizable immediate must be brought in, an
immediate *that I am.*

It is this idea of participation that enables us to
explain the *act of feeling* and it is the *act of
feeling* that is at the basis of the will to participate.

Participation: at one extreme we are in the
objective (to take *my* share of a cake, for instance), at the other extreme all trace of objectivity is gone (participation by prayer, sacrifice.

But on the other hand, the will to participate
can only *act* on the basis of a certain consensus,
which is of the order of *feeling.*

*Participation-feeling* is beyond the traditional
opposition of activity and passivity; to feel is
not to endure, but to receive (in the sense of
receiving into one's self—to receive willingly, to
welcome, to embrace), and to receive is an act.

There is, then, a difference between feeling and
non-feeling, but this difference is probably beyond the grasp of the technician, who is inclined
to conceive the passing from the inert to the alive
according to the processes of fabrication.

The artist alone, the artist with eyes in his head, really participates in the reality of life. Contemplation thus appears as a mode of participation, the highest of all. The *act of feeling* is then a mode of participation, but participation exceeds the limits of feeling.

## VII. BEING IN A SITUATION

Contemplation is a mode of participation in which the oppositions before (in front of) me and within me, outside and inside, are transcended. This being so, recollection is implicit in participation. Recollection (which is not a mode of abstracting one's self) is an act by means of which I over-pass (go beyond) these oppositions, and in which the "turning inward to myself" and "the stretching outward from myself" meet.

But recollection is not abstraction of one's self (from one's spatio-temporal situation); the conditions of recollection are the very conditions of the existence of the being whose circumstantial data cannot appear as contingent.

*My situation, my life,* are not indeed an ensemble of things existing in themselves, to which I am foreign or exterior, though neither can I merge into them and consider them as a fatality or a destiny. In this order the opposition of contingence and necessity must be over-passed (gone beyond), as is shown in the examples of *encounter* (which is not the objective intercrossing of casual series and which supposes interiority) and *vocation* (which is not a constraint but a call); the circumstantial data therefore only intervenes in connection with free activity—called upon to *recognize (know) itself* in this free activity, that is to say, open, permeable (without being strictly speaking influencible), and for which the non-contingence of the empirical 'given' is a call to creative development.

## VIII. 'MY LIFE'

The question: who am I? remains.

Since it is not possible to count on a friend, a party, or a collectivity to decide it for me, the

question becomes an appeal (call), who am I?
Shall I not find the answer by enquiring into my
own life?

*My life* can be considered from two standpoints,
that of: 1. The past. 2. That of the present, the
fact that I am still living it.

1. *In the past.* My life appears to me as something that can, by reason of its very essence, be
narrated.

But to *narrate* is to *unfold*.

It is also to *summarize*, i.e., to totalize schemati-
cally.

My life cannot then be reproduced by a nar-
rative; in as much as it has been actually lived,
it lies without the scope of my present concrete
thought and can only be recaptured as particles
irradiated by flashes of memory.

*Nor is my life* in the notes jotted down day by
day and making up my diary; when I re-read them
they have for the most part lost their meaning,
and I do not recognize myself in them.

*Nor is my work* to be identified with my life;
what judge could sift from my work that which
truly expresses me?

*Finally my acts,* in as much as they are recorded in objective reality, do not tell of that
within me which lies beyond them.

*My life,* in so far as already lived, is not then
an inalterable deposit or a finished whole.

2. *In so far as I am still living it,* my life appears to me as something I can *consecrate* or
*sacrifice,* and the more I feel that I am striving
towards an end, or serving a cause, the more
alive (living) I feel. It is therefore essential to life
that it be articulated on a reality which gives it
a meaning and a trend, and, as it were, justifies
it; this does not signify that life is an available
asset.

To give one's life is neither to part with one's
self nor to do away with one's self, it is to respond
to a certain call. Death can then be life, in the
supreme sense.

My life is infinitely beyond the consciousness
I have of it at any given moment; it is essentially
unequal in itself, and transcendent of the account
that I am led to keep of its elements. Secondary
reflection alone can recuperate that which inhabits
my life and which my life does not express.

## IX. TOGETHERNESS: IDENTITY AND DEPTH

*My life* eludes itself; this being so, should we not say that man is condemned to act a part in a play he has not read, or to improvise without an outline of the plot? Should we not deny that life has a meaning or a trend?

Life is not something found in our path (such as a purse, for example) and of which we decide or not to avail ourselves.

Awareness of one's self as living is indeed to be aware of a former existence, and the role of reflection is here to recognize the prior participation with a reality which consciousness cannot encompass.

This going beyond the consciousness of self is met with particularly in two directions: in relation to others, in relation to one's self.

1. *Relation to others.* Consciousness of self occurs only in the following behaviours: pretentiousness, aggressiveness, humility, i.e., when the living link connecting me and another is broken by over-passing the *I* and *him* opposition.

The ego is the more itself the more it is *with* the other and not directed at itself.

2. *Relation to one's self.* The consciousness of self appears as the breaking of the inner city the ego forms with itself, with its past.

Here again it is intersubjectivity that is first.

My life is then on the far side of the oppositions: I and someone else, unity and plurality.

Abstract identity and historic becoming. It can only be thought from an angle of *depth,* where the now and the then, the near and the far, meet.

## X. PRESENCE AS A MYSTERY

The link of *my life* with the depths of time is an introduction to the mystery of family.

Taken from the angle of *depth,* my life no longer appears as the terminus of various biological series, but as an endowment; the kinship between father and son therefore implies a mutual recognition, and the impossibility of dissociating the *vital* from the *spiritual,* for the *spiritual* is only such on condition that it be bodied forth.

The articulation of the vital and the spiritual, the

common thesis of the lectures of the first series, itself brings in the knowledge of mystery.

This knowledge supposes:

    1. The distinction between object and *presence*.

    2. The criticism of the notion of *problem*.

1. With the object, material communications are maintained without intercommunication: the object is entirely before (in front of) the subject, which thus becomes *another object*.

The being who is present can on the contrary be neither invoked nor evoked; it reveals the other to himself at the same time at it reveals itself to him.

2. The object can then supply information, bring *solutions* to *problems* put regarding it.

The being who is present transcends all possible enquiry, and in this sense is mysterious.

Philosophical research is articulated on mystery.

We must therefore conclude on the *link* between reflection, and presence, and mystery in the trans-historic depth of life.

Mystery coincides with this region of depth which, perhaps, opens out on to eternity.

# REFLECTION & MYSTERY

# CHAPTER I

## INTRODUCTION

First of all, and very sincerely and heartily, I would like to thank the University of Aberdeen for my appointment. As Gifford Lecturer here, I am following in the footsteps of many other thinkers, representing various national cultures, all men of honourable note in the history of philosophy; and as I prepare to make my own contribution, I cannot help being overcome by a feeling almost of awe. Also, of course, I have to get over a certain initial diffidence; is it not a little futile, really, and more than a little rash, to set out to expound one more philosophical doctrine, when there are so many philosophical doctrines already? I fancy that every speculative thinker, however solid he may believe the grounds of his thinking to be, does harbour, somewhere deep down in him, a sceptic—a sceptic to whom the history of philosophy looks rather like the solemn setting up of rows of ninepins, so that they may be neatly knocked down! That way of looking at things is tempting, no more; it is tempting, and for philosophy it is in a sense *the* temptation—just as for man in general suicide is that. It is a kind of suicide, too.

The fact is, moreover, that something systematic; something which would be, strictly speaking, *my*

system; some organic whole of which I could, in
successive lectures, anatomize the structural details,
pointing out its superiorities, to name only two of
my most distinguished forerunners, to the systems
of Bergson and Whitehead—all that is just what I
do *not* intend to lay before you. When I called these
lectures a search for, or an investigation into, the
essence of spiritual reality, I was not choosing
words at random. From my point of view such a
term as search or investigation—some term implying the notion of a quest—is the most adequate description that can be applied to the essential direction of philosophy. Philosophy will always, to my
way of thinking, be an aid to discovery rather than
a matter of strict demonstration. And, if pressed, I
would expand that; I think the philosopher who first
discovers certain truths and then sets out to expound
them in their dialectical or systematic interconnec-
tions always runs the risk of profoundly altering
the nature of the truths he has discovered.

Furthermore, I will not disguise from you the
fact that when I had been nominated by the University of Aberdeen to deliver the Gifford Lectures
in 1949 and 1950, my first reaction was a feeling of
intense inner disturbance. The honour that was being done to me faced me with a serious problem.
Was I not, in fact, being asked to do something
which it had been my constant determination not
to do: namely, to present in a systematic form material which, I repeat, has always remained for me
at the stage of a quest?

All the same, I could not help considering this
nomination as a call upon me. And it has always
been my conviction that, however unexpected such
calls might be, I ought to respond to them with
such strength and skill as I possess—always supposing that they are made by somebody who recognizes the validity of the kind of demand that has
always seemed valid to me. The principle does not

apply, obviously enough, to the appeals that may be made to one by journalists or fashionable hostesses, once one's name has begun to make a certain noise in the world. I am thinking, for instance, of somebody who asked me, a few months ago, to squeeze the core of my philosophy into a couple of sentences. That sort of thing is just silly, and must be answered with a shrug of the shoulders. But on the present occasion, I had the feeling from the first that I could not reject such an offer without becoming guilty of what would be, from my own point of view, an indefensible betrayal.

At the same time, it was clear to me that in answering this call I must continue to respect the specific character of what has always been my own line of development. And, of course, those who made this offer to me would have that line of development in view. Nobody who had any direct knowledge of my writings would dream of expecting from me an exposition in the deductive manner, the logical linking together of a body of essential propositions. My task, therefore, was to try to satisfy whatever expectations I might have aroused, without, however, straining myself to stretch my thought on the procrustean bed of some kind of systematic dogmatism: without, indeed, taking any account at all of whatever modes may prevail at the moment in certain schools of philosophy, without trying to square myself with the Hegelian or the Thomist tradition, for instance. If I was able to accept this offer, and if in the end I felt that I ought to accept it, the reason was that what was being asked of me was, at bottom, merely this: that I should be, that I should remain myself. Now to be oneself, to remain oneself is a trickier matter than most people think. There are always gaps in our personal experience and our personal thought, and there exists a permanent temptation to stop these up with ready-made developments borrowed from some body of pre-existing doctrine. It would be very presumptuous of me to assume that, at certain points, this particular weakness will not come to light in the course of these lectures.

Given all this, my task, as I repeat, could not be that of expounding some system which might be described as Marcelism—the word rings in my ears with a mocking parodic note!—but rather to recapitulate the body of my work under a fresh light, to seize on its joints, its hinges, its articulations, above all to indicate its general direction. And here I would ask your permission to use a metaphor; I shall need such permission more than once, for I share the belief of Henri Bergson in the philosophical value of some kinds of metaphor, those which may be described as structural. The image that imposes itself on me is that of a road. It is just, so it seems to me, as if I had so far been following what tracks there were across a country that appeared to me to be largely unexplored, and as if you had asked me to construct a main road in the place of these uninterrupted paths, or perhaps rather —but it comes to the same thing—to draw up a sort of itinerary.

The metaphor is open to objections of two sorts.

It might be said in the first place that a road implies space; and that the notion of space is something from which a metaphysical investigation, as such, must abstract. One must make the simple answer that if my metaphor must be rejected on this count, so must every kind of discursive thinking; for it is all too evident that the notion of discursiveness implies, and rests on, a simple image like that of walking along a road. Moreover, we shall later on have occasion to recognize the existence and philosophical rights of a sort of spatiality which might be called the spatiality of inner experience; and it may be that this spatiality of inner experience is coextensive with the whole spiritual life.

But the objection may be put in another way, which has a dangerous look of being much more genuinely awkward. To lay down a road in a place where at first there were only tracks, is that not equivalent to fixing in advance a certain destination at which one intends to arrive, and must not that destination, itself, be very exactly located? The underlying image would be that of a grotto, a mine, or a sanctuary whose whereabouts one knew in advance. It would be a matter of showing the way there to those who for one reason or another wanted to have a look at the place, no doubt in order to profit from its riches. But does not this presuppose that the result we are working for has already been achieved, even before we start working for it: does it not presuppose a preliminary or original discovery of the grotto or the sanctuary? Well, looking at the matter in my own way, I must ask whether, in the realm of philosophy, we can really talk about results? Is not all such talk based on a misunderstanding of the specific character of a philosophical investigation, as such? The question raised here at least obliges us to come to much closer grips with the very notion of a result.

Let us take the case of a chemist who has invented and set going some process for obtaining or extracting a substance which, before his time, could only be got hold of in a much more costly and complicated fashion. It is obvious, in this case, that the result of the invention will have a sort of separate existence, or, at all events, that we shall be quite within our rights in treating it as if it had. If I need the substance—let us say it is some pharmaceutical product—I will go to the shop, and I will not need to know that it is thanks to the invention of the chemist in question that I am able to procure it easily. In my purely practical role as customer and consumer, I may have no occasion even to learn that there has been such an invention unless for some out-of-the-way reason; let us say, because a factory has been destroyed and the invention has temporarily ceased to be put into operation. The pharmacist may then tell me that the product is out of stock, or is not to be had at its usual price and quality, but let us get it quite clear that in the ordinary run of affairs the existence of this chemical process will be known only to specialists or to those who are moving in the direction of specialization. Here we have a very simple example indeed of what sort of life a result may lead, cut apart from the methods by which it was achieved. And one could go on to mention many other examples; it is not necessary that a result should always embody itself, as in the instance I have given, as a material commodity. Think of some astronomical forecast, say of a coming eclipse. We welcome that, we make it our own, without bothering ourselves much about the extremely complicated calculations on which it is founded, and knowing quite well that our own mathematical equipment is not sufficient to allow us to do these sums over again in our own heads.

One might note here, in passing, that in our modern world, because of its extreme technical complication, we are, in fact, condemned to take for granted a great many results achieved through long research and laborious calculations, research and calculations of which the details are bound to escape us.

One might postulate it as a principle, on the other hand, that in an investigation of the type on which we are now engaged, a philosophical investigation, there can be no place at all for results of this sort. Let us expand that: between a philosophical investigation and its final outcome, there exists a link which cannot be broken without the summing up itself immediately losing all reality. And of course we must also ask ourselves here just what we mean, in this context, by *reality*.

We can come to the same conclusions starting from the other end. We can attempt to elucidate the notion of philosophical investigation directly. Where a technician, like the chemist, starts off with some very general notion, a notion given in advance of what he is looking for, what is peculiar to a philosophical investigation is that the man who undertakes it cannot possess anything equivalent to that notion given in advance of what he is looking for. It would not, perhaps, be imprecise to say that he starts off at random; I am taking care not to forget that this has been sometimes the case with scientists themselves, but a scientific result achieved, so to say, by a happy accident acquires a kind of purpose when it is viewed retrospectively; it looks as if it had tended towards some strictly specific aim. As we go on we shall gradually see more and more clearly that this can never be the case with philosophic investigation.

On the other hand, when we think of it, we realize that our mental image of the technician—of the scientist, too, for at this level the distinction between the two of them reaches vanishing point —is that of a man perpetually carrying out operations, in his own mind or with physical objects, which anybody could carry out in his place. The sequence of these operations, for that reason, can be schematized in universal terms. I am abstracting here from the mental gropings which are inseparable, in the individual scientist's history, from all periods of discovery. These gropings are like the useless round-about routes taken by a raw tourist in a country with which he has not yet made himself familiar. Both are destined to be dropped and forgotten, for good and all, once the traveller knows the lie of the land.

The greatness and the limitation of scientific discovery consist precisely in the fact that it is bound by its nature to be lost in anonymity. Once a result has been achieved, it is bound to appear, if not a matter of chance, at least a matter of contingence, that it should have been this man and not that man who discovered such and such a process. This retrospective view of the matter is probably in some degree an illusion, but the illusion is itself inseparable from the general pattern of scientific research. From the point of view of technical progress, there is no point in considering the concrete conditions in which some discovery was actually able to be made, the personal, the perhaps tragic background from which the discovery, as such, detaches itself; from the strictly technical point of view all that background is, obviously and inevitably, something to be abstracted from.

But this is not and cannot be true in the same way for the kind of investigation that will be presented in the course of these lectures; and it is essential to see exactly why not. How can we start out on a search without having somehow anticipated what we are searching for? Here, again, it is necessary to make certain distinctions. The notion given in advance, the scientist's or technician's notion, which in a philosophical investigation we must exclude, has to do, in fact, with a certain way of acting: the problem is how to set about it so that some mode of action which is at the moment impracticable, or at least can only be carried out in unsatisfactory and precarious conditions, should become practicable according to certain pre-established standards of practicability (standards of simplicity, of economy, and so on). Let us add, in addition, as a development of what has previously been said, that this mode of action should be of a sort that can be carried out by anybody, at least by anybody within a certain determinable set of conditions, anybody, for instance, equipped with certain indispensable tools.

It is probably not sufficient for my purpose merely

to say that, where a metaphysical investigation is being undertaken, a result of this sort, the arrival at a practicable mode of action within certain determinable conditions, cannot be calculated on in advance, and that in fact the very idea of a metaphysical investigation necessarily excludes the possibility of this kind of practical result. For I might also add that the inaptitude of the run of men for metaphysics, particularly in our own period, is certainly bound up with the fact that they find it impossible to conceive of a purpose which lies outside the order of the practical, which cannot be translated into the language of action.

To get a clearer insight into the matter we must take a real effort to get a more exact definition of the point of departure of this other type of investigation—our own type. I have written somewhere that metaphysical unease is like the bodily state of a man in a fever who will not lie still but keeps shifting around in his bed looking for the right position. But how does this really apply? What does the word 'position' signify here? We should not let ourselves be too much hampered by the spatial character of the metaphor; or, if we are, it can be helped out by another—that of discords in music, with which the ear cannot rest satisfied, but which must be resolved by being transcended in a wider harmony. Let us see if this notion of resolution can be of some use to us here.

Interpreting it in the most general way, we can say that this idea of resolution, of the resolving of discords or contradictions, is that of the passage from a situation in which we are ill at ease to one in which we feel ourselves almost melting away with relief. The general notion of a *situation* is one which is destined to play a great part in my lectures, and I have my reasons for first bringing it to your notice at this point. It will be only much later on that we shall grasp its full significance.

For the moment, let us be content to say that a situation is something in which I find myself involved; but that however we interpret the notion of the involved self, the situation is not something which presses on the self merely from the outside, but something which colours its interior states; or rather we shall have to ask ourselves whether, at this level of discourse, the usual antithesis between inner and outer is not beginning to lose a good deal of its point. The only point that I want, however, to emphasize at this moment is that a philosophical investigation, of the sort in which we are now engaged, can be considered as a gathering together of the processes by which I can pass from a situation which is experienced as basically discordant, a situation in which I can go so far as to say that I am at war with myself, to a different situation in which some kind of expectation is satisfied.

This is still all pretty vague, but already, I am afraid, it begins to raise awkward questions, all centering round this indeterminate notion of the involved self, of my involved self, which I have been forced to take as my reference-point. The really important question that is raised may be framed in the following terms: is there not a risk of the investigation that is being undertaken here reducing itself to an account of the succession of stages by which I, I as this particular person, Gabriel Marcel, attempt, starting off from some state of being which implies a certain suffering, to reach another state of being which not only does not imply suffering but may be accompanied by a certain joy? But what guarantee can I have that this personal progress of mine has anything more than a subjective value? Nevertheless, in the end is it not the case that something more than subjective value is needed to confer on any chain of thoughts what I may describe as a proper philosophic dignity? In other words, are there any means at all of assuring our-

selves whether this indeterminate involved self,
which I have been forced to take as my reference-point, is or is not, for instance, immortal?

In this connection, some remarks which I have
previously made might be of a kind to arouse a certain uneasiness. Have I not seemed to reserve the
privilege of universality in thinking to scientists or
technicians whose method is that of a series of
operations which can be carried out by anybody
else in the world who is placed in the same setting
and can make use of similar tools?

The answer to this very important question will
only clarify itself very gradually, as our thoughts
about it work back upon themselves. I think it
necessary, nevertheless, to indicate even at this moment—partly to allay a very understandable nervous-
ness—in what direction the answer ought to be
sought for.

Let us say, to put it very roughly, that the
dilemma in which this question leaves us—that of
choice between the actual individual man, delivered
over to his own states of being and incapable of
transcending them, and a kind of generalized
thinking as such, what the Germans call *Denken
uberhaupt*, which would be operative in a sort of
Absolute and so claim universal validity for its
operations—let us say that this dilemma is a false
one, and must be rejected. Between these two anti-
thetic terms, we must intercalate an intermediary
type of thinking, which is precisely the type of
thinking that the lecture following this will illustrate. The point should at once be made here that,
even outside the limits of philosophy properly so
called, there are incontestable examples of this type
of thinking. We have only to think, for instance,
of what we describe, rather vaguely indeed, as the
understanding of works of art; it would be better
no doubt, in this connection, to talk of their appre-
ciation—so long as we eliminate from that word its

root reference to a *pretium,* a market price. It would be an illusion and even an absurdity to suppose that the *Missa Solemnis* or some great work of pictorial art is meant for just anybody who comes along; on the contrary, we must in honest sincerity accept the fact that there are plenty of people whose attention is not arrested, and who have nothing communicated to them, by such works. It is none the less certain that when a genuine emotion is felt at the impact of a work of art it infinitely transcends the limits of what we call the individual consciousness. Let us try to clarify this in more detail.

When I look at or listen to a masterpiece, I have an experience which can be strictly called a revelation. That experience will just not allow itself to be analysed away as a mere state of simple strongly felt satisfaction. One of the secondary purposes, indeed, of these lectures will be to look into the question of how we ought to understand such revelations. On the other hand, it is just as incontestably a fact that, for reasons that remain impenetrable to us—if it is right to talk at all about reasons in this connection—such revelations appear not to be granted to other people, people with whom, nevertheless, I have no difficulty at all in communicating on other topics. There would be no point in bringing into play my stores of learning, let me even say my gifts as a teacher; I would never succeed in exciting, in the other person, the thrill of admiration that the great work of art had excited in me. It is just as if the other person were, in the root sense of the word, refractory—one who repels the particles of light—or as if a kind of grace that is operative for me were not operative for him.

The existence of such absolute disparity has something quite indecent about it in a world where the counting of heads has become not only a legal fact but a moral standard. We have got into the habit of thinking statistically, and to do so, at this level, is at bottom to admit that anything which cannot accumulate enough votes in its favour ought not to be taken into consideration, does not count. Obviously, in those parts of the world which have not yet come under the totalitarian yoke, this peculiar logic has not had all its implications worked out. The statistical method is, as it were, dumped down well outside the gates of the palace of art, but for how long? It is permissible, at least, to ask whether in this realm, as in many others, the totalitarian countries, with their brutal way of freezing out the nonconforming artist, have not merely confined themselves to drawing the proper conclusions from premises that are, in fact, accepted by everybody for whom statistics provide a sufficient criterion for the administration of human affairs.

Yet if the conclusions are logical, it may be that the role of the free critical thinker in our time is to swim against the current and attack the premises themselves. That is not our task, here and now: but we must state, simply and flatly, that there do exist ranges of human experience where a too literal, an over-simplified way of conceiving the criterion of universality just cannot be accepted. And, of course, there are still a good many countries in which the idea of taking a referendum on artistic or religious questions would be greeted with hoots of laughter. Let us understand each other: for those who want to study taste and opinion, over a set period, in a given country, the existence of such things as Gallup polls is obviously useful; but there are still a good many people who would refuse to postulate it as a principle that current tastes and opinions, for those countries, ought to have the force of law. The step from 'Such is the case, quite generally' to 'Such ought to be the case, universally' is an obvious *non sequitur*, and that is what matters to us. We ought, in addition, to go on

to a very careful analysis of what kind of question
is really susceptible of being the subject of a referendum. We would then be led to ask if, apart from
questions that can be answered by a simple 'Yes'
or 'No', there are not other infinitely more vital
questions which are literally incapable of embody-
ing themselves in the general consciousness. Of these
questions, the most important are those which present themselves to the philosopher as the first that
have to be answered—though *first* here must not,
of course, be understood in a strictly chronological
sense. The philosopher, of necessity, has begun by
asking himself the ordinary questions; and it is only
at the cost of an effort of reflective thought, which
really constitutes a very painful discipline, that he
has raised himself up from the level of the first
type of question, the type that everybody asks, to
the level of the second, the type proper to philosophy. But I am still drawing the picture with very
crude strokes and in very rough outline. A particular example may make it easier to understand what
I am getting at.

The question, 'Do you believe in God?' is one of
those which, according to the common belief, can
be answered by a simple 'Yes' or 'No'. But a deeper
analysis would enable us to lay bare the invariably
illusory character of these answers. There is a mass
of people who imagine that they believe in God,
when in fact they are bowing down to an idol to
whom any decent theology whatever would undoubtedly refuse the name of God; and on the
other hand there are many others who believe
themselves to be atheists because they conceive of
God only as an idol to be rejected, and who yet
reveal in their acts, which far transcend their professed opinions, a totally inarticulate religious belief.
It follows from all this that the answer to a referendum on the question, 'Do you believe in God?'
ought to be in the great majority of cases, 'I

don't know whether I believe in God or not—and I am not even quite sure that I know what "believing in God" is'. Note, carefully, the contrast between these formulae and those of the agnosticism of the last century: 'I don't know whether there is a God or not'.

Proceeding along these lines we should be brought, undoubtedly, to a definition of the philosopher as the man who asks the true questions. But obviously this formula itself raises a difficulty. The true questions, I have said: true from whose point of view? Or rather, can we give a meaning to the adjective 'true', as it is used here, without bringing in the problem of the point of view of the person to whom the 'true question' is addressed? There is no difficulty, at least in principle, in knowing what the words 'true answer' might mean: 'true questions' are another matter. Perhaps we might bring in Plato's wonderful comparison of the philosophic questioner to the skilful carver. There is a right and a wrong way of carving. But we must take care; the real carver, to whom the philosophic questioner is compared, is exercising his skill on a given structure, let us say the bones of a fowl. Our own skill, in these lectures, has to be exercised on something much less palpable and solid; perhaps not on a structure at all exactly, except possibly in the sense, itself metaphorical, in which we refer to the structure of a play or a poem. From this point of view, the comparison loses much of its aptness. Could we say that the philosopher is a kind of locksmith to whom we turn when we want to open some particular door? Even this is much too simple. In this case door, keyhole, lock, are not given. The task of philosophy, to my mind, consists precisely in this sort of reciprocal clarification of two unknowns, and it may well be that, in order to pose the true questions, it is actually necessary to have an intuition, in advance, about what the true answers might be. It might be said that the true questions are those which point, not to anything resembling the solution of an enigma, but rather to a line of direction along which we must move. As we move along the line, we get more and more chances of being visited by a sort of spiritual illumination; for we shall have to acknowledge that Truth can be considered only in this way, as a spirit, as a light.

It goes without saying that we are here touching on a problem that is going to take up much of our time during this first series of lectures. It is impossible to say anything about the essence of the spiritual life unless one has first succeeded in making it clear what is to be understood by the term 'truth', or at the very least in ascertaining whether the term is one of those which can be univocally defined: that is, defined as having one, and only one, proper meaning, indifferently applicable at all levels of discourse.

So far, it does not seem that all these preliminary points we have been making yet allow us to discern very clearly on whose behalf our investigations are being pursued. I have spoken of an audience that would act as an intermediary between the enclosed subjective self, at one pole of an antithesis, and the generalized thinking of science, with its claims to quite universal validity, at another. I illustrated this middle position from the fine arts, and the way in which they are really understood by some and not understood at all by others; but that illustration does not yet let me see very clearly what set of people this audience might be; and the references to religious belief with which I followed up that illustration may seem to plunge us into even deeper obscurity. What! must I make my appeal, at this point, to an audience of *connoisseurs*? I am using the word in the same sense in whch it is used in artistic circles. Let us stop for a moment, and think about it. The notion of being a connoisseur seems inseparable from that of having a kind of tact or, more exactly, a sensory refinement—a very clear example, for instance, is the really discriminating diner: I am thinking of the kind of expert who can distinguish not only between two very similar wines from neighbouring vineyards, but between two successive years' bottlings from the same vineyard, by means of subtleties that escape the untrained palate. It should be all too clear that the point of view of a connoisseur of this sort is not that at which we should place ourselves if we wish to understand, that is, to take upon ourselves or more accurately to develop within ourselves, the philosophical investigations that will be the subject of these lectures. I would be inclined to say that the audience I am looking for must be distinguished less by a certain kind of aptitude (like, for instance, the discriminating diner's aptitude) than by the level at which they make their demands on life and set their standards.

We shall have to ask ourselves many questions about the nature of reflective thought and about its metaphysical scope. But from the very start we should note how necessary it will be to be suspicious, I will not say of words themselves, but of the images that words call up in us. I cannot enter here into the terribly difficult problem of the nature of language; but from the very beginning of our investigations, we should bear in mind how often it seems to get tied up in knots—or I would rather say in clots, like clots in the bloodstream, which impede the free motion of thought: for that motion, if it is allowed its natural flow, is also a circulation. We get these clots because words become charged with passion and so acquire a taboo-value. The thinking which dares to infringe such taboos is considered, if not exactly as sacrilegious, at least as a kind of cheating, or even as something worse.

Obviously, it is particularly today in the political realm that this sort of thing is noticeable. The term 'democracy', for instance, is one which does block our thinking in a lamentable way. A concrete example of this tendency is the fact that anybody who wants to examine the notion of democracy from a detached point of view is liable to be called a fascist—as if fascism itself were not just democracy which had taken the wrong turning. But the man who stopped short in his thinking for fear of having such labels as 'facist' stuck on him would be inexcusable; and if we are really inspired by that philosophical intention, whose nature I have been trying to make clear, it is certain that we shall be no longer able to feel such fears, or at least we shall be no longer able to take them into consideration. At a first glance, then, it seems that one thing we need for our task is a certain courage, a courage in following out the course of our thoughts where it leads us, a mental courage, about which common experience allows us to say definitely that it is infinitely less widely diffused than physical courage is; and it will be of the utmost importance to ask ourselves why this should be so. For it ought to be a matter of total indifference to me to hear myself called 'fascist' if I know that this accusation rests on an obvious misunderstanding, and even that, at bottom, my antagonist's readiness to make such accusations implies the existence in his mind of some attitudes which are really rather close to that fascist spirit which he pretends to discern in me.

Obviously, this is only an illustration: but it is of set purpose, in this first lecture, that I am multiplying references to various levels of human interest, the technical, the scientific, the artistic, the religious, the political; I want to underline the extremely general scope of the investigations to which all these remarks are leading on.

Now, what exactly lies behind this claim of ours,

this refusal, at any price, to have the free movement of our thinking blocked? What lies behind it is, I think, the philosophical intention seized in its purity; that intention is quite certainly inseparable from what we are accustomed to call freedom. But, as we shall see, freedom is one of these words which need to have their meanings very carefully elucidated; there can be no doubt that, in our own period, the common uses of the word are often very unconsidered and very indiscreet. Let us say simply that if philosophic thought is free thought, it is free first of all in the sense that it does not want to let itself be influenced by any prejudging of any issue. But this notion of prejudice must be here taken in its widest range of application. It is not only from social, political, and religious prejudice that philosophical thinking must be enfranchised, but also from a group of prejudices which seem to make one body with itself, and which, one might say, it has a natural tendency to secrete. I would not hestitate to say, for instance, that philosophical idealism, as that doctrine has long been expounded, first in Germany, then in England and France, rests very largely on prejudices of this sort, and it is obvious that our thinking finds great difficulty in detaching itself from such prejudices. To employ a rather trivial comparison, I would readily admit that philosophy, when she engages in this struggle with the prejudices that are, in a sense, natural to her, must at moments have the impression that she is beginning to tear off her own skin and to immolate herself in a kind of bleeding and unprotected fleshy covering. That metaphor, like so many of the metaphors I have used, is inadequate. Might one not say that in ridding herself of her natural idealistic prejudices, philosophy must, if she looks at the matter from a high moral point of view, fear that she is betraying her own nature, showing herself unfaithful to her proper standards, and assuming in their place the impure, contradictory, vile standards of a renegade, and all this without there being, at a first glance, any visible counterbalancing advantages? I remember very well the periods of anguish through which I passed, more than thirty years ago now, when I was waging, in utter obscurity, this sort of war against myself, in the name of something which I felt sticking in me as sharply as a needle, but upon which I could not yet see any recognizable face.

We shall have to return to this mysterious need, and to expatiate upon it, since it is this need which I am attempting to satisfy in some degree in the course of these lectures, and since it is in danger of appearing completely meaningless to anyone who does not feel it in the depths of his own nature. But at the moment, I would say just this: at bottom, this need is not very different from good will, as that phrase is understood in the Gospels.

It would be folly to seek to disguise the fact that in our own day the notion of 'the man of good will' has lost much of its old richness of content, one might even say of its old harmonic reverberations. But there is not any notion that is more in need of reinstatement in our modern world. Let the Gospel formula mean 'Peace *to* men of good will', or 'Peace *through* men of good will', as one might often be tempted to think it did, in either case it affirms the existence of a necessary connection between good will and peace, and that necessary connection cannot be too much underlined. Perhaps it is only in peace or, what amounts to the same thing, in the conditions which permit peace to be assured, that it is possible to find that content in the will which allows us to describe it as specifically a good will. 'Content', however, is not quite the word I want here. I think, rather, that the goodness is a matter of a certain way of asserting the will, and on the other hand everything leads us to believe

that a will which, in asserting itself, contributes towards war, whether that is war in men's hearts or
what we would call 'real war', must be regarded
as intrinsically evil. We can speak then of men of
good will or peacemakers, indifferently. Of course,
as we go on, these notions will have to be made
more exact and worked out in more detail, and I
dare to harbour the hope that our investigations
will not be without their usefulness if they allow
us to make some contribution towards such a clari-
fying process.

Thus, in seeking to determine for what set of
people this work of ours can be intended, we have
arrived at a distinction between those who feel a
certain inner intellectual need, not unrelated to the
more widespread inner moral need, felt by men
of good will, to seek peace and ensue it, and those
who do not; this distinction needs to be gone into
more deeply. And it is a distinction, as we shall
see in the next lecture, that has to be defined in
relation to a certain general way of looking at the
world.

# CHAPTER II

## A BROKEN WORLD

BEFORE pressing further forward, I feel it necessary
to go back a little, to consider certain objections
that will have undoubtedly occurred to many of
my listeners.

I assert that an investigation of the sort in which
we are engaged, an investigation of an eminently
theoretical kind, can appeal only to minds of a
certain sort, to minds that have already a special
bias. Is there not something strange and almost
shocking in such an assertion? Does it not imply a
perversion of the very notion of truth? The ordinary
idea of truth, the normal idea of truth, surely involves a universal reference—what is true, that is
to say, is true for anybody and everybody. Are we
not risking a great deal in wrenching apart, in this
way, the two notions of *the true* and the *universally
valid?* Or more exactly, in making this distinction,
are we not substituting for the notion of truth some
other notion—some value which may have its place
in the practical, the moral, or the aesthetic order, but
for which truth is not the proper term?

Later in this course of lectures we shall have to
look very deeply into the meaning, or meanings, of
the word 'truth', but we have not yet reached a
stage where such an investigation would have prac-

tical use. We must at this stage simply attempt
to disentangle, to lay bare the presupposition which
is implied in this objection, and to ask ourselves
what this presupposition, as a postulate, is really
worth. What the objection implies, in fact, is that
we know in advance, and perhaps even know in a
quite schematic fashion, what the relation between
the self and the truth it recognizes must be.

In the last two or three centuries, and indeed
since much more remote periods, there has been a
great deal of critical reflection on the subject of
truth. Nevertheless, there is every reason to suppose
that, in our everyday thinking, we remain dominated
by an image of truth as something extracted—extracted, or smelted out, exactly as a pure metal is
extracted from a mixed ore. It seems obvious to
us that there are universally effective smelting processes: or, more fundamentally, that there are established, legitimate ways of arriving at truth; and
we have a confused feeling that the man who steps
aside from these ways, or even from the idea of
these ways, is in danger of losing himself in a sort
of no man's land where the difference between
truth and error—even between reality and dream
—tends to vanish away. It is, however, this very
image of truth as something smelted out that we
must encounter critically if we want to grasp clearly
the gross error on which it rests. What we must
above all reject is the idea that we are forced to
make a choice between a genuine truth (so to call
it) which has been extracted, and a false, a lying
truth which has been fabricated. Both horns of this
dilemma, it should be noted, are metaphorically
modelled on physical processes; and there is, on
the face of it, every reason to suppose that the
subtle labour involved in the search for truth cannot ever be properly assimilated to such physical
manipulations of physical objects. But truth is not
a *thing;* whatever definition we may in the end

be induced to give to the notion of truth, we can affirm even now that truth is not a physical object, that the search for truth is not a physical process, that no generalizations that apply to physical objects and processes can apply also to truth.

Teaching, or rather certain traditional inadequate ways of conceiving the teacher's function, have encouraged the general acceptance of such gross images of truth. In Dickens's novel, *Hard Times,* there is a character called Mr. Gradgrind, for whom anybody and everybody can be treated as a vessel capable of containing truths (such as, 'The horse is a graminivorous quadruped') extracted from the crude ore of experience, divided, and evenly dealt out. Mr. Gradgrind is aware, certainly, that one vessel is not so sound as another; some are leaky, some are fragile, and so on . . . I believe I am not exaggerating when I say that the educational system, even in countries that think of themselves as rather advanced, has still something in common with the coarseness and absurdity of Dickens's satirical picture of it. The interesting question is, under what conditions does this illusory image of truth as a physical substance, even as the stuff contained in a vessel, present itself naturally to the mind? It is obvious that the use of fixed forms of words in teaching plays a prominent part in fostering the illusion. A history teacher, for instance, has to din dates into his pupils. They have to give back just what they have been given, unchanged by any mental process, and they have to memorize the dates in a quite mechanical way. It is very natural in this case to think of the pupil as a vessel, into which a certain measure of liquid is poured, so that it may be poured out again; an even apter metaphor would be that of the gramophone record. Such metaphors, however, cease to apply in the case where, having explained some idea to a pupil, I ask him to explain it back to me in his own words and if possible with his own illustrations; the idea certainly may still be thought of as a content, but it is a content that has to be grasped by the intelligence; it cannot be reduced, like the history master's dates, to some exact, particular formula. It is this irreducibility that we must keep a grip on if we want to get beyond the illusory image of truth as a physical object, a substance, the contents of a vessel, a mere thing, and to recognize the impossibility of adequately representing by material images those processes by which I can both conceive a true proposition and affirm it to be true.

But perhaps there is a principle that we can already postulate (though reserving our right to expatiate more largely on this important topic at a later stage). The principle is this. On the one hand, everything that can be properly called technique is comparable to a kind of manipulation, if not always necessarily of physical objects, at least of mental elements (mathematical symbols would be an example) comparable in some respects to physical objects; and I suggest on the other hand, that the validity for anybody and everybody, which has been claimed for truth, is certainly deeply implied (though even here, subject to certain provisos) in the very notion of technique, as we have conceived that notion here. Subject to certain provisos, I say, since every technical manipulation, even the simplest, implies the possession by the manipulator of certain minimal aptitudes, without which it is not practicable. There is a story, for instance, that I often tell, of how I had to pass an examination in physics which included, as a practical test, an experiment to determine one of the simpler electrical formulae—I forget which now, let us say the laws of electrolysis—and I found myself quite incapable of joining up my wires properly; so no current came through. All I could do was write on my paper, 'I cannot join up my wires, so there is

no current; if there were a current, it would produce
such and such a phenomenon, and I would deduce
. . .' My own clumsiness appeared to me, and it
must have appeared to the examiner, as a purely
contingent fact. It remains true *in principle* that
anybody and everybody can join up the wires, enable the current to pass through, and so on.

Conversely, we must say that the further the
intelligence passes beyond the limits of a purely
technical activity, the less the reference to the
'no matter whom', the 'anybody at all', is applicable; and that in the extreme case there will be
no sense at all in saying that such and such a task
of lofty reflection could have been carried out by
anybody whatsoever. One might even say, as I
indicated in my first chapter, that the philosopher's
task involves not only unusual mental aptitudes
but an unusual sense of inner urgent need; and as
I have already suggested, towards the end of that
chapter, we shall have to face the fact that in such
a world as we live in urgent inner needs of this
type are almost systematically misunderstood, are
even deliberately discredited. Our world today
really gathers itself together against these needs, it
tugs in the other direction like, as it were, a sort of
counterweight; it does so, also, to the very extent
to which technical processes have emancipated
themselves today from the ends to which they ought
normally to remain subordinate, and have staked
a claim to an autonomous reality, or an autonomous value.

Don't you feel sometimes that we are living . . .
if you can call it living . . . in a broken world?
Yes, broken like a broken watch. The mainspring has stopped working. Just to look at it,
nothing has changed. Everything is in place. But
put the watch to your ear, and you don't hear
any ticking. You know what I'm talking about,

the world, what we call the world, the world
of human creatures . . . it seems to me it must
have had a heart at one time, but today you
would say the heart had stopped beating.

That is a speech by the heroine of one of my
plays, and from time to time I shall be quoting
from my own plays in this way. For it is in these
imaginative works of mine that my thought is to be
found in its virgin state, in, as it were, its first
gushings from the source. I shall try later to explain
why this is so and how the drama, as a mode of
expression, has forced itself upon me, and become
intimately linked with my properly philosophical
work. The young woman who makes this speech
is not intended to rank among what we usually
call intellectuals. She is a fashionable lady, smart,
witty, flattered by her friends, but the busy, rush-
ing life that she seems so much at home in obviously masks an inner grief, an anguish, and it is
that anguish which breaks through to the surface
in the speech I have just quoted.

A broken world? Can we really endorse these
words? And are we being the dupes of a myth
when we imagine that there was a time when the
world had a heart? We must be careful here.
Certainly, it would be rash to attempt to put one's
finger on some epoch in history when the unity
of the world was something directly felt by men
in general. But could we feel the division of the
world today, or could some of us at least feel it
so strongly, if we had not within us, I will not say
the memory of such a united world, but at least the
nostalgia of it. What is even more important is
to grasp the fact that this feeling of a world divided
grows stronger and stronger at a time when the
surface unification of the world (I mean of the
earth, of this planet) appears to be proceeding
apace. Some people make a great deal of this

unification; they think they see in it something like the quickening in the womb of a higher conscience, they would say a planetary conscience. Much later in these lectures we shall have to face that possibility, and finally to make a judgment on the real worth of such hopes. But for the moment we have only to ask ourselves about the particular, personal anguish felt today by people like Christiane in my *Le Monde Cassé*. What is the substance of that anguish? And, in the first place, have we any grounds for attributing a general relevance to such personal experience?

There is one preliminary point that must occur to all of us; we live today in a world at war with itself, and this state of world-war is being pushed so far that it runs the risk of ending in something that could properly be described as world-suicide. This is something one cannot be over-emphatic about. Suicide, until our own times, was an individual possibility, it seemed to apply only to the individual case. It seems now to apply to the case of the whole human world. Of course, one may be tempted to say that this new possibility is only part of the price we pay for the amazing progress of our times. The world today is, in a sense, at once whole and single in a way which, even quite recently, it was not. It is from this very unity and totality that it draws its sinister new power of self-destruction. The connection between the new unity and the new power is something we ought to concentrate on very carefully. Let us postpone, for the time being, a consideration of the conditions that make world-suicide possible and their significance; we are still forced to recognize that the existence of the new power implies something vicious in the new unity. It is not enough, I think, to say that the new unity is still mixed with diversity, or at least 'mixed' is a weak and inadequate word for what we mean. Mixture is in itself a certain mode of unity, but we must recognize that it is a mode which in a certain sense betrays the very need that has called it into existence. And this suffices to show, as we shall see by and by much more clearly, that unity is a profoundly ambiguous idea, and that it is certainly not correct to take the scholastic line and to regard unity and goodness as purely and simply convertible terms. There is every reason to suppose that the kind of unity which makes the self-destruction of our world possible (and by possible, I mean perfectly conceivable) cannot be other than bad in itself, and it is easy to perceive where the badness lies. It is linked to the existence of a will to power which occurs under aspects that cannot be reconciled with each other, and which assume opposite ideological characters. On this topic, I cannot do better than recommend to you Raymond Aron's book, *The Great Schism.*\* But it is clear also that from a strictly philosophical point of view we must ask certain questions which fall outside the field of the political writer as such.

From the philosophical point of view, the fundamental question is whether it is a mere contingent fact that the will to power always presents this character of discordance, or whether there is a necessary connection between this discordance and the essential notion of the will to power itself. It should also be our business, indeed, not to content ourselves with a mere analysis of the notion of the will to power, comparing that with the notion of discordance, but to reflect in the light of history, whose lessons, in this instance, have a strict coherence, on the inevitable destiny of alliances, which, when they are instituted for purposes of conquest, are inevitably fated to dissolve and to transform themselves into enmities. It is, alas, true that one can imagine the possibility of a single conqueror's

\**Le Grand Schisme*, Paris, 1947.

gaining possession, today, of the technical equipment that would render both rebellion and opposition futile; and, in principle at least, it seems that a
government based on slavery and terror might last
for an indefinite period. But it is all too clear that
such a government would be only another form of
the state of war, and indeed perhaps the most
odious form of that state that we can imagine.
Besides, if one refuses to let oneself be deceived
by mere fictitious abstractions, one soon sees that
the victor, far from himself being an indissoluble
unity, is always in fact a certain group of men in
the midst of whom there must always arise the
same sort of rupture which, as we have seen, always menaces alliances; so that at the end of the
day, it is still to war, and to war in a more obvious
form than that of a perpetual despotism, that the
triumphant will to power is likely to lead. It could
only be otherwise—and yet this is a real possibility,
and should not be passed over in silence—in a
mechanized world, a world deprived of passion,
a world in which the slave ceased to feel himself
a slave, and perhaps even ceased to feel anything,
and where the masters themselves became perfectly
apathetic: l mean, where they no longer felt the
greed and the ambition which are today the main-
springs of every conquest, whatever it may be. It
is very important to notice that this hypothesis is
by no means entirely a fantastic one; it is, at
bottom, the hypothesis of those who imagine human
society as transformed into a sort of ant-hill. I
would even be tempted to say that the possibility of
such a society is implicit in, and that its coming
into existence would be a logical development of,
certain given factors in our own society. There are
sectors of human life in the present world where
the process of automatization applies not only,
for instance, to certain definite techniques, but to
what one would have formerly called the inner

life, a life which today, on the contrary, is becoming as outer as possible. Only, it must be noticed that in a world of this sort (supposing, which is not proved, that it would really come into existence) it would no longer be proper to speak of the will to power; or rather that expression would tend to lose its precise psychological significance and would in the end stand merely, as in Nietzsche, for some indistinct metaphysical something. Our thinking tends to get lost, in fact, at this point, in the more or less fictitious notion of a Nature considered as the expression of pure Energy. I will quote, on this topic, a very characteristic passage from Nietzsche's great work, *The Will to Power*—a great work which is, in fact, nothing more than a heap of fragments.

And do you know what the world is for me? Would you like me to show you it in my mirror? This world, a monster of energy, without beginning or end: a fixed sum of energy, hard as bronze, which is never either augmented or diminished, which does not use itself up but merely changes its shape; as a whole it has always the same invariable bulk, it is an exchequer in which there are no expenses and no losses, but similarly no gains through interest or new deposits; shut up in the nothingness that acts as its limit, with nothing vaguely floating, with nothing squandered, it has no quality of infinite extension, but is gripped like a definite quantum of energy in a limited space, a space that has no room for voids. An energy present everywhere, one and multiple like the play of forces and waves of force within a kinetic field that gather at one point if they slacken at another; a sea of energies in stormy perpetual flux, eternally in motion, with gigantic years of regular return, an ebb and a flowing in again of all its forces, going from the more simple to the more complex, from the more calm, the more fixed, the more frigid, to the more ardent, the more violent, the more contradictory, but only to return in due course from multiplicity to simplicity, from the play of contrasts to the assuagement of harmony, perpetually affirming its essence in the regularity of cycles and of years, and glorying in the sanctity of its eternal return as a becoming which knows neither satiety, nor lassitude, nor disgust . . . Do you want a name for this universe, an answer to all these urgent riddles, a light even for yourselves, you of the fellest darkness, you the most secret, the strongest the most intrepid of all human spirits? This world is the world of the Will to Power and no other, and you yourselves, you are also the Will to Power, and nothing else.

To whom is Nietzsche addressing himself here, if not to the Masters whose advent he is announcing? Certainly, these masters, as he conceived them, are far from resembling the dictators we have known, or know still. The case really is, as Gustave Thibon has shown beautifully in the fine book on Nietzsche he brought out a few months ago, that a confusion tended to arise in Nietzsche's thinking between two categories which cannot really be reduced to each other.* Let us put it this way, that he was hypnotized by a role, a purely lyrical role, which he wished however to assume as his own role in real life, but with which he was incapable of effectively identifying his actual self. This purely personal yearning was enough to vitiate his philosophy of history; nevertheless there is something, in the sort of glimpse of an imaginary cosmos which I have just quoted, that does retain its worth and its weight. Otherwise, I would not have quoted that page. It does remain true that, in the 'broken world' we live

*Nietzsche, Lyons, 1949.

in, it is difficult indeed for the mind to withdraw itself from the dizzying edge of these gulfs; there is a fascination in that absolute dynamism. One would be tempted to call Nietzsche's picture of the world 'self-contained', in the sense that his 'monster of energy' does not refer outwards to anything else that sustains or dominates it; except that for Nietzsche this 'self-contained' world is essentially a mode of escape from the real self, in its pure ungraspability. Let us note also in passing that if our world really were such a world as Nietzsche here has described it to be, one has no notion at all of how it could give birth to the thinker, or the thought, which would conceive it as a whole and delineate its characteristics. It always seems to happen so; when a 'realistic' attitude of this sort is pushed to the very limit with brutal, unbridled logic, the 'idealistic' impulse rises to the surface again and reduces the whole structure to dust. But let us notice that, at the level of dialectics, it is this very process which makes manifest the disruption of the world. The world of the Will to Power, as Nietzsche describes it—and it would be easy to show that this world today provides the obscure and still indistinct background of everything in contemporary thought that rejects God and particularly the God of Christianity—that world cannot be reconciled with the fundamental direction of the will that underlies every investigation bearing upon what is intelligible and what is true. Or rather, when, like Nietzsche, one does attempt to reconcile the intention of the philosopher and that picture of the world, one can only succeed in doing so by a systematic discrediting and devaluation of intelligibility and truth as such; but in discrediting these, one is undermining oneself, for, after all, every philosophy, in so far as it can be properly called a philosophy at all, must claim to be true.

These general remarks may help us to see in

what sense the world we live in today really is a broken world. Yet they are not enough to enable us to recognize and acknowledge how deep and how wide the break really goes. The truth of the matter is that, by a strange paradox and one which will not cease to exercise us during the course of these lectures, in the more and more collectivized world that we are now living in, the idea of any real community becomes more and more inconceivable. Gustave Thibon, to whom I referred just now in connection with Nietzsche, had very good grounds indeed for saying that the two processes of atomization and collectivization, far from excluding each other as a superficial logic might be led to suppose, go hand in hand, and are two essentially inseparable aspects of the same process of devitalization.

To put it in quite general terms, and in simpler language than Thibon's, I would say that we are living in a world in which the preposition 'with'— and I might also mention Whitehead's noun, 'togetherness'—seems more and more to be losing its meaning; one might put the same idea in another way by saying that the very idea of a close human relationship (the intimate relationship of large families, of old friends, of old neighbours, for instance) is becoming increasingly hard to put into practice, and is even being rather disparaged. And no doubt it is what lies behind this disparagement that we ought to bring out. Here I come to one of the central themes of these lectures; but I shall confine myself, for the moment, to treating the matter merely in terms of a superficial description of the known facts.

It is, or so it seems to me, by starting from the fact of the growingly complex and unified social organization of human life today, that one can see most clearly what lies behind the loss, for individuals, of life's old intimate quality. In what does this growingly complex organization—this sociali-

zation of life, as we may call it—really consist?
Primarily, in the fact that each one of us is being
treated today more and more as an agent, whose
behaviour ought to contribute towards the progress
of a certain social whole, a something rather distant, rather oppressive, let us even frankly say rather
tyrannical. This presupposes a registration, an enrolment, not once and for all, like that of the new-
born child in the registrar's office, but again and
again, repeatedly, while life lasts. In countries like
ours, where totalitarianism so far is merely a threat,
there are many gaps in this continuous enrolment;
but there is nothing more easy than to imagine it
as coextensive with the whole span of the individual
life. That is what happens in states governed by a
police dictatorship; in passing, I should like to make
the point that a police dictatorship is (for many
reasons, there is not time to go into them now)
merely the extreme limit towards which a bureaucracy that has attained a certain degree of power
inevitably tends. But the essential point to grasp now,
is that in the end I am in some danger of confusing
myself, my real personality, with the State's official
record of my activities; and we ought to be really
frightened of what is implied in such an identification. This is all exemplified in a book called *The
Twenty-Fifth Hour* by a young Rumanian called
C. Virgil Gheorgiu. In this extraordinary novel, we
see a young man who has been falsely denounced
to the Germans by his father-in-law and is sent to
a deportation camp as being a Jew; he has no means
of proving that he is not a Jew. He is labelled as
such. Later on, in another camp in Germany he
attracts the attention of a prominent Nazi leader,
who discovers in him the pure Aryan type; he is
taken out of the camp and has to join the S.S. He
is now docketed as 'Pure Aryan, member of the
S.S.' He contrives to escape from this other sort of
camp with a few French prisoners and joins the

Americans; he is at first hailed as a friend, and
stuffed with rich food; but a few days later he is
put into prison; according to his passport, he is a
Rumanian subject. Rumanians are enemies; ergo . . .
Not the least account is taken of what the young
man himself thinks and feels. This is all simply
and fundamentally discounted. At the end of the
book, he has managed to get back to his wife,
who has meanwhile been raped by the Russians;
there is a child, not his, of course; still, the family
hope to enjoy a happy reunion. Then the curtain
rises for the Third World War, and husband, wife,
and child are all put into a camp again by the
Americans, as belonging to a nation beyond the
Iron Curtain. But the small family group appeals
to American sentimentality, and a photograph is
taken. 'Keep smiling', in fact, are the last words
of this interesting novel, * which summarizes graph-
ically almost everything I have tried to explain in
this lecture.*

The point, here, is not only to recognize that the
human, all too human, powers that make up my life
no longer sustain any practical distinction between
myself and the abstract individual all of whose
'particulars' can be contained on the few sheets of
an official dossier, but that this strange reduction
of a personality to an official identity must have an
inevitable repercussion on the way I am forced
to grasp myself; what is going to become of this
inner life, on which we have been concentrating so
much of our attention? What does a creature who
is thus pushed about from pillar to post, ticketed,
docketed, labelled, become, for himself and in himself? One might almost speak, in this connection, of

*La Vingt-cinquième Heure, Paris, 1949.
*George Orwell's Nineteen Eighty-four, which I read
only a few months ago, is of course another illustration, even more striking than The Twenty-fifth Hour
of this set of ideas.

a social nudity, a social stripping, and one might
ask oneself what sort of shame this exposure is
likely to excite among those who see themselves
condemned to undergo it?

To be honest, it does not seem to me that there
is any real deep analogy between this social nakedness and actual physical nakedness, with the sense
of slight shame which normally accompanies such
nakedness in man—a sense of shame on which the
Russian thinker, Soloviev, has some deep and original
observations. On the other hand, it is, I think, highly
significant to compare the state of a man in his
social nakedness—stripped, by society, of all his
protections—to that in which a man finds himself
who believes himself exposed to the observation of
an omnipresent and omniscient God. This comparison is all the more necessary and important because
the Moloch State of totalitarian countries does tend
to confer on itself a sort of burlesque analogue
of the Divine prerogatives. Only the essential is
lacking (that is to say, the State is not in fact God,
or a God), and this fundamental lack lies at the
basis of the evils from which any society must
suffer that seeks to enchain itself by submitting to
the yoke of the Moloch State. The common factor
in the two types of nakedness—nakedness under the
eyes of the State, nakedness under the eyes of
God—is, most assuredly, fear. But in the presence
of a real God, I mean a God who is not reduced
to the status of a mere savage idol, this fear has a
note of reverence, it is linked to our feeling for the
sacred, and the sacred only is such in and through
our adoration of it. In the case of nakedness under
the eyes of the State, it is clear, on the other hand,
that an adoration, worthy properly to be called
adoration, is impossible, unless it attaches itself to
the person of a Leader; it is then pure fanaticism,
and it is enough to recall the hysterical cult of
which Hitler was the object to understand what

fanaticism means, and what great gulfs of temptation are masked by that word. But between the
Moloch State and such figures as Hitler the relationships that can be established are uncertain,
unstable, threatening either to the Leader or the
State—if only because of the envy and hate that
Leaders must arouse in others who either would
covet their position for themselves or at any rate
could not think of somebody other than themselves
enjoying it without impatience and rage. It is all
too clear that the state of universal continuous
registration and enrolment, from birth to death, to
which I have already alluded, can only be brought
into being in the bosom of an anonymous bureaucracy; now, such a bureaucracy cannot hope to in-
spire any other sentiment than a vague fear—the
same feeling that takes possession of me personally
every time I have to deal in a government office
with some impersonal official who identifies himself
with his job. One cannot avoid, at this point, bringing in the familiar metaphor of the administrative
*machine*: but it is important to notice that the workings of this machine are not something I can contemplate, its presence is simply something I feel:
if I could contemplate its workings, I might be
forced to feel a certain reluctant admiration for it
—as it is, as a person who is being governed,
who is being taxed, for instance, my sentiments
when the machine has been in contact with me
must be purely negative. To make them positive
I would need a chance to get to the other side of
the counter and become myself one of those
privileged beings who contain a morsel of this
mysterious power. Thus it is quite natural that, in
countries where a bureaucratic system prevails,
there should be a tendency towards the general
bureaucratization of life; that is to say, really, towards the abandonment of concrete and creative
activities in favour of abstract, depersonalized, un-

creative tasks and even—one could illustrate this
point easily—an active opposition to all kinds of
creativity.

Let us take it, though it is by no means certain,
that in such a bureaucratized world a certain social
equality would prevail. It would be an equality
obtained by levelling *down,* down to the very level
where the creative impulse fails. But this kind of
equality—and perhaps every kind of equality—is
(though in my own country the opposite has for
long been thought to be the case) in the last analysis
rigorously incompatible with any sort of fraternity;
it appeals to a different need, at a different level of
human nature. One could prove this point in various ways. In particular, it is easy to see that the
very idea of fraternity implies the idea of a father,
and is not really separable, indeed, from the idea
of a transcendent Being who has created me but
has also created you. It is exactly at this point
that we see the yawning central gap, which I mentioned earlier, in the claims of the Moloch State
to be treated as a sort of God. One can see clearly
enough that the State can in no case be treated as a
creator or a father. Yet almost unconsciously here I
have stumbled on an ambiguity. There are different
levels at which men understand the word God. It
is true that the State in our time, even in countries
where it has not reached the totalitarian phase, has
become more and more the engrosser and dispenser
of all sorts of favours, which must be snatched from
it by whatever means are available, including even
blackmail. In this respect the State *is* properly comparable to a God, but to the God of degraded
cults on whom the sorcerer claims to exercise his
magic powers.

From the moment, however, when the ties of
fraternity are snapped—and there is nothing that
can take their place except a Nietzschean 'resent-
ment' or, at the very best, some working social

agreement strictly subordinated to definite materialistic purposes, as in the social theories, say, of the early English utilitarians—the state of social atomization, of which I spoke earlier, inevitably tends to appear. All this, of course, cannot be taken literally as the expression of a state of affairs which has been, by now, established for once and for all. In different countries, this state of affairs is established to different degrees, and even sometimes in different parts of the same country; and in any case, wherever there are men, there are certain vital persisting elements. Using the histological simile which always seems to crop up in this sort of discussion, I would say that there are some kinds of tissue that have a good resistance to this contagion, or rather to this malignant growth. But the main point is to see that here we have what is really the general prevailing tendency today in most countries that we usually think of as civilized. I am not talking merely about the states, for instance, that follow in the path of Soviet Communism. We can show, and in fact it has already been shown (I am thinking particularly of the remarkable books by Arnaud Dandieu and Robert Aron *) that large-scale capitalism exposes the countries in which it is a controlling factor to similar risks. In any case, it is not the usual antithesis between the Communists and the enemies of the Communists that is our point here; no doubt I shall come back to this at the end of these lectures, when I shall try to make clear the conclusions towards which this investigation has led us.

'But', you may feel inclined to say to me at this point, 'we do not see exactly in what sense our world can be called a broken world, since you yourself admit that it is on the way to being unified,

* Arnaud Dandieu, *Décadence de la Nation française*, Paris, 1931. Robert Aron, *La Révolution nécessaire*, Paris, 1933.

though you have added that the unification is probably the pleasing stamp on a coin that rings false.'
The answer, it seems to me, is that—even given
a degree of atomization of which we have as yet
no direct experience, and which can only be conceived entirely in the abstract—it seems impossible
that man should reduce himself to that mere expression of an official dossier, that passive enrolled
agent, with which some seek to confuse his essential
nature.

Let us notice this fact: even if, as is certainly
the case, there should be a tendency for a sinister
alliance to be concluded between the masters of
scientific technique and the men who are working
for complete state-control, the real conditions under
which a human creature appears in the world
and develops there remain, in spite of everything,
out of reach of this strange coalition—even though
certain experiments which are now being carried
out in laboratories give us reason to fear that this
relative immunity may not be of long duration.
But what we can affirm with absolute certainty is
that there is within the human creature as we know
him something that protests against the sort of rape
or violation of which he is the victim; and this torn,
protesting state of the human creature is enough to
justify us in asserting that the world in which we
live is a broken world. That is not all. Our world
is more and more given over to the power of words,
and of words that have been in a great measure
emptied of their authentic content. Such words as
*liberty, person, democracy,* are being more and
more lavishly used, and are becoming slogans, in a
world in which they are tending more and more to
lose their authentic significance. It is even hard to
resist the impression that just because the realities
for which these words stand are dwindling away, the
words themselves are suffering an inflation, which is
just like the inflation of money when goods are

scarce. It may be, indeed, that between the development of tokens of meaning, and that of tokens of purchasing power, there is some obscure connection, easier to feel in a general and indistinct way then to work out in detail. But certainly that break in the world which I have been trying, all through this lecture, to make you feel, is broad and gaping here. The depreciation, today, both of words and of currency corresponds to a general failure of trust, of confidence, of (both in the banker's sense of the word and in the strongest general sense) *credit*.

There is, however, one more question which we must examine, and which might be put from a strictly religious point of view. If anybody accepts the dogma of the Fall, is there not implicit in that acceptance an admission that the world is, in fact, broken? In other words, is it not the case that the world is *essentially* broken . . . not merely *historically* broken, as we have seemed to be saying, basing ourselves, as we have done, on a certain number of facts about the contemporary world? Does not our talk about a broken world imply that there have been periods when the world was intact, though this implication contradicts both the teachings of the Church and all the showings of history?

For my own part, I would certainly answer, without any hesitation, that this break in the world cannot be considered as something that has come about in recent years, or even during recent centuries, in a world originally unbroken. To say so would not only be contrary, I repeat, to all historical likelihood but even metaphysically indefensible. For we should be forced in that case to admit that some incomprehensible external action or other has been brought to bear on the world; but it is all too clear that the world itself must have already continued the possibility of being broken. But what we can say, without contradicting either the recorded facts of history or the more obvious principles of metaphysics, is that in our time the broken state of the world has become a much more obvious thing than it would have been for, say, a seventeenth-century philosopher. In general, such a philosopher would have recognized that broken state only on a theological plane; a man like Pascal, who came to such a recognition through a long process of psychological and moral analysis, anticipating the thought of a much later day, was an exception. In the eighteenth century, the optimism which was common among non-Christian philosophers suffices to show that this feeling of living in a broken world was not, on the whole, widely diffused; even those who, like Rousseau, insisted that the time was out of joint, felt that a certain combination of rationality and sensibility might set them right. It is clear enough that this belief in the possibility of benevolently readjusting human affairs persisted throughout the nineteenth century among various schools of rationalists, and that it has not entirely disappeared even today. Marxism itself might be considered, in its beginnings, as an optimistic philosophy, though today the general darkening of the historical horizon makes that element of optimism in it less and less perceptible. Besides, it is becoming more and more clear that there is nothing in Marxism that would serve to dissipate that deep sense of inner disquiet that lies at the very roots of metaphysics. At the most, the Marxist can hope to numb that, as one numbs a pain. There is nothing easier than to imagine an analgesic technique for this purpose; metaphysical uneasiness would be considered as a psychosomatic malady and would be treated according to the appropriate medical rules. Thus, for Marxists in general, the problem of death as such must no longer be faced, or rather they consider that the problem will cease to have its present agonizing character for an individual who is fully integrated with his community.

But integration conceived after this fashion runs the risk, as we shall see later on when we discuss the nature of liberty, of reducing itself to mere automatization.

Why, it may be well asked at this point, have we lingered so long, in this lecture, over topics which at first glance seem quite foreign to the proper themes of a metaphysical investigation? Simply because it was necessary to describe those conditions, in our life today, which are the conditions most unpropitious to such an investigation; so unpropitious, indeed, that in countries where these conditions are fully operative, metaphysical thinking loses its meaning and even ceases to be a practicable possibility. Perhaps it may not be wholly useless to enlarge a little on this point.

The world which I have just been sketching for you, and which is tending to become the world we live in, which is already indeed the world we live in, in so far as that world is exposed to the possibility of self-destruction, rests wholly on an immense refusal, into whose nature we shall have to search much more deeply, but which seems to be above all the refusal to reflect and at the same time the refusal to imagine—for there is a much closer connection between reflecting and imagining than is usually admitted. If the unimaginable evils which a new world war would bring upon us *were* genuinely imagined, to any extent at all, that new world war would become impossible. But do not let us be led into supposing that this failure to reflect and to imagine is merely the fault of a comparatively few individuals in positions of power and responsibility; these few individuals are nothing at all without the millions of others who place a blind trust in them. But this failure to reflect and imagine is bound up, also, with a radical incapacity to draw conclusions from the sort of thing that has been happening for at least fifty years. Was it not already incredible, in 1939, that men should be found ready to launch another war when the ruins piled up by the previous war had not yet been wholly rebuilt, and when events themselves had demonstrated in the most peremptory fashion that war does not pay? Possibly somebody may feel that such remarks smack of journalism and are hardly worthy of a qualified philosopher. But I fear that any such criticism would merely be an expression of a gravely erroneous conception of philosophy, a conception which for too long has weighed heavily on philosophy itself, and has helped to strike it with barrenness; this erroneous conception consists in imagining that the philosopher as such ought not to concern himself with passing events, that his job on the contrary is to give laws in a timeless realm, and to consider contemporary occurrences with the same indifference with which a stroller through a wood considers the bustlings of an ant-hill. One might be tempted, indeed, to suppose that both Hegelianism and Marxism have considerably modified this traditional way of looking at philosophy; but that is true only up to a certain point, at least in the case of present-day representatives of these doctrines. An orthodox Marxist accepts without any real criticism the daring extrapolation by which Marx treated as quite universal those conditions which had been revealed to him by an analysis of the social situation of his own time in those countries which had just been transformed by the Industrial Revolution. Let us add that the Marxist sets out to criticize existing societies using as his yardstick the indeterminate and psychologically empty idea of a classless society. In this respect, it would be no exaggeration to say that the Marxist places himself in the worst sort of timeless realm, an historical timeless realm, and that it is his stance on this non-existent point of vantage that enables him to decide so confidently whether such and such an event, or such and such an institution, is or is not in keeping with 'the meaning of history'. I, for my part, think on the contrary that a philosophy worthy of the name ought to attach itself to a given concrete situation in order to grasp what that situation implies; and I think it should not fail to acknowledge the almost inconceivable multiplicity of combinations of events that may arise from the factors it has laid bare by its analysis.

In a very general way, one may say that the refusal to reflect, which lies at the root of a great many contemporary evils, is linked to the grip which desire and especially fear have on men. On this topic, of the baleful effect of the passions if the reasonable will does not control them, it is all too sadly clear that the great intellectualist doctrines of philosophy (those, above all, of Spinoza) are being grimly borne out. To desire and fear we ought, certainly, to add vanity, above all the vanity of specialists, of those who set themselves up as experts. This is true, for instance, in the educational world; in France to my own knowledge, but not only in France. I have often said that if one were rash enough to ask what will remain, under any form at all, in the minds of children, of all that has been painfully taught them, what will be the final positive result of the effort that is demanded from them, the whole system would fall to bits, for it is absolutely certain that as regards most of the subjects taught this final positive result will be precisely nothing. Those who are responsible for our educational programmes have not the elementary shrewdness of the industrialist who, before undertaking a new enterprise, ascertains what will be the initial outlay, what are the probable yearly profits, and whether the proportion between these two figures makes the whole thing worth his while. One is careful not to ask such a question of educational experts; would one not be insulting a noble profession? Yet fine words butter no parsnips. They are simply taking advantage of the fact that in teaching the outlay is less visible, less easily definable than in the case of an industrial enterprise; hence a waste of time and strength whose remoter consequences are beyond all calculation.

We shall be starting off, in the lectures that are to follow, from the double observation that nothing is more necessary than that one should reflect; but that on the other hand reflection is not a task like other tasks; in reality it is not a task at all, since it is reflection that enables us to set about any task whatsoever, in an orderly fashion. We should be quite clear about the very nature of reflection; or, to express myself in more exact terms, it is necessary that reflection, by its own efforts, should make itself transparent to itself. It may be, nevertheless, that this process of reflective self-clarification cannot be pushed to the last extreme; it may be, as we shall see, that reflection, interrogating itself about its own essential nature, will be led to acknowledge that it inevitably bases itself on something that is not itself, something from which it has to draw its strength. And, as I said above, it may be that an intuition, given in advance, of supra-reflective unity is at the root of the criticism reflection is able to exert upon itself.

# CHAPTER III

## THE NEED FOR TRANSCENDENCE*

THIS sort of circular panorama of our subject has not yet made very clear to us the real significance and nature of this investigation. We have found out what it is not; also, what conditions are likely to freeze its growth. We must now seek to grasp more directly what such an investigation *is*: and first of all we must ask ourselves what is the nature of that urgent inner need, of which I have spoken so often as being, in a way, the mainspring of such investigations.

I should like to call it a need for transcendence. Unfortunately, that word has been lately much abused both by contemporary German philosophers and some of their French pupils. I should like to lay it down in principle that 'transcendence' cannot merely mean 'going beyond'. There are various ways of 'going beyond', for instance, for which 'transcendence' is an inappropriate word. There is going beyond in space: encroaching, as the explorer does, on some surface that lies beyond a commonly accepted limit. But there is also going beyond in time: I am thinking particularly of the notion of the 'project', the sort of moral claim upon the

*The word 'need' does not convey the meaning of the French word *exigence;* the German equivalent would be *Forderung.*

48

future, which plays such an important part in Sartre's thinking. If we call these 'transcendence', we are extending the meaning of the word in a way which may be grammatically permissible, but which is philosophically confusing. I would rather cling to the traditional antithesis between the immanent and the transcendent as it is presented to us in textbooks of metaphysics and theology. And, though I know there will be objections to this, I should even like to make a distinction between a horizontal and a vertical 'going beyond', the latter of which is more truly transcendence. We have already met with the main objections; they have to do with the use in an abstract metaphysical argument of categories that seem to belong exclusively to our individual perception of space. But really our way of evaluating certain experiences as 'high' and others as 'low' appears in a sense to be a fundamental thing, linked, as it were, to our very mode of existence as incarnate beings. I should like to mention in passing the important researches on such spatial metaphors that have been carried out separately by Dr. Minkowski and M. Robert Desoille. Their level of approach is rather different; both are psychiatrists, but Dr. Minkowski has the advantage of being specially trained in philosophy and the phenomenologic method, as M. Desoille is not.*

*In his extremely interesting book, *Vers une Cosmologie,* (Paris, Fernand Aubier, 1936), Dr. Minkowski speaks of a primitive space of experience in which our thoughts and ideas, as well as our bodies, can be said to move. The nature of this primitive space varies according to exactly what is moving through it; thus Dr. Minkowski suggests that we can contrast our inner with our outer, our mental with our physical space. He gives an example that perhaps may make his drift clearer. I am saying goodbye on a station platform to someone I care for deeply; the train moves off, my friend is still leaning out of the window, and instinctively I run after the train,

I think, however, that these objections should not simply be thrust aside, but rather taken up, and transformed into an argument on our own behalf. The argument might also be illustrated by an analysis bearing on the inevitable ambiguity which attaches, today, to the notion of 'the heavens above'. In France, we have known rationalists who have expended a great deal of exuberant irony in lucid demonstrations of the pre-copernican character of the theological idea of heaven: they have insisted at length, and in a rather laborious way, on the absurdity of clinging to the traditional notions of an absolute 'height' and an absolute 'depths', a real 'up' and a real 'down', in a world that has been enlightened by mathematical physics. But strangely enough, it is the rationalists who in the end seem simple-minded; they fail, it seems, to grasp that there are categories of lived experience that cannot be transformed by any scientific discoveries, even those of an Einstein. We feel the earth below us, we see the sky above; the ways of expressing

---

stretching out my hands towards him. At the end of the platform, as the train disappears from sight, I do actually stop running, but nevertheless, in my inner space, I am still pursuing it; my thought follows the train and participates, so to speak, in the movement which is carrying away part of my being. Dr. Minkowski observes that, according to our usual way of thinking, the only real motion is bodily motion; but this, he says, is a false way of thinking, for thought moves, too. And possibly, on my way out of the station, lost in the thought that is still following my friend as he is carried away from me, I may bump into somebody. 'I am sorry,' I shall say, 'I didn't notice where I was going, my thoughts were *somewhere else* . . .' This is a striking illustration of what inner space, lived space, the space of experience, means; and later in this series of lectures we shall have, I fancy, to remember this notion and to make use of it.

ourselves that derive from that situation could be changed only if the actual mode of our insertion into the universe could be changed; and there is no chance at present of that. When we are dealing, indeed, with such a simple matter as the correspondence of certain postures of the human body to certain contrasting emotions, we have to clench our minds to grasp what the problem is. I am using the rather vague word 'correspondence' on purpose in order not to bring in the questionable idea of a strictly causal relationship. When we think, for instance, of the quite precise and concrete emotional realities that translate themselves in French into a noun like 'abattement' and in English into a phrase like 'feeling cast down', is it not by an unnatural and, indeed, by a barren effort that we try to separate the facts themselves from the metaphor, rooted in language and hardly any longer felt as a metaphor, that fits them like a glove? I may add that the whole drift of such remarks will become clear only when we have got further on our way.

Therefore, we have now to ask ourselves what this urgent inner need for transcendence exactly consists of. I think we must first of all try to map it out in relation to life as it is concretely lived, and not to outline its shape in the high void of 'pure thought'; for my method of advance does invariably consist, as the reader will have noticed already, in working my way up from life to thought and then down from thought to life again, so that I may try to throw more light upon life. But it would be a hopeless undertaking, I think, to attempt to ensconce oneself, once and for all, in the realm of pure thought. Or rather such an attempt is not legitimate except in one or two quite specialized disciplines, above all, of course, in the mathematical sciences; even so, it is a moot and rather troublesome question whether the mathematician can develop his speculations in a world quite totally cut off from experience, that is to say, fundamentally, from life. We shall have, later on, to go in more detail into the exact relations between these two important notions of 'experience' and of 'life' and to dissipate a confusion about these relations which prevails in certain realms of philosophic thought.

Let us notice in the first place that the need for transcendence presents itself above all, is deeply experienced above all, as a kind of dissatisfaction. But the converse does not seem to be true, it does not seem that one would be in the right in saying that every kind of dissatisfaction implies an aspiration towards transcendence. It is important, I think, at this point to be as concrete as possible, that is to say to dramatize, that is, to imagine, as precisely as possible, the situation, the sort of situation in which I may find myself involved. The personal pronoun 'I' should, in addition, be taken here in its widest sense. For it is not a matter only of that finite individuality that I myself am, but of every individuality with which I can sympathize in a lively enough way to represent its inner attitudes to myself. I have no difficulty for instance in putting myself in the place of somebody who suffers from having to lead a narrow life, a life whose development is embarrassed because all its expenses have to be kept at the lowest level, and who dreams of an easier and larger existence; let us imagine the case for instance of a young girl who, so that she may obtain the satisfactions of which she feels herself deprived, marries for money. Let us notice clearly that she perhaps frees herself from certain religious and moral prejudices, and in this sense one might, it seems, properly speak of a 'going beyond'. On the other hand, we have a very clear sense indeed that the need to which the girl has yielded cannot properly be called a need for transcendence. That is enough to justify the distinction which I made at the beginning of the lecture.

We can now imagine a quite different case: the dissatisfaction of somebody who is on the contrary leading an easy life, full of material satisfactions, but who wants to break with this existence in order to commit himself to some spiritual adventure. We should have to go on to an analysis of these two types of dissatisfaction. The first, the girl's, is linked to the idea or, more exactly, to the image of a certain number of goods to which it seems to me that I have the right, or of which I feel myself deprived. Yet it is not, as it seems to me, the idea of possession as such which one should here chiefly stress. I would say, roughly and generally, that the person who suffers from poverty aspires above all to a liberty of movement which is denied to him. Whatever he wants to do, he is brought up short by the question of what it costs, and always he sees himself forced to renounce his purpose. It would be quite unjust to suppose that the girl who marries for money is necessarily inspired by cupidity, that she loves money for its own sake. Perhaps she is even a generous being who suffers particularly from not being able to help those she loves. In this connection, it is thus possible to conceive an hierarchy of satisfactions, some low and vulgar, others on the contrary highly spiritual. Let us note in passing that at this point the antithesis between the 'high' and the 'low' has cropped up again. These satisfactions, though hierarchically arranged, have, however, a common characteristic. They are all organically linked with the fact of possessing a certain power which does not fundamentally belong to me, a power which is not, strictly speaking, myself. The dissatisfaction has to do with the absence of something which is properly speaking external to me, though I can assimilate it to myself and in consequence make it mine. Let us not, at this point, bring in any moral judgments; we have not to ask ourselves whether marrying for money is in fact equivalent to selling oneself, or if it ought to be considered as blameworthy. We are moving at the level of description, and at that level only.

It seems to me then that the first type of dissatisfaction ceases at the moment when I have obtained the external help that assures for me that freedom of movement that I need. But the strange thing is, or so it seems, that the other type of dissatisfaction is directed precisely against satisfactions of this first type. It is just as if—and we shall have to remember this point later on—this liberty of movement which has been granted to us were to reveal itself as meaningless or quite worthless. Perhaps meaningless or worthless, just because its principle lies not in the self, but outside the self. From that moment, it is as if another sort of yearning arose in me, directed not outwards, but inwards. Naturally, the first example of this sort of yearning that presents itself to our minds is the yearning for sanctity; but it is not the only example, and we can also think, at this point, of the case of the creative artist. We can reflect upon the weariness that grips the man who has read *too many* books, heard *too many* concerts, visited *too many* galleries. If there is still enough life left in him, that weariness will tend to transform itself into a desire to create. Certainly, there is no guarantee that this new yearning will be satisfied. It does not lie within my own choice to be a creator, even if I genuinely aspire to creation. In other words, one would be guilty of an indefensible simplification if one asserted that the first kind of dissatisfaction is linked to the absence of something that does not depend on me—such as wealth—but that in the case of the second kind of dissatisfaction, it is up to myself to put an end to it. The truth is infinitely more subtle and complicated, and we cannot fall back here on the famous Stoic distinction —between things that lie within our power, and

things that fall outside it—at least in its simple
original form.

We shall have to come back to this point later
on when we shall be trying to discern in what sense
man is in the right in considering himself as a free
agent, but even now we can see that the fact of a
man's managing to fulfil his vocation, however high
(and this is even truer, the higher his vocation is)
could not be explained away as being the result of
a simple decree of his will. There is, on the contrary, every reason to suppose that this fulfilment
of a high vocation involves a kind of co-operation
from a whole swarm of conditions over which the
person with the vocation has no direct control. This
is a point of the greatest importance and it shows
that the problem of the vocation is essentially a
metaphysical one, and that its solution transcends
the scope of any psychological system whatsoever.
It is not by mere chance that the verb 'to transcend' has here intruded itself, quite unexpectedly,
into our discussion. We are already caught up, as it
were, within the poles of that transcendence which
we attempted to define in the first part of this lecture. Might it not be said that to create is always
to create at a level *above* oneself? And is it not
exactly, also, in this sort of connection that the
word 'above' assumes its specific value?

It is true that the great Swiss novelist, Ramuz,
in whom we must salute a thinker of profound
power, seems, in his memories of Stravinsky, to
say precisely the contrary. 'I do not know why,'
he says, 'but I was reminded of that sentence of
Nietzsche: "I love the man who wants to create
something higher than himself and so perishes."
But what I loved at that time in you was the man
who, on the contrary, creates something lower than
himself and does not perish.' But there is, it seems
to me, a confusion here, a confusion of which Jean
Wahl is also perhaps guilty in attempting to dis-

tinguish, in one of his essays, between transcendence and transdescendence. What Ramuz is trying to say here, and what he has asserted many times, for instance in his book *Salutation Paysanne\** is that one can only make poetry with the antipoetic, that art must be grafted on a wild stock, or rather that the artist must start off from the rawest and most familiar reality, contemplated in all its thickness, its primitive density. It is extremely probable that Ramuz is right in saying this. But there is no reason at all for denying a certain character of transcendence to this raw, familiar reality, always allowing that we insist on one point, which is as follows, and which is very important. There would be no meaning in treating transcendence as a sort of predicate which could belong to one determinate reality and not to another. On the contrary, the reference of the idea to the general human condition is fundamental; but it must be added that it is not a reference arrived at by way of abstract thought, but rather one that is grasped through intimate lived experience—experience, in the sort of case I am talking about, intimately lived in the inner awareness of the poet or the artist. We should notice, however, that we have now raised a difficulty which we must not evade. From the moment when the idea of transcendence is evoked in relation to the human condition in general, is it not negated *as* transcendence and in some sense absorbed back into experience, that is to say, in a word, brought back to the status of immanence? But in that case what becomes of the urgent inner need for transcendence, properly so called?

Let us proceed in this case as we always ought to in cases of this sort; that is to say, reflectively, asking ourselves whether the objection does not presuppose a postulate or rather an implicit image

\*Paris, 1929.

which ought to be erased? What is in question here is the very idea that we form of experience; have we not an unjustifiable tendency to think of experience as a sort of given, more or less shapeless substance, something like a sea whose shores are hidden by a thick fog, and we have just been speaking as if the transcendent was a sort of misty cloud which would by and by melt away; but we have only to reflect upon what experience really is, to realize that this metaphor is grossly inadequate. But we must, I think, go further still, and this remark will apply, in a certain sense, to all our future investigations. One cannot protest too energetically not only against this particular way of representing the idea of experience, but against the claim that experience can possibly be represented, in any way at all. Experience is not an *object,* and I am here taking the word 'object', as I shall always be taking it, in its strictly etymological sense, which is also the sense of the German word *gegenstand,* of something flung in my way, something placed before me, facing me, in my path. We must ask ourselves if some confused representation of experience as an object is not really involved when, in the manner of the Kantian philosophy if that is taken quite literally, one speaks of what lies outside, what lies beyond the limits of, experience. That, in the last analysis, can mean nothing, since the judging of something to be *outside* experience is itself empirical, that is to say it is a judgment made *from within* experience.

These very simple remarks lead us to an important conclusion, one of which we must never lose sight, especially during the second series of these lectures, when we shall be touching on more strictly metaphysical questions. Not only does the word 'transcendent' *not* mean 'transcending experience', but on the contrary there must exist a possibility of having an experience *of* the transcendent as such, and unless that possibility exists the word can have no meaning. One must not shirk the admission that, at a first glance, such an assertion runs the risk of appearing to contradict itself. But may not this be due to the fact that we tend, without realizing it, to form far too restrictive an idea of experience? A typical example of experience, taking the idea of experience in a narrow sense, would be a sensation of taste; in that case, experience appears to be linked to the presence of something for me, and in me, and we interpret it as part of the act of ingesting something. But it is obvious that this act of ingestion is not part of the essence of experience as such, and that in other cases, experience is not so much an absorbing into oneself of something as a straining oneself towards something, as when, for instance, during the night, we attempt to get a distinct perception of some far-off noise. I am still confining myself to examples belonging to the field of sensation. But we know very well that experience goes far beyond the domain of the external senses; and it is also very obvious that in what we call the 'inner life' experience can express itself through attitudes that may be diametrically opposed to each other.

Moreover, I am not allowing myself to forget that in the language of contemporary phenomenology the word 'transcendence' is understood in a much wider sense than that in which, up to the present, I have been understanding it; every object, as such, being considered, in that system, as a transcendent object. However, as I have already said, I prefer to stick to the traditional sense of the word, probing into it, however, more deeply than it has been usual to do. Let us admit, for that matter, that for a topic of this kind it is always very difficult to find an adequate vocabulary. To say that the transcendent is still immanent in experience, is to persist in objectifying experience and in imagining it as a sort of space of which the transcendent would be, so to say, one dimension. One can avoid such confusions only by keeping continually present to one's thought the spiritual meaning which one is stressing. Naturally, there is no possibility of doing without symbols; nevertheless, symbols should always be recognized as such and should never encroach on the ideas that one is straining to elucidate through their use.

Thus, I repeat, the urgent inner needs for transcendence should never be interpreted as a need to pass beyond all experience whatsoever; for beyond all experience, there is nothing; I do not say merely nothing that can be thought, but nothing that can be felt. It would be much more true to say that what is our problem here is how to substitute a certain mode of experience for other modes. Here again we have to battle against a distorting symbolization which would represent these modes of experiences as physical spaces separated by some kind of partition. But it is sufficient, if we want to get rid of this misleading picture, to turn to a concrete and precise example: let us think, if you are willing, of the kind of inner transformation that can take place within a personal relationship. Here, for instance, is a husband who has begun by considering his wife in relation to himself, in relation to the sensual enjoyments she can give him, or even simply in relation to her services as an unpaid cook and charwoman. Let us suppose that he is gradually led into discovering that this woman has a reality, a value of her own, and that, without realizing it, he gradually comes to treat her as a creature existing in her own right; it may be that he will finally become capable of sacrificing for her sake a taste or a purpose which he would formerly have regarded as having an unconditional importance. In this case, we are witnesses of a change in the mode of experience which provides a direct illustration of my argument. This change revolves upon the centre

of an experiencing self; or, to speak more exactly,
let us say that the progress of the husband's thought
gradually substitutes one centre for another; and of
course the word 'thought' is not quite exactly the
right word here, for we are dealing with a change
in the attitude of a human being considered as a
whole, and with that change, also, in so far as it
embodies itself in that human being's acts. I hope
this example gives us a glimpse, at least, of the
direction in which we must set ourselves to move if
we want to give a meaning to these words that are
certainly obscure in themselves: *urgent inner need
for transcendence.*

It will be objected, nevertheless, that the term
'transcendence' taken in its full metaphysical sense
seems essentially to denote an otherness, and even
an absolute otherness, and people will ask how an
experience of otherness as such can even be conceived. Does not the other, *qua* other, fall by definition outside my experience? Again, in this case, we
must ask ourselves whether the objection does not
mask a preconceived idea which we must bring to
the surface before we can expose it to criticism.
Here again it is our conception, or again I would
rather say our image, of experience that is in question. The point is so important at this juncture that
we must be allowed to insist on it.

It may be said that the philosophy of the last
century was in a very large measure dominated by
a prejudice which tried to assume the dignity of a
principle. The prejudice consisted in admitting that
all experience in the end comes down to a self's
experience of its own internal states. Let us notice,
in passing, that what we have here is a paradoxical
conjunction, or osmosis, of two contrasting elements—on the one hand a philosophy which had
originally been based purely on the reality of sensation, and on the other hand an idealism whose
nature was essentially different. The first of these

philosophies, so long as it remained faithful to its first roots, was forced, for that matter, to deny to the self all autonomous reality; one can even say, it seems to me, that from this point of view (the point of view of Hume, for instance) the self is built up out of its own states, or out of something which is only an abstract and uncertain outcome of these states. It was quite another matter for idealism (and Descartes is the obvious name to mention in this connection), for which, on the contrary, the thinking self possesses an indubitable existence, and even a real priority. I mean that for idealism the thinking self stands as the necessary postulate without which any kind of experience at all is inconceivable. One might be tempted to say that for idealism it was rather the self's states of consciousness that had a wavering and doubtful metaphysical status. Moreover, in this connection, one recalls, of course, the difficulties that arise in Kant's doctrine about the relation between transcendental awareness and ordinary, everyday psychological awareness. How can the *Ich denke* become an *Ich fühle* or an *Ich erlebe*? It could not be a matter, in this case, of course, of postulating a separateness, like the separateness of physical objects, between the thinking self and the feeling self, that is, of claiming that the one was not the same thing as the other. Such an affirmation would result in the end in idealism's once more *thingifying* the self. To avoid that impasse, idealism will be forced to speak of functional differences between the self that thinks and the self that feels. But by this sort of schematism does one not risk distorting the nature of experience as a single lived reality? This is a serious problem, to which we shall have to come back. Can feeling be properly considered as a function of the self? Or is it not rather the case that every function presupposes feeling as anterior to it and other than it?

This mass of difficulties is bound to make us

reflect, and to force us to call in question the whole notion of 'a state of consciousness'. But we must get a clear grasp of the meaning of this problem.

The notion of a state, taken in its most general sense, is one that we cannot do without when we are thinking of bodies submitted to all sorts of modifications that appertain to their physical nature. I am not at this moment seeking to raise the difficult metaphysical problem of just what the relations between a body, considered in itself, and its modifications are, or more exactly whether the phrase 'considered in itself' can in such an instance have a precise meaning. That question, for the moment, is not relevant. What is beyond doubt is that we cannot afford to dispense with the idea of a state, if we want to describe the modifications suffered by any body whatsoever under the influence of external agencies. But then, when we speak of states of consciousness, is it not the case that, without being aware of it, we are treating consciousness as a sort of bodiless body which is capable of suffering an analogous series of modifications? Let us understand each other; in so far as I am myself a body —later, we shall have to consider at length the implications of this equivocal assertion—it is all too clear that I pass through an infinity of successive states. In so far as I am a body: but not at all in so far as I am a consciousness. For, in a word, whatever the ultimate nature of consciousness may be, it obviously cannot be considered as a body, even a bodiless one. On this point, Descartes was right and with him all the forms of idealism that are derived from his thinking. Consciousness is essentially something that is the contrary of a body, of a thing, of whatever thing one likes to imagine, and given that fact it is permissible to think that the expression 'state of consciousness' involves a contradiction in terms.

One might be tempted to resolve the contradiction, as Spinoza resolved it, by formulating the following observations: might not one say that what we call a state of consciousness is the state of a body at a given moment in so far as it is *represented*? Represented, in this technical sense, means something like *seen in a mirror*. Consciousness, on this theory, would be nothing else than the fashion in which a body looks at itself. But this solution raises innumerable difficulties and insoluble difficulties, too. The most serious of these have to do with the word 'consciousness' itself. The word implies something permanent which can only exist ideally, and it does not seem that one can attribute this permanence to body as such. What seems to be proper to a body, by reason of its very mutability, is to have no self. It is selfless by definition. But that is not all: we must be wary of the tendency that leads us to place ourselves as it were outside consciousness in order to represent it to ourselves (here, as a mirror), for all this can only be an illusory advance, since it is an intrinsic quality of consciousness that it cannot be detached, contemplated, and considered in this way. What we believe we are looking at from the outside is no longer consciousness, and perhaps it is not even anything at all. It is necessary then to reject at this point the conception according to which the so-called states of consciousness would be simply bodily states looking at themselves or becoming objects for themselves. But this refusal entails important consequences; it is not difficult to see, for instance, that it must lead us to reject the theory of psycho-physical parallelism. I do not think, for that matter, that Bergson's criticism of that theory has ever been refuted.

We are led, then, to this negative but very important conclusion that it is not possible to treat all experience as coming down in the end to a self's experience of its own states. The path that we should follow here is rather that first

explored and mapped out by phenomenologists
of the school of Husserl. I shall therefore lay it down
as a principle, to be accepted in the whole of my
subsequent argument, that, before it is anything
else, consciousness is above all consciousness *of*
something which is other than itself, what we call
self-consciousness being on the contrary a derivative
act whose essential nature is, indeed, rather uncertain; for we shall see in the sequel how difficult it
is to succeed in getting a direct glimpse of whatever
it is that we mean by *self*. Even at this point, let us
notice that I cannot know myself or even make an
effort to know myself without passing beyond this
given self which I claim to know, and this 'passing
beyond' appears to be characteristic of consciousness, which is enough in itself to dispose of the idea
of consciousness as a mere mirror. Perhaps there
are reasons for supposing that epiphenomenalism,
that is, the idea of consciousness as a mere surface
encrustation on matter, has penetrated today far
beyond the bounds of materialism properly so
called, and that all modern minds need to make
a painful effort if they are free themselves of this
theory. Science and technique in general have, after
all, stressed very strongly in our time the idea of
a purely objective reality, a reality to which we all
tend to attribute, though falsely, an internal
coherence.

But from the moment when one has understood
that consciousness is consciousness of something
other than itself, we can easily overcome the temptation of epiphenomenalism, and at the same time
the objection against which the idea of transcendence was hammering loses all its massive strength.
It is necessary also, at this point, to notice how
much we must be on our guard against all these
metaphors which have been incorporated into the
very flesh of language and which consist in assimi-
lating the fact of being conscious to modes of

physically gathering or taking. Such verbs as 'seize' and 'grasp' are very revealing from this point of view. Of course, it is not merely an unlucky chance if, even in an investigation of this sort, we find ourselves making a spontaneous use of them; we can hardly prevent ourselves from practising this sort of transposition of elusive notions into familiar, palpable terms, but it is important that we should not be deceived by the habit, and that we should be able to recognize within what limits this kind of transposition can be properly and legitimately exercised—limits outside of which it becomes illegitimate and degenerates into something meaningless.

I should be inclined to say in a very general fashion that the closer we get to the topic of intellection properly so called, the more these metaphors centred on the acts of plucking, taking, or grasping become really useless. One might admit that they are suitable enough for all those acts of the mind which will partake of habit. To form a habit is really to take, or seize, or grasp something, for it is an acquisition; but to discover an intelligible relation, for example some mathematical relation whose eternal validity one suddenly recognizes, that is not in any sense to grasp something; it is to be illuminated, or rather, to have a sudden access to some reality's revelation of itself to us. What we should notice here, however, is the impossibility of making a radical distinction between acquisition and illumination; for if illumination is to be communicated it must inevitably become language, and from the moment it has passed into a sentence it runs, in some degree, the risk of blinding itself and of sharing in the sad destiny of the sentence itself, which in the end will be repeated mechanically, without the person who repeats it any longer recognizing its meaning. Let us observe, moreover, that this danger is not only one which attends a communication from myself to another person, but that it also attends, if I may be allowed to put it in this way, a communication from me to myself. There is always the risk of the hardened, transmissible expression of the illumination growing over the illumination like a sort of shell and gradually taking its place. This is true at all levels, true wherever anything has been revealed, for instance about a work of art, a landscape, and so on . . . It is just as if the initial, living experience could survive only on condition of degrading itself to a certain extent, or rather of shutting itself up in its own simulacrum; but this simulacrum, which should only be there on sufferance, as a kind of *locum tenens,* is always threatening to free itself from its proper subordinate position and to claim a kind of independence to which it has no right; and the serious danger to which thought itself is exposed is that of starting off from the simulcrum, as an existing basis, instead of referring itself perpetually to that invisible and gradually less and less palpable presence, to indicate which (and to recall it to our memories) is the sole justification of the simulacrum's existence. This is a very general observation and it opens out in all sorts of diverse directions. For the moment, I will illustrate it by a single example which anticipates a good deal that we shall see more clearly later on.

Here is a person of whom we have a detailed knowledge, with whom we have lived, whom we have seen in many different situations. But it may happen that we are asked to say something about him, to answer questions about him, to offer a necessarily simplified opinion of his character; we offer a few adjectives, ready-made, rather than made to measure. This summary, inexact judgment of our friend then, within ourselves, begins to form what I have called a simulacrum. For it may paradoxically happen that this simulacrum obstructs or dims the fundamentally far more concrete idea we have formed of this person, an idea fundamentally incommunicable, an idea which we cannot even communicate in its pure essence to ourselves. And it is quite possible for the simulacrum we have formed of our friend to change our attitude to him, and even our behaviour towards him, for the worse. Though it may be, of course, that some circumstance will arise which will enable us to thrust aside this obstacle we have placed in the path of a true human relationship, without realizing we have done so.

There is, unfortunately, all too much reason to think that many a philosophy of the past—before Bergson's time, who in this field was a liberator whose beneficent activities can never be too highly celebrated—has been built up not on experience but on a waste product of experience that had taken experience's name. For a philosopher worthy of the name there is no more important undertaking than that of reinstating experience in the place of such bad substitutes for it.

But, it will be asked, what is the relationship— or is there even a relationship?—between the urgent inner need for transcendence and such a preoccupation? On a first impulse, one would be tempted to answer in the negative: but why? Because one would like to imagine, in accordance with a vicious fashion of philosophizing, that transcendence is fundamentally the direction in which we move away from experience. But the views that have been put forward in the first part of this lecture have prepared us to understand that this is false and that it presupposes an idea of experience which robs experience of its true nature.

Here, it seems to me, is the anatomy of this error. One cannot insist too strongly that what traditional empiricism failed to see was that experience is not, in any sense, something which resembles an impermeable mass. I would rather say that experi-

ence is receptive to very different degrees of
saturation; I employ this expression from chemistry
(where one talks, for instance, of a saturated solution, meaning one into which no new substance can
be dissolved) with regret, and I shall seek for other
expressions, so that our thought may not become
fixed on a necessarily inadequate simile. One might,
say, for example, that experience has varying degrees of purity, that in certain cases, for example, it
is distilled, and it is now of water that I am thinking.
What I ask myself, at this point, is whether the
urgent inner need for transcendence might not, in
its most fundamental nature, coincide with an aspiration towards a purer and purer mode of experience. I can quite see, of course, that the two
metaphors of which I have made use appear to be
contradictory—the metaphors of saturation and
purity. But it is just this kind of opposition, linked
to the material world, that tends to disappear at
the spiritual level. We have only, if I may put it so,
to dematerialize the initial comparison to see how
it can fit in with the second. Let us think, for instance, not of a heavy body like salt, saturating a
solution, but of radiations; one can imagine some
liquid at once very pure and very radioactive; and,
of course, even the notion of radioactivity is still
borrowed from the physical world. Let us now
imagine in an even vaguer fashion whatever sort
of thing an intelligible essence might be, and we
can easily conceive that the experience most fully
charged with these imponderable elements, intelligible essences, might at the same time be the
purest. We shall have to bear in mind the connection between plenitude and purity when we attempt
to throw light, later on, upon how we ought, and
above all upon how we ought not, to conceive an
essence.

But even if we cling to the notion of saturation,
we should have no difficulty in understanding that

two completely opposite kinds of saturation of experience can be imagined. An experience can be saturated with prejudices: but this means that the prejudice which obstructs it at the same time prevents it from being fully an experience. Often, for instance, when we are travelling in a strange country, it is precisely so; we are unable to free ourselves from a certain number of preconceived ideas which we have brought with us without being distinctly aware of having done so; they are like distorting spectacles through which we look at everything that is presented to us. The other type of saturation is the opposite; one might say, to recall an old notion of the Greeks, that the eye must become light in order to comport itself properly in the face of light, and that this is not true only of the eye; the intelligence must become at once pure ardour and pure receptivity. It is necessary to put these two words together, the process I am imagining is a simultaneous one. If we put the stress exclusively on ardour, we cease to see how the intelligence is able to understand things; it seems that it is no longer properly intelligence, but merely enthusiasm; but if we insist only on receptivity, we are already the dupes of that material image which I have already taken note of; we persuade ourselves falsely that to understand, for the mind, is like, for a vessel, being filled with a certain content. But the intelligence can never be properly compared to a content, and it is of this that we shall convince ourselves in our next lecture when we attempt to sound the depths of what is to be understood by the notion of truth.

# CHAPTER IV

TRUTH AS A VALUE:

THE INTELLIGIBLE BACKGROUND

IN THIS lecture, which will be taken up entirely
with an investigation bearing upon the question of
what we have in mind when we talk about truth,
I shall have to refer to the essay by Martin
Heidegger, *Vom Wesen der Wahrheit*. I shall only
do so, however, in a rather wary fashion. The
largely novel vocabulary of this German philosopher
cannot fail to arouse, in many of his readers, a
grave uneasiness. In passing, I would like on this
topic to remark that when he coins new words,
a philosopher is often the victim of an illusion.
The strange and surprising impression produced on
him by his new word often prevents him from seeing that there is nothing strange or surprising about
the thought it expresses. What lies behind the creation of such words is often the shock which the
philosopher has felt in rediscovering, on his own
account, something that was already discovered long
before him. This rediscovery is not discovery, in
the proper sense of the word.

It is my own intention, on the other hand, to
use, with one or two exceptions, the simplest words
I can find. But it will be hard for my listeners, I
know, to determine, without a wide margin of uncertainty, the relation between the comparatively
everyday language which I shall be using and that

of the German philosopher; though the Belgian philosopher, Alphonse de Waehlens, did a great deal to elucidate Heidegger's terminology in his French translation of Heidegger's* essay which appeared at Louvain in 1948.

One of my pupils observed to me the other day that there is more material in my plays than in my speculative writings that could be used for the working out of a doctrine of truth. And when I had thought it over carefully, I thought his remark basically sound. But if this is so, is it mere chance that it is so? Obviously not. The fact is simply the indirect confirmation of the more general fact that when we set out to speak about truth, as when we set out to speak about God, we are in danger of speaking about something which is not truth, but is merely its simulacrum; here again is that word which played such an important part in our last lecture. We must ask ourselves, then, whether truth is something which can only be alluded to, in a glancing way. The role of the drama, at a certain level, seems to be to place us at a point of vantage at which truth is made concrete to us, far above any level of abstract definitions. Let us see whether this reflection serves, or does not serve, to confirm our preliminary assumptions.

In order to throw more light on the direction of our quest, I should like to insist strongly that what matters for us is to elucidate our own meaning when we say, for instance, that we are guided by the love of truth, or that somebody has sacrificed himself for the truth. Let us ask ourselves what condition, even and perhaps above all what negative condition, such assertions must satisfy if they are to have a meaning. It is obvious at a first glance that a traditional formula, such as 'truth is the

*De L'Essence de la Verité, par M. Heidegger, Louvain, 1948.

adequation of the thing and the intellect', whatever
its theoretic value may be, is by no means suited
to throw light on such assertions. There would be
no meaning in saying that somebody had died for
the adequation of the thing and the intellect. This
in itself serves to show that the idea of truth has a
fundamental ambiguity. Let us take it for the present that we are applying ourselves to the consideration of truth in so far as truth is a value; it is only
under this aspect that truth can become 'something
*at stake*'.

I shall start off with a very simple example, and
from my point of view a very instructive one. We
have all been taught from our earliest years that
we must not confuse what we should like to be
the case and what is the truth. A great Doctor of
the Church has even declared that this confusion
is a perversion of the understanding. But, first of
all, is there any difference at all here between what
is the truth and what simply *is*? Is it not obvious
that what is true is nothing other than what is, what
exists, what is the case; from a certain point of
view, the difference between them is non-existent.
But only from a certain point of view, and more
precisely from the perspective of a kind of thinking turned at once towards the object and towards
possible action on the object, that is to say, a thinking along the lines of technique. What, then, is the
other perspective, within which a distinction between what is true, and what is, must in spite of
everything be maintained? On what will it lay its
stress? I will quote here an important passage
from Bradley in his *Essays on Truth and Reality*.
We shall have to ask ourselves if it throws some
light on our problem:

> Truth is the whole Universe realizing itself in
> one aspect. This way of realization is one-sided,
> and it is a way not in the end satisfying even its

own demands, but felt by itself to be incomplete. On the other hand the completion of Truth itself is seen to lead to an all-inclusive Reality, which Reality is not outside Truth. For it is the whole Universe which, immanent throughout, realizes and seeks itself in Truth. This is the end to which Truth leads and points, and without which it is not satisfied. And those aspects in which Truth for itself is defective, are precisely those which make the difference between Truth and Reality.

In other words, Truth distinguishes itself from Reality in the measure in which it is only a single aspect among others, or is unilateral, while Reality is in essence omni-comprehensive.

But, for reasons which will appear more clearly in the sequel, I shall refrain from bringing in, as a solution of this problem that is occupying us, the notion of an omni-comprehensive reality; for though the latter idea dominates all Bradley's thinking, I am afraid it is by no means invulnerable to all criticism. What we should notice here is that the operation of including (and Bradley builds up his Absolute by an hierarchy of inclusions) is one which can only be carried out within the bosom of a relatively, not absolutely, complete system or totality which is then stretched out to gather in the new element that has to be included; more precisely, I would say this method of inclusion is suitable only for a pattern of philosophical thought which is in motion, which is in the process of completing itself. It is obvious that such an inclusive system of thought can only, at any time, be *provisionally* rounded off; there is always a tension between the system in itself, considered as a whole, and the elements of experience that have still to be absorbed in it. It remains to be shown, and most probably it cannot be shown, that we have the right to pass the ideal limiting case, where nothing more need be ab-

sorbed; and that the act of inclusion remains possible or conceivable where the level of thought on
the move, let us say of discursive thought, has been
transcended, and where we profess to have established ourselves at a point *beyond* all development.

It seems to me that it would be better to set out
on a more modest path, that is to say that of the
phenomenologists, and to ask ourselves just what
we have in mind when we talk about the difference
between *being* and *being true*.

One solution presents itself naturally to the mind,
which has been adopted by numerous philosophers:
it consists of saying that truth has to do exclusively
with judgments. A judgment is true or false, but
one cannot talk of truth or falsity in the case of a
sensation or a sentiment. Sensations and sentiments,
in all the judgments we make about them, appear to
be merely themselves.

This distinction, however, must be treated with
more caution than is commonly thought necessary.
For in affirming the self-identity of sensations and
sentiments, in saying that within all judgments and
for all judgments they are simply what they are,
am I not forgetting their real nature? Or rather
—for if they had a real nature, it would not be necessary to assert that self-identity—am I not mistaken
in supposing that they have a nature in this sense?
They are fugitive, they are elusive it may be said,
thought cannot fix them, and it is only where
thought can fix something that we can properly talk
of its having a nature. Obviously, at this point, we
are getting rather close to a certain aspect of
Platonism: the notion that the world of the senses
and feelings is somehow unreal unless it is transformed into a higher world of concepts. However,
before we can accept such a position, we have to
face a serious difficulty. After all, to take a quite
elementary example, a flavour, for instance, does
appear to bear witness to the presence of something

that has a nature, a self-identity. There must be
something there, after all, if there is something that
I can talk about. I can say, for instance: I like, or
I do not like, the taste of raspberries, the smell of
tar. And what testifies to the self-identity of that
taste or that smell is that I have only to experience
them afresh, after a gap of years, to be carried
back into a distant past which is essentially *my* past.
The most we can say is that there is a sense in
which I can confidently affirm that my companion
and I are talking about the same sensation when
we discuss the taste of raspberries, I saying I like it,
he that he does not. What, however, makes the
question really obscure is that it is almost impossible
to distinguish sharply between the kernel of the
sensation and the kind of array of emotional over-
tones that encloses it, and that inevitably varies with
each individual because the background of experience as a whole, for each individual, is different.
Thus the taste of raspberries may be linked in my
case with walks in the Vosges woodlands with people I love, and for somebody else with a house and
a garden in the Paris suburbs where he spent his
childhood holidays under the care of a bad-
tempered grandfather. Yet in principle the distinction between the kernel and its shell remains valid,
and the notion of the kernel of sensation retains its
theoretic validity. Thus, after all, it does not seem
to be quite that sensations and sentiments are always
too fugitive to be fixed by thought; or that thought
cannot refer to them without transforming them
into something other than themselves, something
essentially, as sensations and sentiments are not,
objective.

But on the other hand we ought to notice that as
soon as we admit the existence of this kernel, we
admit also the possibility of a certain congruousness
between my own grasp of it and another person's;
this congruousness cannot be accidental, but it is

by no means guaranteed. For instance, I once knew a man who thought raspberries had no taste; there can be a sort of taste-blindness, and the same sort of thing is true over the whole range of possible sensations. There are many people who cannot tell the difference between the great vintages and very ordinary wines. It would be a fallacy to draw negative or even relativist conclusions from such facts. In every realm of sense-experience there are connoisseurs; their gifts are real and cannot be denied without absurdity. Let us add, to round off this argument, that the non-connoisseur is in no position to deny the connoisseur's status; in fact the non-conoisseur ought to recognize his own condition, which is that of being shut off from certain realities. Realities, I say. Could I not say truths? After what seemed a digression, we have come back to our original problem.

It may be objected, indeed, that whether we talk of truths or realities here depends on how we choose to define our terms. But there is an important point that hangs on that 'how we choose': whether we seize on this word, or on that word, to fix a real distinction which we have perceived, the distinction must be, as it were, in the long run accepted and sustained by the common idiom of language. The non-connoisseur is keeping within the bounds of truth when he recognizes that he is a non-connoisseur; he is falling outside these bounds when he fails to recognize that fact. But it would be absurd to say that he is falling outside the bounds of reality. Whatever truths he fails to recognize, he himself remains perfectly real. And if he is a conceited man, for instance, his refusal to recognize his deficiency may reflect his real nature excellently well, unless indeed we are using 'real nature' in a non-psychological sense—a point which leads us back to a path we have trodden before. What we are aiming at, in fact, when we grope for the idea of truth, is not the kind of rounded and complete positive experience that we might be aiming at if we were groping for the idea of reality. On the contrary, one can be within the bounds of truth and one's reality can be suffering from a denudation, a lack; I am thinking, for instance, of the case of a deaf man who wishes at all costs to take a part in social life, that is, to refuse to adopt the kind of behaviour that seems to go with being deaf, to refuse to draw the usual conclusions from the premise of his infirmity. In a word, this deaf man refuses to shut himself in—he refuses to draw the blinds against a certain kind of light. But what is this light? And where does it come from? . . . May not this metaphor of light help us to grasp the very essence of what we mean by truth? But I will emphasize, in the first place, that it is more than a metaphor; or if it is one, it is a metaphor woven into the texture of my argument, part of the pattern of the argument, not a mere incidental illustration of a point, as the other metaphors have been which I have used so far, but of which I soon had to rid myself, since, after easing its path for a moment, they soon obstructed the progress of pure thought. Truth can dazzle and wound us as a bright light does when we turn our eyes full on it; and in ordinary language, we speak of men making themselves deliberately blind to the truth, and so on. . . .

It is nevertheless clear that we should pause at this point to analyse just what we have in mind when we think of truth as light. There would naturally be no sense in imagining, in a grossly realistic fashion, that facts as such throw out a kind of light which is the light of truth. The chief error of the philosophers of the empiricist tradition has been, in fact, a failure to recognize what a confused notion that of a fact is; we may at any moment be forced to treat as a fact, as we have seen only a short time ago, something which is pure absence, like the fact

of the non-connoisseur's being shut off from certain
realities. But it is time to seek for another illustration of that idea, since the illustration to which one
clings too long tends to grow stale.

Let us think of somebody who has decided to
enter a religious community, to become a monk.
But he has never been clear in his own mind about
what causes have led him to this decision. He is on
the eve of taking his final vows, there is still time
for him to renounce his purpose. It would be essential at such a time that he should ask himself
whether his vocation is in fact an authentic one,
whether he has really the sense of being called by
God to be God's servant. But in fact he dare not
ask that question directly, since he is afraid of the
answer. In reality, his decision has been taken after
a long succession of purely worldly disappointments
—perhaps because a woman he loved had deceived
him, or because he had failed in a difficult examination; perhaps also because he sees the obscure
chance of obtaining, as a monk, the respect of his
family, who have so far always thought him incapable of carrying through any design successfully.
But all this has obviously nothing to do with a
vocation; and before taking an irrevocable step, he
ought to open himself to the light. But we are back
to our problem: what is this light? Where does it
come from? Of the data which I have just enumer-
ated, not one can be regarded as being in itself a
source of light. But under what conditions might
such a datum become one?

Let us note well, before going further, that the
great majority of human beings grope about during
their whole lives among these data of their own
existence rather as one gropes one's way between
heavy chairs and tables in a darkened room. And
what is tragic about their condition is that perhaps
only because their lives are passed in this shadowy
gloom can they bear to live at all. It is just as if

their seeing apparatus had become finally adapted
to this twilight state: it is not a question of what
Ibsen in *The Wild Duck* calls the 'life-lie', it is a
state of non-vision which is not, however, a state
of quite complete non-awareness. It can also be
said that the attention of such people is not directed
towards the data of their own existence, that they
even make a point of directing it elsewhere, and,
indeed, this 'making a point' is as it were the hidden
spring that makes their lives tick on reasonably
bearably. One might express this in another way:
all of us tend to secrete and exude a sort of protective covering within which our life goes on.

But to express oneself thus is still to postulate
the existence of a light which comes from outside
and which it would be possible to intercept. And
yet we have seen distinctly that this idea is absurd.
It is necessary, however, to see just where its absurdity lies.

It seems to me to consist in the first place in
treating what we call fact, whatever that may really
be, as if it were something placed *outside me*, in
the sense in which some material body is, in its
case, outside my body, and placed, indeed, at a
measurable distance from that. It is against this
idea of the fact as external to me that we must
direct our polemic. We must not hesitate to affirm
that the coherence of a fact, of any fact, is conferred on it by the mind that grasps it, by the understanding self. There is therefore every reason to
suppose that if this fact, or this collection of data,
should possess the strange power of irradiation of
which I have spoken, it would be from the understanding self that it had borrowed the power, rather
than possessing such a power intrinsically itself:
the latter supposition, I repeat, is absurd. But at this
point it seems that we are falling into an inextricable confusion. How can I, as an understanding self,
shut myself against a light which, as we have just

seen, does not come strictly speaking from the facts themselves, but from myself who have conferred upon them this strange power of radiation? If this is the case, we must acknowledge that what we call a fact is only an inert, neutral element, and that everything that really seems to be a relation between my understanding and the facts is really a relation between me and myself. Only at this point we are once more forced to recognize the ambiguity of the term 'self', its profound lack, in fact, of self-identity; the self which confers what I shall henceforth call a reverberatory power on facts does not seem to be identical with the self which refuses to let itself be penetrated by that power. But they are both *my* self.

Yet again, at this juncture, let us beware of being deceived by language. When I speak of a non-coincidence between the self which confers a power and the self which refuses to be penetrated by the power, I do not really mean that I have two selves. As I have already observed, that would be the case only if we were dealing with objects, and in consequence could treat what we are discussing here as a matter of elements that could be labelled and numbered off: this self, that self. But that is just what is obviously impossible. We are forced once more to make a distinction here between the notions of *difference* and *duality,* and to protest against everyday language, which, having to do above all with physical objects, inevitably contributes to the confusion of difference with duality. This is not all; we must also beware of interpreting what has been said about the reverberatory power of facts and its source in causal terms. All that I have said needs to be written out again with more care or, if you like, transposed into a key that will leave no room for any misunderstanding.

It might be interesting to go back, for the sake of clarity, to the case of the religious novice which

I brought up a short time ago. If we wanted to treat that example adequately, it would have to be in the manner of a novelist; for it would be the novelist's business to make concrete, and to give their proper respective weight to, the various data which I presented in a schematic fashion. But to achieve this the novelist would have to present the surroundings in which such a character has lived, and make clear the exact kind of pressure these surroundings have exercised on him; that is how we would be enabled to understand how in this case a failure or a romantic disappointment, which in somebody else's case might have been incidents hardly worth mentioning, have in this case assumed a tragic importance. How can we apply this with precision to what I have said earlier on in a more abstract fashion about the fact's not being external? It is quite clear that the fact only acquires its value *as* a fact because it is referred to that living centre, the character in our imaginary novel. Referred, I say: the term 'represented', which is generally current in idealist philosophy, is inadequate. It may be that the would-be monk in our story suffered because of realities which he had *not* managed to represent to himself; these realities had nevertheless become digested into the tissue of his life. Only it is a question here of what I may call a dematerialized digestion, comparable to the allusions to or reminiscences from other poems which a poet may introduce into an original work: a good example is Mr. T. S. Eliot's *The Waste Land*.

A question, or rather an objection, can hardly fail at this moment to spring to the reader's mind. I have turned my novice into a character in a novel: but is it not, in fact, only at the level of the work of imagination, such as the novel is, that the totality of facts is really referred to a sort of living centre and thus appears to be, as it were, interiorized? But I reply that the proper function of the novelist consists exclusively of enabling us to get a more distinct grip on that unity which, of course, existed in life before it existed in fiction, and which makes fiction possible. The novelist communicates directly to us something which ordinary conditions of life condemn us merely to glance at. But the novelist is in no sense the inventor of this sort of unity; and the greater a novelist is, the more he gives us the sense that he is not making anything up. I quote Charles Du Bos on Tolstoy's *War and Peace*: 'Life would speak thus, if life could speak'. I have no hesitation for my own part in saying that it is through the novelist's power of creation that we can get our best glimpse of what lies behind and under the reverberatory power of facts.

Could it not be said that this power implies the existence of a certain uncompleted structure—a structure essentially uncompleted since its foundations are in space and time? This structure extends on all sides beyond such a direct awareness as the self can have; and that awareness—a point on which we shall expatiate later—is not and cannot be shut in on itself. The less, in fact, we think of the self as a monad, the more we shall emphasize the importance of this uncompleted structure extending beyond the self. We shall also have to acknowledge the intimate affinities that exist between this structure and the body in the ordinary sense of the word, in so far as for the self the body is *this* body, *my* body. It is in connection with this structure that the problem of truth can and must be raised; I mean that if we were to do something that cannot be done, and sweep the idea of this structure away, the idea of truth would at the same time lose its meaning. We have now reached a central point in our investigation. But perhaps it will not be unprofitable to recur here to the traditional notion of the relation between truth and judgment and to see how it looks in the light of the preceding explanations.

Let us first of all notice that from this point of view, what I have called 'fact' can be regarded as a property of our postulated structure; it is in some sense integrated into the structure, and it is for this reason that it can become radiant—always allowing, as we have seen, that the self disposes itself in relation to the radiant fact so as to receive the light that streams from it. I have already had occasion to remark how much we are in danger of being misled by the use of verbs like 'receive' in such a connection. The difficulties, indeed, that have accumulated round the notion of truth are in a large part due to the embarrassment we feel when we seek to define this essential act of the 'reception' of truth. Let us say in a very general way that at this level the contrast between activity and passivity —between reception, say, considered as taking, and reception considered as being given something —loses a great deal of its meaning; in the dimension in which we now find ourselves, we must move beyond such categories.

Once again I shall choose an illustration that will enable us to see exactly what the place of judgment is. Think of a mother and father who, after deceiving themselves for a long time about their son, are forced to admit that he is abnormal; so far, in every particular case, they have made an effort to find explanations for his behaviour that would allow them to believe that, fundamentally, he is just 'like other children'. But there comes a moment when they are brought face to face with the painful truth. When we say that somebody is forced to 'face' the truth, the expression we use is extraordinarily full of meaning, and it is important to bring out all its implications. It is obvious that the notion of 'facing' the truth implies a kind of activity;

we talk, for instance, about people having the *courage* to face the truth. But nobody will admit that courage can be anything else but active: and this is true, of course, even of the courage which consists of bearing some misfortune patiently. But at the same time—and it is here the paradox lies—the idea of courage is intimately linked to that of 'having no alternative', an idea which, if it were presented in isolation, would be equivalent to an idea of mere and pure constraint. The mother and father, for instance, in the illustration I have just given, 'have no alternative but to . . .' But if the parents, in this case, are obliged to recognize their child's deficiency, do not let us forget that an obligation is always something which can be evaded to some degree. I would recall to you the character Rose Deeprose, in Sheila Kaye-Smith's fine novel of that name, who refuses to the last to admit that her child is an idiot, since, if she did make this admission, she would be obliged to put the child in an institution. In extreme cases, we are forced to ask ourselves—but it is a point on which psychiatrists would be able to enlighten us—whether what we call madness may not be, in some instances, a sort of flight from necessity.

The truth is that an obligation is something that always ought to be recognized, and that this recognition is an act. But on the other hand it does not look as if an act of this sort can ever be what is properly called a spontaneous act. It is necessary, one might say, that the facts should exercise a sort of dumb pressure on the self which will force the self, if I may put it so, to recognize the obligation which lies upon it to recognize the facts themselves. . . .

There is thus an extremely subtle reciprocal interlinking between facts and self that comes into existence every time we recognize a mortifying truth. And obviously I am far from claiming that

every truth has necessarily a mortifying character;
but for the purposes of this analysis it is interesting
to concentrate on truths of this sort, if only because it is in such cases that it is most difficult to
understand how truth can be loved.

But there is one obvious point that can be made
here; it is that after I have shirked for a long time
the recognition of a painful truth, I can find a real
consolation in opening my mind to it; the essential
quality of this consolation lies in the fact that, by
opening my mind to the truth that hurts me, I have
put an end to a long and exhausting inner struggle.
But what sort of struggle was it? Let us recall some
points we have previously made. We cannot properly talk of a struggle against the facts; for let me
repeat it, the facts have no existence or power
that is intrinsic to themselves; we ought to talk,
rather of a struggle against oneself. Here again
we find that ambiguity in the notion of the self
which I have so often remarked on: the self that is
all desire has been fighting against what I shall from
now on call the spirit of truth.

But what is it in the self that feels this consolation,
this sense of liberation, which is certainly felt when a
painful truth has been recognized? Can we think
of this spirit of truth as itself capable of feeling
joy—or of feeling pain? And on the other hand
is it not a contradiction in terms that the desiring
self, which has in a sense been conquered in the
battle, should feel a strange satisfaction in its own
defeat? Must we at this point insert some third,
mediating term—shall we speak of a self which is
neither the desiring self nor the spirit of truth? But
who can fail to recognize that this dissociation
within the self is artificial and that we cannot isolate,
in order to transform them into distinct entities,
the various aspects of a single life, which is, precisely, the life of *one* self? What we have to grasp—
and we can only succeed in doing so by exorcizing

every deceptive metaphor—is that, in the light of truth, I succeed in diminishing that permanent temptation that assails me to conceive reality, or to represent it to myself, as I should like it to be. In the light of truth, in the presence of truth; it is just—however obscure this may seem—as if this truth possessed a stimulating power, as if it were able to purify me, as a sea wind can or the piney tang of the forests. But these are only comparisons and they cannot really help us. The essential question remains and it obviously has a dominating part to play in this dark and difficult investigation. It is this: has truth a substance that is proper to it? Are we in the right in considering it, as our most recent metaphors have suggested, as a distinct power which can be given or lent to us in exchange for the difficult and praiseworthy act of opening ourselves to it? It is very clear that if this were the case we should grasp much more clearly than we have so far succeeded in doing, just how it is possible to love truth, and even to sacrifice oneself for truth. But after all, if we conceive truth in this way, are we not falling into a sort of mythology, and in our recent investigations into the idea of a structure have we not prepared ourselves to form a wholly different idea of truth—an idea of truth as strictly immanent?

However, this is just the moment to remind ourselves of what we said earlier about the impossibility of accepting, in these lectures, the opposition between the ideas of the immanent and the transcendent in its elementary form. It follows that there may perhaps be no absolute contradiction between the two aspects of truth with which we are here confronted.

Heidegger, in that essay to which I alluded at the beginning of this lecture, has emphasized the importance of the notion of openness for any theory of truth—or the notion perhaps of being opened.

His German word is 'Offenständigkeit', and the
French translators have coined 'apérité' as an equivalent. What he is really trying to do is to find a basis in
possibility for that adequation of the mind and the
thing which constitutes a true judgment as such.
Here is a piece of metal: I describe it correctly
when I say that such is its shape, such its colour,
such its market value, and so on. Allowing that
my description is an exact one, the meaning of
'exactness' in this sense is just what Heidegger is
out to define. A judgment about a thing, in so far
as it is an adequate judgment, establishes in regard
to the thing the particular relation that can be expressed by the formula: *such . . . that . . .* (It is
*such* a thing *that* it has certain qualities, it is *such*
an X *that* it is also a Y.) The essence of this
relation is what Heidegger calls, not representation,
but appresentation. To appresent is 'to allow the
thing to surge up before us in the guise of this or
that object, but in such a fashion that the judgment
lets itself be led by the thing and expresses it
just as it has presented itself. It is a necessary condition of all appresentation that the appresentating
being should be placed in the middle of a light
that will allow something to appear to that being,
be to made manifest to it. This "something" must
span or traverse a domain open to our encounter'.

The fundamental agreement between these views
and those that I have been previously expounding
should be obvious. What we have still to discover
is whether our explanations meet the whole case,
and whether they enable us to make a definitive
judgment on the possibility of treating truth as an
effective power. We must be wary here, since we
are exposed to the old danger of creating fictitious
entities out of phrases. It is all too clear on the
basis of my assumption that there is something
called the love of truth, that I shall be tempted to
give it the status of an entity: I may try to link

up the love of truth in my mind, for instance, with
the love of God. There is a whole theological background there, that is likely to affect our thinking
without our wanting it to and without our even
being distinctly aware that it is doing so; and we
should be very wary of its intrusions. I do not
say that, after a long divagation, we may not have
to rediscover this background in the end. But would
it not be very rash, for instance, to attribute to the
love of truth, as it exists in the ordinary learned
man, a religious character?

On the one hand, it seems pretty certain that the
learned man—I am thinking particularly of the
scientists, with the possible exception of the mathematical scientist—does postulate the identity of
what is and what is true; his task really is, in fact,
to discover what is, what is the case, for instance
what is the constitution of matter. But, on the
other hand, though truth and being are identical
for him from that point of view, is his love of
truth really a love of being? Does not the love of
being always have a note about it of reverence?
Is it not a love of what is created in so far as
that is the veiled expression, or the token, of the
presence of the creator? It would, I think, be quite
arbitrary to attribute to scientists and learned men
generally a reverent attitude of this sort; one would
have to admit that if this attitude does exist in
most scientists, not only are they not aware of it,
but, more often than not, it is in opposition with
their professed beliefs, or rather non-beliefs. It
seems to me that in the scientist's own eyes his
love for truth can be reduced to a passionate interest in research as such, and also, as a rather
more remote consideration, an unbounded confidence in the social utility of research. Let us suppose,
however—and unfortunately in our world today no
supposition is more plausible—that the scientist is
called upon by the State or the Party to deny

or renounce some conclusion to which his researches have led him; let us suppose that he refuses and risks being sent to a concentration camp; what exactly will be the mainspring of the heroic stand he is taking? There we have the problem that has been worrying us all along, stated as concretely as can be. The problem is harder to solve in this case because there is something, most probably, in the structure of the scientist's mind (as a non-philosopher's, a non-believer's mind) that prevents him from asking himself this question; reflection in our sense of the word is something deeply alien to him. As philosophers, or students of philosophy, we are in danger of solving his problem for him by bringing in something which runs against the very grain of his mind.

What he refuses to do is to recant. But what exactly are we to understand by that? A superficial mind will say that this is a mere matter of self-respect, or even of pride, though no doubt proper pride; if he were to recant, he would be humiliating himself. But this is certainly a false interpretation, by which I mean that it is not true to the scientist's own experience. For him, it *is not himself* that is at stake, but *truth*: the truth of which he is an interpreter and to which in a certain sense he bears witness. If he were to recant, he would be perjuring himself. But it is just the nature of this treason that he shrinks from, that we must make clear. He would be betraying truth; but, or so it would seem, we can only betray a person; is truth a person, can it be compared to a person? We do talk indeed of sinning against the light, but has this any meaning outside that world of religious experience, which we wish, as I have said, to exclude for the moment from our discussion?

Ought we not to recur here to one of the deepest notions of the Californian philosopher, Josiah Royce, and to say that the man who is engaged in

the search for truth enters into an ideal community? He becomes a citizen of a city that is not
built with stones and that is cemented only with
thought. But is it not against this city that the scientist is committing a treason when, out of fear or
out of self-interest, he recants the conclusions that
he reached in the days when he served truth loyally?

That conclusion cannot be lightly set aside; it will
obtain the support of many thinkers who have little
taste for metaphysics as such. Nevertheless, I think
it takes us only half-way to the truth. The notion
of this ideal city is only a halt, or a ledge, on a
steep, stony mountain path that must lead us much
further on. For we are still left with the problem
of how such a city is possible and what are its
foundations. Is it not the main note of this city
that it has been constructed with truth in mind and
for the purposes of truth? But that leaves the whole
problem where it was. It may be, however, that if
we can once more probe through mere words and
images, this notion of an ideal city will help us
upwards on the path towards a more distinct conception than we have yet obtained of our destination.

What are we to understand by an ideal city? Let
us put aside every characteristic that belongs specifically to a material city. What remains is the idea
of a place where people live together and where
exchanges of goods and services of all sorts take
place. Certainly, when we talk of such exchanges,
we evoke once more an image of physical trans-
actions. I bring along some banknotes and I buy
an object which has a stated price. But, after all,
there are other exchanges of an infinitely more
subtle kind. I go into a museum, for instance, and
I bring with me a certain number of ideas, or rather
a preliminary grounding of experience, which enables me to understand, or rather to appreciate,
works of art that might otherwise have left me in-

different. It may be objected that it is improper to speak of an exchange in this instance, since I 'give' nothing to the work of art; but that is only true from a grossly material point of view. There is a deeper sense in which one can say that the work is enriched by the admiration it inspires and that it undergoes, in a sense, a real growth and development. This mysterious phenomenon—which cannot, of course, leave any palpable traces—belongs, in a way, to the ideal city. Let us notice, in passing, that a town, when it deserves the name of a town, and is not a mere juxtaposition of buildings, has itself something of the function of the museum; it offers spiritual nourishment to those who live in it, and they in their turn help on the growth of what one might call its spiritual substance.

Let us see how these very simple remarks can throw some light on the notion of the ideal city itself and on its connections with the notion of truth.

As always, we have been tempted to cling to a physical representation. Just as the city of stone or wood is laid out to get the best light available, so we have imagined the ideal city as constructed in such a fashion that it can be illuminated by a truth that is external to it. But the relationship is not the same in both cases; where the city of stone or wood seems to have a prior existence in itself without the light being a necessary constituent part of that existence, the ideal city, as we have glimpsed, does draw its very existence from that other light which is truth. This certainly gives us only a very abstract and general grasp of what we are talking about, but it is enough to show how impossible it would be to represent the ideal city in an objective fashion. The best image, indeed, that we can here evoke that city by, is the simple one of a discussion about ideas in which both the conversationalists are so interested in their topic that each forgets about

himself, which is to say, really, about the personal
impression he is making on the other; for the
tiniest touch of self-complacency would lower the
tone of the discussion. The very soul of such dis-
cussions is the joy of communicating, not necessarily the joy of finding that one's views agree
with another's; and this distinction between communication and agreement has great importance. It is
just as if two climbers were tackling the same hill,
up different approaches; allowing that the climbers
can communicate directly with each other, at any
moment, through portable radio or television sets.

But there is something paradoxical in this situation, even when our imagination has grasped it
properly. Truth is at once what the two conversationalists, or the two climbers, are aware of striving
towards—and it is also what pushes them up their
hill; which is to say that it is at once in front of
them and behind them, or rather that, at this level
of discourse, this spatial contrast has no reality.

Has all this brought us nearer to the discovery of
what truth is? My reflections on what I have called
the ideal city, or merely on what is involved in the
notion of a sincere discussion between two persons, should lead us to acknowledge, it seems to
me, that when we talk of truth—just because we
are *talking* of it—we run a grave risk of placing
ourselves just at the most unfavourable standpoint
for grasping what truth may be. You will notice
that in the illustrations which have taken up so
much of this lecture I have always been anxious
to flow in the direction of a sort of current, without
asking myself precisely what the current is, what
are its characteristics, for instance whether it is a
continuous current—as Bergson seems to have
thought, who in this instance does seem to me to
have taken a large leap beyond the given facts of
experience. And this notion of a 'current', taken in
isolation, does not seem to me a completely satis-

factory notion. What I mean is that I have been
dealing with thought in so far as thought is committed to some task or other, and I have not been
asking myself exactly how thought gets such tasks
suggested to it. But all this comes down to saying
that to me it does not appear permissible to isolate
a judgment and to ask what truth is in relation to
that judgment. We have been led in this lecture,
and we shall be led more and more in subsequent
lectures, to give weight to the idea of a sort of
intercourse, which can take place both between distinct personalities and within what we call the same
personality. This will become clearer later on,
when we shall have to define the specific characteristics of intersubjectivity. We have already got a
glimpse, however, of the fact that all intercourse
takes place against what I would call a kind of
intelligible background; there would be everything
to lose if we were tempted to transform this notion
of an intelligible background into the image of a
material background; though that temptation is, in
our case, with us all the time. But though this notion of an intelligible background, or setting, is
still a misty one, does it not permit us to give a
certain body of meaning to the phrase 'within the
bounds of truth' which we used earlier in this lecture? Even more, might we not have a basis for supposing that what we call the love of truth may be
a sort of mysterious joy in moving against this
intelligible background, within this intelligible setting? Though the joy certainly is a precarious and
threatened one.

For if it is the case that we have access to this
region only under rather difficult conditions, and
under conditions on which we cannot concentrate
our attention too firmly, we can certainly not say
that we are 'native to the place', that we *naturally*
belong there. This intelligible region is not our natal
soil. It is not so, at least, unless we can conceive a

double mode of belonging, or unless, in a quite different fashion, we can think of ourselves, as Plato did, as linked to this region by mysterious threads of reminiscence. But at a first glance we have to admit that this is a strange notion, and that we cannot yet attribute to it anything more than a negative content; we see what it is not, much rather than grasp what it is.

We are thus led to the world we do naturally belong to, the world of our sense experiences, the world that constitutes us as existing creatures. And it is only very much later that we shall be able to return to the difficult notions which, towards the end of this lecture, had begun to beckon us with a distant gleam.

# CHAPTER V

## PRIMARY AND SECONDARY REFLECTION:

### THE EXISTENTIAL FULCRUM

THE questions about the nature of truth that took up our whole attention during the last lecture were certainly difficult and involved, and at a first glance it may seem strange that we should have raised them at all before turning to our present topic. But it seemed to me that a first examination of how we ought to understand the notion of truth was a necessary preliminary to everything else. That intelligible background or setting, of which we spoke towards the end of our last lecture, however hard it may be to grasp it in its essential nature, is nevertheless, (since it is not merely a place of encounter, but, as we shall gradually see more and more clearly, communication and will to communicate,) the setting against which our investigation must spread itself out. It may be objected that it is also the setting for every kind of thought that is worthy of the name of thought. Agreed: but the distinctive note of philosophic thought, at least according to my conception of it and I have many authorities for that conception, is that not only does it move towards the object whose nature it seeks to discover, but at the same time it is alert for a certain music that arises from its own inner nature if it is succeeding in carrying out its task. We have already said that the point about philosophic thought is that it is reflective; and it is into the nature of reflection, as an activity, that we must now probe more deeply than we have done so far.

As usual, I shall start with the simplest examples I can find, to show how reflection has its roots in the daily flow of life.

I put my hand, let us say, into my pocket to take my watch out. I discover that my watch is not there; but it ought to be there; normally my watch *is* in my pocket. I experience a slight shock. There has been a small break in the chain of my everyday habits (between the act of putting my hand in my pocket and that of taking out my watch). The break is felt as something out of the way; it arrests my attention, to a greater or a less degree, according to the importance I attach to my watch; the notion that a valuable object may be lost arises in my mind, and this notion is not a mere notion but also a feeling of disquiet. I call in reflection to help me . . . but let us be careful here not to fall into the errors of an out-of-date psychology which isolated one faculty of the mind from another. It is very clear in the example I have chosen, and in every similar example, that reflection is nothing other than attention, in the case where attention is directed towards this sort of small break in the daily chain of habit. To reflect, in this kind of case, is to ask oneself how such a break can have occurred. But there is no place here for the kind of purely abstract speculation which, of its very nature, can have no practical outcome; what I have to do is to go back in time until I recall the moment when the watch was last in my possession. I remember, let us say, having looked at the time just after breakfast; therefore at that moment everything was still all right. Between then and now something must have happened to the watch. My mental processes are rather like—there is no avoiding the comparison—the actions of a plumber who is trying to trace a leak. Was there perhaps a hole in my pocket? I look at my pocket and discover that there is no hole. I continue with my task of alert recapitulation. Say that I succeed in recalling the fact that there was a moment when I put the watch down on a table; I shall go, of course, to see whether it is still on the table; and there, let us say, the watch still is. Reflection has carried out its task, and the problem is solved. . . . Let us notice, however, even in connection with this almost childishly simple example, that I have made my mental effort because something real, something valuable, was at stake. Reflection is never exercised on things that are not worth the trouble of reflecting about. And, from another point of view, let us notice that reflection in this case was a personal act, and an act which nobody else would have been able to undertake in my place, or on my behalf. The act of reflection is linked, as bone is linked with bone in the human body, to living personal experience; and it is important to understand the nature of this link. To all appearances, it is necessary that the living personal experience should bump into some sort of obstacle. One is tempted to use the following sort of metaphor. A man who has been travelling on foot arrives at the edge of a river where the bridge has been carried away by a flood. He has no option but to call a ferryman. In an example such as that which I have just cited, reflection does really play the part of the ferryman.

But the same sort of thing can happen, of course, at the level of the inner life. I am talking to a friend, and somehow I let myself be drawn into telling him something which is an actual lie. I am alone with myself again, I get a grip on myself, I face the fact of this lie; how was it possible for me to tell such a whopper? I am all the more surprised at myself because I have been accustomed to think of myself, up to the present, as a truthful and trustworthy

person. But then what importance ought I to attach
to this lie? Am I forced to conclude that I am not
the man I thought I was? And, from another point
of view, what attitude ought I to take up towards
this act of mine? Ought I to confess the lie to my
friend, or on the other hand would I make myself
ridiculous by doing so? But perhaps I ought to make
myself ridiculous, to let my friend laugh at me, as a
sort of punishment for having told him the lie in the
first place?

As in the previous example, what we have here
is a kind of break; that is to say, I cannot go on just
as if nothing had happened; there really is something
that necessitates an act of readjustment on my part.

But here is a third example that will give us an
easier access to the notion of reflection at the
properly philosophical level. I have been disappointed
by the behavior of somebody of whom I was fond.
So I am forced to revise my opinion of this friend
of mine. It seems, indeed, that I am forced to
acknowledge that he is not the man I believed him
to be. But it may be that the process of reflection
does not halt there. A memory comes back to me
—a memory of something I myself did long ago, and
suddenly I ask myself: 'Was this act of mine really
so very different from the act which today I feel
inclined to judge so severely? But in that case am
I in any position to condemn my friend?' Thus
my reflections, at this point, call my own position
into question. Let us consider this second stage.
Here, again, I cannot go on as if nothing had
happened. Then, what has happened? There has
been this memory and this sort of confrontation
that has been forced upon me, of myself and the
person I was judging so harshly. But what does
'myself' mean here? The point is that I have been
forced to ask myself what I am worth, how true
I ring. So far I had taken myself, so to speak, for
granted, I quite naturally thought of myself as quali-

fied to judge and eventually to condemn. Or perhaps
even that is not quite the case: I used to behave
or, what comes to the same thing, I used to talk
like a man qualified to judge others. In my heart
of hearts, I did not really think of myself as such
a man . . . Here, for the moment at least, this
process of reflection may terminate. Such reflections
may leave me in a mood of anguish, and nevertheless I have a certain sense of being set free, the
sense of which I spoke in the last lecture: it is as
if I had overturned some obstruction in my way.

But at this point a twofold and important reali-
zation is forced upon me; on the one hand, I am
now able to communicate at a broader level with
myself, since I have, as it were, introduced the self
that committed the dubious act to the self that did
not hesitate to set itself up as the harsh judge of such
acts in others; and on the other hand—and this
cannot be a mere coincidence—I am now able to
enter into far more intimate communication with
my friend, since between us there no longer stands
that barrier which separates the judge on the bench
from the accused man in the dock.

We have here a very striking illustration of that
important notion of intercourse, on which I was
expatiating the other day, and no doubt we shall
later have to remember this illustration when we
begin to disucss the topic of intersubjectivity properly so called.

But meanwhile there are certain other observations on the relations between reflection and life
that are pertinent at this point. There is a kind of
philosophy, essentially romantic, or at least romantic in its roots, which very willingly contrasts reflection and life, sets them at opposite poles from each
other; and it is permissible to notice that this contrast, or this opposition, is often stated in metaphors
of heat and cold. Reflection, because it is critical,
is cold; it not only puts a bridle on the vital impulses,

it freezes them. Let us, in this case too, take a concrete example.

A young man has let himself be drawn into saying rash things to a girl. It was during a dance, he was intoxicated by the atmosphere, by the music, the girl herself was a girl of unusual beauty. The dance is over, he comes home, he feels the intoxication of the evening wearing away. To his sobered mood, reflection does present itself, in such a case, as something purely and merely critical: what is this adventure going to lead to? He has not the sort of job that would make marriage a reasonable proposition; if he were to marry this girl, they would have to lead a narrow, constricted life; what would become of love in such sordid circumstances? And so on, and so on . . . It is obvious that in such cases reflection is like the plunge under an icy shower that wakens one from a pleasant morning dreaminess. But it would be very rash to generalize from such examples, and even in regard to this particular example we ought to ask ourselves rather carefully what real relationship between reflection and life it illustrates. For I think we must be on our guard against a modern way of interpreting life as pure spontaneity. For that matter, I am not sure that spontaneity is, for the philosopher, a really distinct notion; it lies somewhere on these shadowy borders where psychology and biology run into each other and merge. The young Spanish philosopher, Julian Marias, has something relevant and useful to say about this in his *Introduction to Philosophy*.* He says that the verb 'to live' had no doubt a precise meaning, a meaning that can be clearly formulated, when it is applied, say, to a sheep or a shark: it means to breathe by means of this organ and not that (by lungs or gills, as the case may be), to be nourished in such and such a fashion (by preying on other fish, by cropping grass), and so on. But

*Introduction à la Philosophie. Madrid, 1947.

when we are talking about human life the verb 'to
live' cannot have its meaning so strictly circum-
scribed; the notion of human life cannot be reduced
to that of the harmonious functioning of a certain
number of organs, though that purely biological
functioning is, of course, presupposed in the notion
of human life. For instance, a prisoner who has
no hope of getting out of jail may say without exaggeration—though he continues to breathe, to eat,
to perform all his natural functions—that his existence is not really a life. The mother of an air-
man might say in wartime, 'While my son is risking
his life, I am not really living'. All this is enough
to make it clear that a human life has always its
centre outside itself; though it can be centred, certainly, on a very wide and diverse range of outside
interests. It may be centred on a loved one, and
with the disappearance of the loved one be reduced
to a sad caricature of itself; it may be centred on
something trivial, a sport like hunting, a vice like
gambling; it can be centred on some high activity,
like research or creation. But each one of us can
ask himself, as a character in one of my plays does,
'What do I live by?' And this is not a matter so
much of some final purpose to which a life may be
directed as of the mental fuel that keeps a life
alight from day to day. For there are, as we know
only too well, desperate creatures who waste away,
consuming themselves like lamps without oil.

But from this point of view, from the human point
of view, we can no longer think of life as mere and
pure spontaneity—and by the same token we can
no longer think of reflection as life's antagonist. On
the contrary, it seems to me essential that we should
grasp the fact that reflection is still part of life, that
it is one of the ways in which life manifests itself, or,
more profoundly, that it is in a sense one of life's
ways of rising from one level to another. That, in
fact, is the very point of the last few examples we

have been taking. We should notice also that reflection can take many different shapes and that even
conversion can be, in the last analysis, a sort of reflective process; consider the hero of Tolstoy's *Resurrection* or even Raskolnikov in *Crime and Punishment*. We can say therefore that reflection appears
alien to life, or opposed to life, only if we are reducing the concept of human life to, as it were, a manifestation of animality. But it must be added that if
we do perform this act of reduction, then reflection
itself becomes an unintelligible concept; we cannot
even conceive by what sort of a miracle reflection
could be grafted on mere animality.

So much for the relations between reflection and
life; we would reach similar conclusions about the
relations between reflection and experience, and this
links up with what has been previously said. If I take
experience as merely a sort of passive recording
of impressions, I shall never manage to understand
how the reflective process could be integrated with
experience. On the other hand, the more we grasp
the notion of experience in its proper complexity,
in its active and I would even dare to say in its
dialectical aspects, the better we shall understand
how experience cannot fail to transform itself into
reflection, and we shall even have the right to say
that the more richly it is experience, the more, also,
it is reflection. But we must, at this point, take one
step more and grasp the fact that reflection itself
can manifest itself at various levels; there is primary
reflection, and there is also what I shall call secondary reflection; this secondary reflection has, in fact,
been very often at work during these early lectures,
and I dare to hope that as our task proceeds it will
appear more and more clearly as the special high
instrument of philosophical research. Roughly, we
can say that where primary reflection tends to dissolve the unity of experience which is first put before
it, the function of secondary reflection is essentially

recuperative; it reconquers that unity. But how is such a reconquest possible? The possibility is what we are going to try to show by means of the quite general, the (in the parliamentary sense) privileged, example on which we must now concentrate our attention. We shall soon see that what we have to deal with here is not merely, in fact, an illustration or an example, but an actual way of access to a realm that is assuredly as near to us as can be, but that nevertheless, by a fatality (a perfectly explicable fatality, however), has been, through the influence of modern thought, set at a greater and greater distance from us; so that the realm has become more and more of a problematic realm, and we are forced to call its very existence into question. I am talking about the self, about that reality of the self, with which we have already come in contact so often, but always to be struck by its disquieting ambiguity.

We are now embarking upon the question on which, really, all the other questions hang: it is the question I put when I ask myself who I am and, more deeply still, when I probe into my meaning in asking myself that question.

There is a remark which, in such a setting, may appear trifling and even farcical; yet it is interesting, one must say it, at this point to remind ourselves of how very often nowadays we are called upon to fill in forms establishing what is called our identity. The multiplication of such forms today is significant, and its causes should be looked into; it is tied up, of course, with that growth of bureaucracy we have already spoken of. That growth has a sinister, metaphysical significance, though that significance, apart from such a writer as Kafka and his more thoughtful readers, is not yet generally recognized. My point now is that when one fills in such a form one has a silly feeling—as if one were putting on fancy dress, not to go to a costume ball, but to set about one's daily labours. The most precise fashion in which I can express this feeling in general terms is as follows: I have not a consciousness of *being* the person who is entered under the various headings thus: *son of, born at, occupation,* and so on. Yet everything I enter under these headings is strictly true; I should be guilty of telling a lie if I varied the entries from form to form, and, besides that, I would be risking serious trouble. If this form-filling is a game, it is a game I am forced to play. But what is really remarkable is that the filling in of any such form whatsoever would give me the same silly feeling, unless, for a single moment, I could exercise my creative faculty by inventing an identity of my own choice; only the strange thing is that after a short time this invented identity, if I were forced to stick to it, would give me a feeling of peculiar, intimate disgust—like some shabby garment, not my own, that I was forced to drag around with me everywhere. It is, in fact, against the existence of such garments that I have to protest: *I* am not this garment. . . . A mental specialist might say that we are here on a dangerous path that can lead to mythomania or even actual insanity. But such a remark has a merely practical value, and is irrelevant to our present speculative discussion. The point I want to make now is that this feeling about identity forms that I have been talking about is no doubt completely foreign to many people: but why? Must we say that such people quite lack the sense of fantasy? I think we can go further and say that the absence of this uneasiness must be linked to a total deficiency as far as the faculty of creation is concerned. Later on, we shall see more clearly why this is so.

Let us try to imagine, now, the sheer dumbfoundedness of the civil servant who, on asking me, 'So you are Mr. So-and-so?' received the curt reply 'Certainly not'. He would arrive at only one of two conclusions: either this person is insane, or he is

passing under a false identity. But what is quite
certain is that he would never begin to suspect that
for me and him the verb 'to be' in that sentence—
'*Are* you Mr. So-and-so?'—has a quite different
meaning. If I am a person of common sense, therefore, I shall try not to step outside the very narrow
limits in which what such a creature calls his mind
functions, and to stick loyally to his categories, to
the headings on the form which he wishes me to
fill up, however rudimentary these categories may
appear to me to be.

But in compensation there is nothing to stop me
personally from facing up to the strange duality
which seems to be implied in the uneasiness with
which I regard an identity form, and asking myself certain direct questions: if I cannot satisfy myself
by saying, 'I am Mr. So-and-so, the son of Mr.
So-and-So, living in Paris or wherever it may be',
what then is the urgent inner need which makes me
aware of this dissatisfaction? *Really*, who am I?

I should like to observe, in the first place, that
the question put by the civil servant—'So you', let us
say, 'are Mr. So-and-so, and these are your particulars?'—has to do with somebody or other, or
rather with some one definite somebody, of whom
one might say that he springs to attention, as a
soldier does, when his number is called out. It is
just as if somebody had said to me: 'State the identity
of Number 98', and as if I had the job of answering
for this unfortunate Number 98—as if Number 98
were illiterate for instance, and so could not fill in
the form, or were deaf, and so could not hear the
question. But I, who am forced to answer for Number 98, who am I, really? The real fact, the thing
that complicates the whole business, that is, the truth
of it, is that I am myself and not somebody else;
if I were somebody else, the question would be put
again, when my turn came up, but it would still be
exactly the same sort of question. There is thus,

or so it seems to me, a sense in which I am not a definite somebody; from the moment when I start to reflect, I am bound to appear to myself as a, as it were, non-somebody linked in a profoundly obscure fashion, with a somebody about whom I am being questioned and about whom I am certainly not free to answer just what I like at the moment when I am being questioned.

These are the conclusions at which we can arrive after a first examination of our topic. We shall certainly have to go beyond them. Nevertheless, they throw some light on an aspect of the situation which we cannot pass over without some further comment.

It is only in so far as I assert myself to be, in one sense, not merely a somebody, that I can acknowledge two facts; firstly, that there is another sense in which I *am* a somebody, a particular individual (though not merely that), and secondly that other somebodies, other particular individuals, also exist. Let us point out that a solipsistic type of idealism would never be able to grasp the fact of my existence, in so far as it is a somebody's existence, neither do I possess any particular ontological privilege in relation to all the other somebodies; indeed, one may go further, it is obvious that if I am a somebody, a particular individual, I am only so at once in connection with and in opposition to an indefinite number of other somebodies; and this enables us to solve *a priori,* and without any trouble at all, a problem which the philosophers of the past have woven into wantonly intricate tangles: the problem of how I can be certain that anybody, or anything, other than myself, exists.

In compensation, we have still a paradox of our own to play with, the central fact that I appear to myself both as a somebody and not a somebody, a particular individual and not a particular individual, and at this point we must probe a little more deeply into that paradox. Can we get a closer grip on this experience of the self as not being a somebody? Can we assign a positive character to this experience? The experience consists, it seems to me, in recognizing that the definite characteristics that constitute the self in so far as I grasp it as a particular individual, a somebody, have a contingent character— but contingent in relation to what? Can I really truthfully say that, at the same time as I grasp myself as a somebody, I also grasp myself as universal mind? In spite of some testimonies, like those of Amiel in his *Journal*, it would, I think, be rash to claim this. This mysterious reality in relation to which I see the definite characteristics of my particular individuality as contingent is not really an object for me—or if it is an object, it is one completely hidden by a veil, which seems self-contradictory, for it is part of the notion of an object that it is at least partly unveiled. I shall feel tempted to say, therefore, that it is in relation to myself as subject that these definite characteristics of my particular individuality are felt to be, and acknowledged to be, contingent. But will the introduction of the term 'subject' get us out of the wood here? In what sense can I grasp myself as a subject without, to the very degree that I do grasp myself, turning myself into an object? But we should not allow ourselves to be halted here by difficulties which arise, in the last analysis, from an attempt to interpret philosophical thought as springing from the grammatical structure of language; the accusative case being linked, in that structure, to the object, and to the process of objectivization. One, in fact, of the most serious weaknesses of philosophy up to our own times seems to me to have consisted in an outrageous over-simplification (I have already made such a point and we shall have to go into the whole topic much more closely) of the relationships that bind me to myself a failure to see that an indefinite, perhaps an infinite, number of such relationships can be specified; for I can behave to myself as a master, as a friend, as an antagonist, and so on . . . I can treat myself as a stranger and, on the other hand, as somebody with whom I am intimate. But to treat myself as somebody with whom I am intimate is to be in touch with myself as a subject. That feeling, which has always been so strong, not only among Christian mystics, but in, for instance, a Stoic like Marcus Aurelius, of a certain sacred reality in the self cannot be separated from an apprehension of the self in its subjectivity.

Nevertheless, if we push our analysis a little further, we cannot fail to strike upon a disconcerting fact. Of this self, felt and recognized as *not* being the self of some particular individual, can we strictly say that it exists? Of course, the answer will be that it primarily depends upon what one means by 'exists'; nevertheless, I am forced to take account of very numerous cases in which I do not hesitate to say, without running any risk of contradiction, that somebody or something exists; the real question is whether the current use of the verb 'to exist' (quite apart from all the notional elaborations of the idea of existence in recent philosophy) permits us to say that this 'veiled reality' also exists. I have no doubt about the answer: it is in the negative. In the usual sense of the verb 'to exist', a sense, of course, which we shall have to define by and by, this reality, taken in isolation, does not exist—which does not necessarily mean that it is imaginary, for there is no *a priori* reason for postulating a relationship between the actual and the imaginary, such that what is not actual must be imaginary, and what is not imaginary must be actual.

But we must now ask ourselves, still holding back from any attempt to define the notion of existence, if there is any touchstone of existence, or rather any existence that will itself serve as a touchstone, that we can put a name to: to be as precise as possible, do I know of an existence such that, if I were to deny it, any assertion by me that anything else at all existed would become quite inconceivable? Let us notice that we are here at the level of phenomenology and not of ontology; in the old-fashioned terms, of appearance and not reality, of manifestation and not ground. The question I am asking myself is by no means a question of the following order: whether in the hierarchy of being there is an absolute existent—which could only, of course, be God—such that it confers existence, that the derivative existence of everything else proceeds from it. No, I am talking merely about myself, in so far as I make a judgment that something or other exists, and I am asking myself whether there is some central significance of existence, or some centrally significant existence in relation to which all these judgments are arrayed and organized. If there is, I would call it an existential indubitable. Now this centrally significant existence, my denial of which entails the inconceivability of my asserting any other existence, is simply, of course, myself, in so far as I feel sure that I exist. But the exact implications of that statement must be carefully elicited; for I risk, at this point, a head-on collision with total or modified scepticism.

Total scepticism would consist in saying: 'I am not sure either that something exists or what sort of a something it would be that could exist'. But to assert, in this way, that perhaps nothing exists implies the previous taking up of two positions; firstly, I lay down a criterion, no doubt a vague, inexplicit criterion, failing to satisfy which nothing can be said to exist; secondly, I ask myself whether anything I am directly acquainted with satisfies that criterion, and come to the conclusion that I am not quite sure. I will risk saying that a question framed in such hazily defined terms lacks even metaphysical significance; but at the phenomenological level, at least, it is quite obviously meaningless. From our phenomenological point of view, we have only to consider that for us, in the everyday experience we start from, there is that which exists and that which does not exist, and to ask ourselves what meaning we attach to this distinction; we need not ask ourselves whether this existence of everyday experience is or is not an absolute existence, nor whether these two terms, absolute and existent, are congruous with each other, that is whether the notion of an absolute existent conveys anything to the mind. That is a problem which we must tackle much later, in the context of all our other problems.

Relative or modified scepticism, on the other hand, would consist in saying: 'Possibly I myself do not really exist, I who am asking questions about existence'. Here, I think, we do really run our heads against the existential indubitable. But we must remember that a certain caution is necessary even at this point. If, in the question, 'Do *I* exist?' I take the 'I' separately and treat it as a sort of mental object that can be isolated, a sort of 'that', and if I take the question as meaning: 'Is or is not existence something that can be predicated of this "that"?' the question does not seem to suggest any answer to itself, not even a negative answer. But this would prove simply that the question had been badly put, that it was, if I may say so, a vicious question. It was vicious for two reasons: because the 'I' cannot in any case whatsoever be treated as a 'that', because the 'I' is the very negation of the 'that', of any 'that' whatsoever and also because existence is not a predicate, as Kant seems to have established once and for all, in the *Critique of Pure Reason*.

If therefore the 'I exist' can be taken as an indubitable touchstone of existence, it is on condition that it is treated as an indissoluble unity: the 'I' cannot be considered apart from the 'exist'.

It seems necessary, however, to probe more deeply still, for I think a discussion about the nature of this pure immediacy—the pure immediacy expressed by the 'I exist'—must inevitably intrude at this point. One might, in particular, be tempted to say that the self's immediate certitude of its existence pertains essentially to its sense-experience; and some modern philosophers might be tempted to substitute for the *Cogito, ergo sum* of Descartes a *Sentio, ergo sum.* It would be easy, to be sure, to show that this change is a mere change in appearance; for from the moment that, in a mental process, there intervenes anything resembling the process of inference (like the *ergo* in *Sentio, ergo sum*), there we have thought; the *sentio* masks a *cogito*, or rather it is itself a *cogito* in an enshrouded and indistinct state. On the other hand the *sum* itself, the affirmation, 'I exist', seems to lie at another level; above, as it were, and on the banks of every possible current of inference. This is what Claudel expresses with peculiar pungency in the opening lines of his *Tête d'Or*:

Here am I,
Weak, ignorant,
A new man in the face of unknown things,
And I turn my face to the year and the rainy
    arc, my heart is full of weariness,
I lack knowledge or force for action. What shall
    I utter, what shall I undertake? How shall I use
    these dangling hands, these feet of mine that
    draw me on like dreams?

In such lines, we are up against existence in all its nakedness. But I would rather evoke another image, that of the small child who comes up to us with shining eyes, and who seems to be saying: 'Here I am! What luck!' As I wrote a few years ago in my *Diary* (1943:) 'When I say, not that I am, but that I exist. . . . I glimpse more or less obscurely the fact that my being is not only present to my own awareness but that it is a manifest being. It might be

better, indeed, instead of saying, "I exist", to say,
"I am manifest". The Latin prefix *ex*—meaning
*out, outwards, our from*—in "exist" has the greatest
importance. I exist—that is as much as to say: I have
something to make myself known and recognized
both by others and by myself, even if I wear borrowed plumes.' There is, to be sure, one difficulty
that seems to arise in this connection; we may be
tempted to make a distinction between the fact of
existing and that of saying, to others or to oneself,
that one does exist. But in such a context perhaps
the verb 'to say' is ambiguous. To clear away that
ambiguity as far as possible, let me say that this impossibility of doubting one's own existence of which
we have been talking seems to be linked to a kind of
exclamatory awareness of oneself; this awareness is
expressed in the small child (and, indeed, perhaps
already at the level of consciousness of the higher
animals) by cries, by leaps, and so on, though naturally with the adult its expression is more measured
and restrained—more and more so, the more, for
the adult, that immediacy of self-awareness is crusted
over by habits and by all the superstructures of an
official, compartmentalized life; it is pretty certain,
in fact, that we are all tending to become bureau-
crats, and not only in our outward behaviour, but
in our relations with ourselves. This is as much as to
say that between ourselves and existence we are
interposing thicker and thicker screens.

But even if this is the case, we must still say,
quite peremptorily, that existence and the exclamatory awareness of existence cannot be really separated; the dissociation of the two can be carried
out only at the cost of robbing the subject of our
investigation of its proper nature; separated from
that exclamatory self-awareness (the child's, 'Here
I am! What luck!), existence tends to be reduced to
its own corpse; and it lies outside the power of any
philosophy whatsoever to resuscitate such a corpse.

But what we should specially notice here, and what cannot be too much underlined, is the massive character of this self, this existential indubitable. If we are, as I think we are, in the presence here of a key datum, or rather a datum on which everything else hinges, we should also acknowledge from the first that this datum is not transparent to itself; nothing could bear a smaller likeness to the transcendental ego, which already in a certain sense in Kant's case, but much more noticeably among his successors, had taken its stance, as it were, at the very heart and center of the philosophical arena. This non-transparency is implied in the fact, which I mentioned earlier, that I postulate myself as existing both for myself and for others; and when I do so, whatever I am asserting cannot be considered apart from the datum which is now going to take up our attention, I mean, my body; my body in so far as it is *my* body, my body in so far as it has the character, in itself so mysterious, which we are expressing here by saying it is something I *possess*, something that belongs to me.

Let us note at once that there could be no clearer example than that which we are now beginning to consider of the special part played in thought by secondary, by what I have called recuperative, reflection. Primary reflection, on the contrary, for its part, is forced to break the fragile link between me and my body that is constituted here by the word 'mine'. The body that I call my body is in fact only one body among many others. In relation to these other bodies, it has been endowed with no special privileges whatsoever. It is not enough to say that this is objectively true, it is the precondition of any sort of objectivity whatsoever, it is the foundation of all scientific knowledge (in the case we are thinking of, of anatomy, of physiology, and all their connected disciplines). Primary reflection is therefore forced to take up an attitude of radical detachment, of complete lack of interest, towards the fact that this particular body happens to be *mine;* primary reflection has to recall the facts that this body has just the same properties, that it is liable to suffer the same disorders, that it is fated in the end to undergo the same destruction, as any other body whatsoever. Objectively speaking, it is non-privileged; and yet spontaneously, naively, I do have a tendency to delude myself about it, and to attribute to it—in relation to this malady, or that—a sort of mysterious immunity; sad experience, however, in most cases dissipates such an illusion, and primary reflection forces me to acknowledge that the facts must be as I have stated them.

Let it be clearly understood that secondary reflection does not set out flatly to give the lie to these propositions; it manifests itself rather by a refusal to treat primary reflection's separation of this body, considered as just a body, a sample body, some body or other, from the self that I am, as final. Its fulcrum, or its springboard, is just that massive, indistinct sense of one's total existence which a short time ago we were trying, not exactly to define (for, as the condition which makes the defining activity possible, it seems to be prior to all definition) but to give a name to and evoke, to locate as an existential centre.

It is easy to see that the dualism of body and soul, as it is postulated, for instance, in the Cartesian philosophy, springs from primary reflection, though in one peculiarly obscure passage, indeed, Descartes was led into talking of the union of body and soul as a third substance; but what I propose to do here is not, in fact, to comment on such well-known philosophical doctrines, but to get directly to grips with that non-transparent datum, which is constituted by my body felt as *my* body, before primary reflection has performed its task of dissociating the notion of body from the notion of what is intimately mine. But how will secondary reflection proceed in this case? It can only, it might seem, get to work on the processes to which primary reflection has itself had recourse; seeking, as it were, to restore a semblance of unity to the elements which primary reflection has first severed. However, even when engaged in this attempt at unification, the reflective process would in reality still remain at the primary stage, since it would remain a prisoner in the hands of the very oppositions which it, itself, had in the first instance postulated, instead of calling the ultimate validity of these oppositions into question.

Everything, however, becomes fairly clear if we set the matter in the following perspective, keeping within the limits of that traditional logic, the logic not of the process but of the thing, which remains faithful to the age-old distinction between the subject and the predicate. With the categories of such a logic in mind, we shall be led either to consider the body and soul as two distinct things between which some determinable relationship must exist, some relationship capable of abstract formulation, or to think of the body as something of which the soul as we improperly call it, is the predicate, or on the other hand of the soul as something of which the body, as we improperly call it, is the predicate. The arguments that tell against the two latter interpretations have been put forward so often, and besides are so obvious in themselves, that I do not think there would be any point in going over them again now. Besides, they are implied in the whole general drift of our investigation. There remains to be considered a dualism of body and soul which can, however, take extremely different forms; we can have psycho-physical parallelism, as in Spinoza, or we can have psycho-physical interactionism. But in both cases, body and soul, at least, are treated as *things*, and things, for the purposes of logical discourse, become *terms*, which one imagines as strictly defined, and as linked to each other by some de-

terminable relation. I want to show that if we reflect
on what is implied by the datum of my body, by
what I cannot help calling *my* body, this postulate
that body and soul are *things* must be rejected; and
this rejection entails consequences of the first importance.

We should notice, in the first place, that to say
'my body' is to reject psycho-physical parallelism;
for it is to postulate a certain intimacy of relation
ship between me (whatever exactly I mean by 'me'
here) and my body for which the parallelist schema
has no place. I may be told that my belief in the
existence of this intimacy is a simple illusion on
my part, which it is the business of the philosopher,
as such, to clear out of the way. But let us remember,
once more, that we are proceeding, throughout the
whole of this discussion, in a strictly phenomenological fashion; that is to say, we are accepting our
everyday experience, and asking ourselves what implications we can draw from it. From this phenomenological point of view we have to ask ourselves
where the philosopher, who is eager to clear this
illusory belief out of the way, is taking his stand.
He is taking his stand on some height where he has
abstracted from his own experience, where he has
put aside, as unworthy of consideration, the fact that
he himself has this feeling of an intimate connection
between himself and his body; but it is surely permissible to think, in that case, that for the richness
of experience he is substituting mere abstract
schemas, and that, far from transcending experience,
he has not yet reached the stage of grappling with
it. From my own point of view, all I have to bear
in mind is that my own experience implies the
possibility of behaving in a various number of definite ways towards my own body; I can yield to its
whims, or on the other hand I can try to master it.
It can become my tyrant, but I can also, or so it
seems, make it my slave. It is only by sheer prodi-

gies of acrobatic sophistry that I can fit these facts
into the framework of the parallelist thesis; and at
the point in our discussion we have now reached,
I can see no worthwhile reason for trying to do so.
In compensation every experience of this kind does
presuppose, as its basis, that opaque datum: *my*
body. What we must now see is whether an analysis
of the notion of ownership in general—of whatever the 'my' of 'my body' implies—can set that
datum in a clearer and more penetrating light.

Is my body *my* body, for instance, in the same
sense in which I would say that my dog belongs to
me? The question, let us first of all notice, of how
the dog originally came into my hands is quite irrelevant here. Perhaps I found it wandering wretch-
edly about the streets, perhaps I bought it in
a shop; I can say it is mine if nobody else puts in
a claim for it—though this is still quite a negative
condition of ownership. For the dog to be really,
not merely nominally, mine there must exist between us a more positive set of relations. He must
live, either with me, or as I, and I alone, have
decided he shall live—lodged, perhaps, with a servant or a farmer; whether or not I look after him
personally, I must assume the responsibility for his
being looked after. And this implies something reciprocal in our relations. It is only if the dog recognizes me, obeys me, expresses by his behaviour towards me some feeling which I can interpret as
affection or, at the very least, as wholesome fear,
that he is really mine; I would become a laughing-
stock if I persisted in calling an animal that completely ignored me, that took no notice of me at all,
*my* dog. And the mockery to which I would be exposed in such an instance is very significant. It is
linked to a very positive idea of how things must be
between my dog and me, before I can really say,
'This dog is mine'.

Let us now try to see what relationship there may

be between such a mode of ownership and the link between myself and my body that makes my body mine. We are forced to recognize that the analogy is rather a full and exact one. There is first of all my indisputable claim to my body, as to my dog. I recall, in this connection, the title of a very bad novel that came out in Paris a few years ago: *My Body is My Own*. This claim, this right to one's own body, this instinctive feeling that my body belongs to me, can be held in check only under slavery. The slave's master thinks, on the contrary, that the slave's body belongs to him; because he has bought that body, or for some other reason that has to do with a particular historical situation. But it must be pointed out that even where slavery exists as a social fact, it is always more or less obscurely resented by the slave himself as essentially unjust and not to be justified, as incompatible with a human right written, as it were, into the very build of the slave's own nature; and I would even go as far as to say that a creature who had lost even the very obscurest awareness of the rape committed on him by slavery would no longer be quite human. But that is a limit which, so long as life itself persists, can never be quite reached; the slave really cannot rid himself of the feeling that his body is his own.

When it comes to the question of looking after my dog, or my body, the analogy is still relevant. Thinking of my body, I am bound to envisage the inescapable responsibility laid upon me to provide for its subsistence. Here, too, there is a limit, though this time an upper limit, that implied by a total asceticism; but here too we are leaving life, though leaving it at a more elevated level (it is the yogi, of course, rather than the Christian Fathers of the Desert, that I have in mind). We should notice, also, that these two ideal limits, these two possibilities—that the slave might say, 'This body is not mine', and the yogi, 'Looking after this body is not

my responsibility'—are in the highest degree characteristic of our situation or our condition, call it
what you will. This is a fact we must never lose
sight of.

Finally, what I have said about the dog's obedience applies also to my union with my body; my
body is only properly mine to the degree to which
I am able to control it. But here, too, there is a
limit, an inner limit; if as a consequence of some
serious illness, I lose all control of my body, it tends
to cease to be *my* body, for the very profound
reason that, as we say in the common idiom, I
am 'no longer myself'. But at the other extreme,
possibly as a yogi I also cease to be myself, and
that for the opposite reason, because the control
exercised by the yogi over his body is absolute,
whereas in the mean position which is that of what
we call normal life, such control is always partial,
always threatened to some degree.

Having recognized the fulness and exactness of this
analogy, we must interpret it, but not without first
recognizing that, in spite of its fulness and exactness, it has its specious side; my dog, like, to be sure,
any other object that belongs to me, presents itself
to me as something distinct from that spatio-temporal being that I am, as external to that being.
Literally speaking, it does not form part of that
being, though after a long association between my
dog and myself a special and mysterious link may be
created, something that comes very near, and in a
rather precise fashion, to what we shall later call
intersubjectivity.

But our central problem here has to do with the
idea of *having* as such. It is not, I think, very
difficult to see that my link with my body is really
the model (a model not shaped, but felt) to which
I relate all kinds of ownership, for instance my
ownership of my dog; but it is not true that this
link can *itself* be defined as a sort of ownership. In

other words it is by what literally must be called
a paralogism that I seek to think through my relationship with my body, starting off with my relationship
with my dog. The truth is rather that *within* every
ownership, every kind of ownership I excercise, there
is this kernel that I feel to be there at the centre;
and this kernel is nothing other than the experience
—an experience which of its very nature cannot
be formulated in intellectual terms—by which my
body is mine.

We can throw at least a little light on our argument at this point by making the following observation. The self that owns things can never, even in
thought, be reduced to a completely dematerialized
ego. It seems to me impossible even to conceive
how a dematerialized ego could have any claim,
or any care, to possess anything; but the two notions
of claiming and caring are implied, of course, in
every case of something's being possessed.

In the second place—and this observation derives
from, and may throw light on, that previously made
—my possessions, in so far as I really hold to them,
or cling to them, present themselves to me as felt
additions to, or completions of, my own body. This
becomes extraordinarily clear at any moment when,
for whatever reason, the link between myself and my
possessions is snapped or even threatened. I have
at such moments a sort of *rending* feeling which
seems quite on all fours with my feeling when the
actual wholeness of my body is threatened in some
way; and indeed such words as 'rending' or 'wrenching', which are quite commonly used to express people's feelings about losing their possessions, are
themselves very significant in this connection.

I shall say once more that *having,* possessing, owning, in the strong and exact sense of the term, has to
be thought of in analogy with that unity, a unity
*sui generis,* which is constituted by my body in so far
as it is *my* body. No doubt, as I have already said,

in the case of external having, possessing, ownership, the unity is imperfect; the object that I possess
can be lost, can be stolen, can be damaged or de-
cayed—while I, the dispossessed possessor, remain.
I remain, but affected by my loss, and the more
affected the more deeply, the more strongly I was,
if I may coin the term, a *haver*. The tragedy of all
having invariably lies in our desperate efforts to make
ourselves as one with something which nevertheless
is not, and cannot, be identical with our beings; not
even with the being of him who really does possess
it. This, of course, is most strikingly so in the case
where what we want to possess is another being who,
just because he or she *is* a being, recoils from the
idea of being possessed. That, for instance, is the
point of Molière's *L'Ecole des Femmes*, a comedy
which strikes us even today as one of the world's
imperishable masterpieces; while the penultimate sec-
tions of Proust's great novel, with their account
of Marcel's desperate attempts to hide Albertine
away, and thus make himself feel sure of her inside
himself, provide a tragic illustration of the same
theme.

But in relation to this whole matter of possession,
what is at once characteristic and exceptional about
my own body is that, in this solitary instance, it
does not seem that we can assert, in the case of
the thing possessed, the usual relationship of independence of the being who possesses. More precisely, rather, the structure of my experience offers
me no direct means of knowing what I shall still
be, what I *can* still be, once the link between myself and my body is broken by what I call death.
That is a point to which we must return, to deal
with it at length, in my second volume; and we
shall then have to ask ourselves whether there is
any way of getting out of this metaphysical blind
alley. But for the moment we must simply admit
that, swathed up, as it were, in my situation as

an incarnate being, there is this riddle, which, at a
purely objective level, appears to admit of no answer
at all.

To explore this situation more thoroughly, we
must tackle it from yet another angle, and naturally
it is still secondary reflection that we are calling
on to help us.

I cannot avoid being tempted to think of my
body as a kind of instrument; or, more generally
speaking, as the apparatus which permits me to act
upon, and even to intrude myself into, the world.
It does look, for instance, as if Bergson's philosophy implied a doctrine of the body-soul relationship of this sort; though this cannot be taken as a
definitive interpretation of that philosophy. What
we must do in this case, however, is just what we
did when we were examining the notion of having,
owning, possessing; we must ask ourselves what being an instrument implies, and within what limits
instrumental action is feasible.

It is obvious that every instrument is an artificial
means of extending, developing, or reinforcing a
pre-existing power which must be possessed by
anyone who wants to make use of the instrument.
This, for instance, is true of the simplest tool, for
instance of the knife or the hoe. It is equally, however, true of the most complicated optical apparatus
conceivable. The basis of such an apparatus is our
power of seeing and the possibility of extending that.
Such powers are what one might call the very
notes of an organized body's activity; it might even
be contended that, considered realistically—that is
to say, dynamically, functionally—such a body consists merely of its assembled powers. The word
'assembled', however, seems to convey in a very
inadequate fashion the *kind* of totality which we
have here in mind; so it might be better to say
that each of the body's powers is a specific expression of its unity—and I am thinking of the unity of

an apparatus, an apparatus adaptable to many purposes, and considered, by us, from the outside.
Only let us remember that it is not *a* body, but *my*
body, that we are asking ourselves questions about.
As soon as we get back to this perspective, our
original perspective, the whole picture changes.

My body is *my* body just in so far as I do *not*
consider it in this detached fashion, do not put a
gap between myself and it. To put this point in
another way, my body is mine in so far as for
me my body is not an object but, rather, I *am*
my body. Certainly, the meaning of 'am' in that
sentence is, at a first glance, obscure; it is essentially, perhaps, in its implications, a negative meaning. To say that I *am* my body is to negate, to deny,
to erase that gap which, on the other hand, I would
be postulating as soon as I asserted that my body
was merely my instrument. And we must notice
at this point that if I do postulate such a gap, I am
involved at once in an infinite regress. The use of
any instrument whatsoever is, as we have seen, to
extend the powers of the body, or in a sense to
extend the body itself. If, then, we think of the
body as merely an instrument, we must think of
the use of the body as being the extension of the
powers of some *other* body (a mental body, an astral
body, or what you will); but this mental or astral
body must itself be the instrument that extends the
powers of some third kind of body, and so on for
ever. . . . We can avoid this infinite regress, but
only on one condition: we must say that this body,
which, by a fiction modelled on the instruments
that extend its powers of action, we can think of
as itself an instrument, is nevertheless, in so far as
it is *my* body, not an instrument at all. Speaking
of my body is, in a certain sense, a way of speaking
of myself; it places me at a point where either I
have not yet reached the instrumental relationship
or I have passed beyond it.

But let us walk warily at this point. There is a way of conceiving the identity of myself and my body which comes down to mere materialism, and materialism of a coarse and incoherent sort. There would be no point in asserting my identity with the body that other people can see and touch, and which for myself is something other than myself, in so far as I put it on the same level as any other body whatsoever, that is, at the level of the body as an object. The proper position to take up seems, on the contrary, to be this: I *am* my body in so far as I succeed in recognizing that this body of mine *cannot*, in the last analysis, be brought down to the level of being this object, *an* object, a something or other. It is at this point that we have to bring in the idea of the body not as an object but as a subject. It is in so far as I enter into some kind of relationship (though relationship is not an adequate term for what I have in mind) with the body, some kind of relationship which resists being made wholly objective to the mind, that I can properly assert that I am identical with my body; one should notice, also, that, like the term 'relationship', the term 'identity' is inadequate to our meaning here, for it is a term fully applicable only in a world of things or more precisely of mental abstractions from things, a world which our incarnate condition inevitably transcends. It goes without saying, by the way, that the term 'incarnation', of which I shall have to make a frequent use from now on, applies solely and exclusively in our present context to the situation of a being who appears to himself to be linked fundamentally and not accidentally to *his* or *her* body . . . In a former work of mine, my *Metaphysical Diary*, I used the phrase 'sympathetic mediation' to convey the notion of our non-instrumental communion with our bodies; I cannot say that I find the phrase wholly satisfactory, but even today, that is to say, twenty-five years later, the phrase seems to me the least inadequate way, if only that, of conveying the slippery notion. To elucidate the meaning of the phrase, we should recall the fact that my body, in so far as it is properly mine, presents itself to me in the first instance as something felt; I am my body only in so far as I am a being that has feelings. From this point of view it seems, therefore, that my body is endowed with an absolute priority in relation to everything that I can feel that is other than my body itself; but then, strictly speaking, can I really feel anything other than my body itself? Would not the case of my feeling something else be merely the case of my feeling *myself* as feeling something else, so that I would never be able to pass beyond various modifications of my own self-feeling?

But this is not the end of our difficulties: I shall be tempted to ask myself whether I am not forced to make use of my body in order to feel my body— the body being, at one and the same time, what feels and what is felt. Let us notice moreover that at this point the whole question of instrumentality intrudes itself once more surreptitiously into our argument. My postulate has been simply that feeling is a function which can be exercised only thanks to some apparatus or other—the apparatus, in fact, of my body—but by postulating this I have once more committed myself to all the contradictions, with which we are already well acquainted, of the instrumental view. Ought we not therefore to conclude from this that feeling is not really a function, that there is no instrument that enables us to feel? Was it not, really, just this fact that feeling is not instrumentally based that my rather obscure expression, 'sympathetic mediation', was intended to convey?

However that may be, we have certainly at this point laid upon ourselves the duty of enquiring into the fundamental nature of feeling. We shall not start by criticizing philosophical explanations of feelings; but by criticizing, rather, our common, everyday ways of grasping at the fact of feeling, of representing feeling to ourselves, long before we have reached the stage of philosophical reflection.

# CHAPTER VI

I SHALL start off, today, by going rapidly over the stages that have brought us up against the problem of the nature of feeling.

In our last lecture, our point of departure was a very general question: Who am I? We were led to ask just what connection my being—and by 'my being' I mean here just what I would mean by 'my way of existence'—has with what I call my body. I sought to prove, in regard to two typical notions (my body as a possession of mine, and my body as an instrument of mine), that when I seek to imagine some external relationship between me and my body I am invariably led into a self-contradictory position, that betrays its absurdity by implying an infinite regress. This induced me to assert (in a negative sense, a sense whose main purport was the *denial* of such external relationships) that I *am* my body. We noticed, however, the ambiguity of this assertion; it must not be interpreted, in our context, in materialist fashion. I *am* my body only in so far as for me the body is an essentially mysterious type of reality, irreducible to those determinate formulae (no matter how interestingly complex they might be) to which it would be reducible if it could be considered merely as an object. Let us remind ourselves of exactly what the notion of

127

being an object implies; the body is an object in so far as it can be scientifically known, gives scientific knowledge something solid to get to grips with, and gives a whole range of techniques, from hygiene to surgery, derived originally from scientific knowledge, something equally solid to work upon. It is also obvious, though I did not think it necessary to press home this point in our last lecture, that my body can be an object for *me*; my situation as an incarnate being implies an ability on my part to consider my body just as if it were any other body whatsoever. And it is certainly very necessary that I should be able to consider my body in this detached way; the necessity has a connection with what I said in my fourth chapter about truth, about the intelligible setting or background, against which minds are able to communicate with each other and, I should like to add at this point, with themselves.

So much for body as object: it seems, on the other hand, impossible to insist on what is specifically mine in my body without putting one's emphasis on the notion of feeling as such. Feeling, my feeling, is really what belongs only to me, my prerogative. What I feel is indissolubly linked to the fact that my body is *my* body, not just one body among others. I am out, let us say, for a walk with a friend. I say I feel tired. My friend looks sceptical, since he, for his part, feels no tiredness at all. I say to him, perhaps a little irritably, that nobody who is not inside my skin can know what *I* feel. He will be forced to agree, and yet, of course, he can always claim that I am attaching too much importance to slight disagreeable sensations which he, if he felt them, would resolutely ignore. It is all too clear that at this level no real discussion is possible. For I can always say that even if what he calls 'the same sensations' were felt by him and not by me, still, they would not really be, in their new setting, in the context of so many other sensations and feelings that I do not share, the *same* sensations; and that therefore his statement is meaningless.

But here we are up against a difficult question, a question that one has a tendency to dodge. What, after all, *is* feeling, and what makes it possible for us to feel?

We have already noticed that in trying to grasp what I mean when I talk of my body as something felt, or of myself having the feeling of my body, I run into difficulties. It does seem that I must postulate the body as the necessary instrumental condition of bodily feeling, unless, on the other hand, I am willing to admit that feeling is something that cannot be given an instrumental base, that it is by its nature irreducible to the functioning of an apparatus.

We may see our way more clearly here if we change the terms of our question and ask ourselves what makes it possible for us, not merely vaguely to feel, but more precisely to have sensations. How is sensation in general a possibility? (I am taking up here an argument that I developed formerly in my first *Metaphysical Diary* and rather later, merely in a more elaborate but not in an essentially altered form, in my essay, *Existence and Objectivity*.) *

In so far, then as we cling to the data of primary reflection, we cannot help thinking of sensation as some stimulus sent from an unknown source in outer space and intercepted by what we call a 'subject', but a subject, in this case, thought of objectively, that is, as a physical receiving apparatus; in other words we think of sensation on the model of the emission and reception of a message. It is difficult, almost impossible, for a mind at the stage of primary reflection to deny that what is sent out at point *x* (that is to say, somewhere or

*Printed as an appendix to the *Journal*.

other), then transmitted through space under conditions of which physics claims to give us an intelligible picture, *is* finally received and transcribed by the sensitive subject—transcribed, of course, in the key of the sense concerned. In short, we can hardly avoid thinking of sensation as the way in which a transmitter and a receiver communicate with each other and in this case—as in that of telepathy, to which we shall come back later—the imaginary model that conditions our thinking is that of a system of radio telegraphy. Let us notice, however, that the communication between emission post and reception post will be conceived, and even imagined, in a quite different manner, according to whether one does or does not adhere to a panpsychist doctrine—a doctrine that leaves, clouds, stones, roses, too, have in a sense their souls—like, for instance, that of Feschner. Those who reject panpsychism will not be willing to admit that more than one of the posts (the reception post, in fact) knows itself for what it is. The emission post, on this theory, does not know that it is an emission post, and is only grasped as such at the reception post. The rose and the stone are such for us, and not for themselves. They send out no conscious message. The panpsychists on the other hand (who are certainly a much smaller party) believe that the emission post itself already has a certain awareness, however tenuous or diffuse one may suppose it to be, of the message which it is addressing to us. The most suggestive example might be that of an odour, a scent; between the flower-bed whose scents are now reaching me and my own organism, something is travelling, something is being transmitted to me, which the physicist would consider to be a mere shaking pattern of waves; but for the panpsychist, at the beginning of this journey between the flower-bed and my nose, something must already exist, a smell not yet smelt, which must, in its essential nature, be comparable to an element of actual awareness, comparable, perhaps, to a confused joy at mere existence.

But what everybody admits, without asking how this is possible, is that this shaking of the atmosphere once it reaches its destination, my nose, is translated into the language, or transcribed in the key, of the sense of smell. What we must notice very carefully is that, for an investigation of our sort, this is the only thing that matters. The conjectures, the finally unverifiable conjectures, on the original nature of such a thing as a smell—on what it is, in itself, before we smell it—pass beyond the limits of the phenomenological method. It would be only from a strictly ontological point of view that one would be led to take up a position for, or against, the panpsychist hypothesis. It must therefore, fascinating as it may be in itself, no longer detain our attention; and in any case, if there is such a thing as the presence of the flower to the flower itself—a wavering, ghostly presence, one imagines it!—perhaps it would reveal itself only to the intuition of a poet. On the other hand, for the purposes of our own more prosaic investigation, it is of the greatest importance that we should ask ourselves whether there is any point at all in telling ourselves this little story about a so-called message (and the alleged origins of the message are irrelevant) which is transcribed in the key, or translated into the language, of the senses. Just as in our last chapter we probed critically at the notion of the body as an instrument, so we must now probe at the notion of sensation as transcription or translation of a message; and following a path now well known to us, we shall arrive, naturally enough, at a familiar kind of destination.

What does translation really consist of? Of the substitution of a set of given elements for another set of given elements, at least partly different in kind; however many differences there may be between the two sets, we should specially notice that both sets must be objective, that is, fully accessible to the mind. This is as true of the simple rendering of a piece of plain prose out of one language into another as of the deciphering of a cryptogram. In both cases, the translator must have access to a *code*, even though in the former case the code is nothing more than an ordinary dictionary. In the code the elements of both sides of the transaction, equated with each other, are fully accessible to the mind.

Now in the case of sensation, just nothing at all of this sort, or even remotely comparable to this, takes place. If I want to exercise the activity of a translator, I must start with a given something to work on, the text I am to translate from. This is a sort of prior datum: but the physical event prior to sensation, which I am supposed to be translating into the language of sensation, cannot be said to be a datum of mine in any sense whatsoever. If we do not at first acknowledge this fact, it is because we are spellbound by physical science's picture of some distant stimulus travelling towards the organism and shaking it up, and we confuse that conceptual picture with the fact of having an objective datum. What we are really doing is to project, in physical terms, the mysterious relationship which the term *datum* implies. But if we feel we must be more stringent in our reasoning than this, we are soon caught in a dilemma: either on the one hand, we must acknowledge that the physical event as such is not a datum of ours, is not, whatever modifications it may exercise on our bodies in so far as the latter too are considered in a purely objective fashion, *literally* given to us in any sense at all, in which case it seems impossible that this non-given physical event should ever be transformed into sense data; or on the other hand we shall have to

bridge the gap between physical events and sense
data by postulating the existence of an intermediary order of sensibilia, or unsensed sensa—of things
that are like sensations in all respects, except that
nobody is aware of them. This way out of our difficulty will not stand up to critical examination. At
the most, it pushes our troubles one stage farther
back. How are we to understand the notion of a
sensation which is a sensation in all respects, except
that nobody is aware of it? If we stick to the general
lines of the interpretation we started with, we shall
have to treat the unsensed sensum as itself a message
sent out from an emission post (but missing, in this
case, its destination at the reception post), and
then we are back where we started. Or, on the
other hand, we can, of course, treat the unsensed
sensum, or the sensibilium, as something primary
and unanalysable; in that case, of course, it cannot
be a message, and so the interpretation of sensation we started with has foundered. Moreover, if
we have technically solved our problem in this
latter instance, we have done so, quite obviously,
by a piece of trickery; the *sensibile* or unsensed,
sensum, whose existence we are assuming as our
starting point, is something about whose nature,
by the very notion of the thing, nobody can know
anything at all.

But is there any way at all, then, out of this
labyrinth? Secondary reflection is forced to recognize that our primary assumptions must be called
in question, and that sensation, as such, should
certainly *not* be conceived on the analogy of the
transmission and reception of a message. For, and
this is our basic reason for rejecting the analogy,
every kind of message, however transmitted or received, *presupposes* the existence of sensation—
exactly in the way in which, as we have already
seen, every kind of instrument or apparatus presupposes the existence of my body.

Let us see, now if we can form a less strictly negative idea of the conclusions to which our argument has led us, always bearing in mind that what we are looking for is an answer to the question that started us off on our enquiries into body, feeling, and sensation: the question, 'Who am I?' on which, of course, there depends the other question of what exactly I mean when I ask who I am.

Every transmission of a message, indeed every instrumental act of any sort at all, can be regarded as a kind of *mediation*. By mediation, of course, I mean, here, in the broadest sense, any operation at all that consists of reaching some final terminus by making use of intermediary stages. We are talking about mediation whenever we use such phrases as 'by means of', 'by way of', 'passing through', 'at the present stage', and so on.

From the point of view of pure thought, as Hegel saw with incomparable strength and clarity, everything that is immediate can be considered as mediatizable *ad infinitum*; and this is true above all of the two determinants that constitute immediate experience as such, the 'here' and the 'now'. 'Here', when I say, 'Here I am', is a particular determinate spatial locus which, by definition, has its place in the infinite network of determinate spatial loci in general: 'now', similarly, when I say, 'Now I see it', is a moment of time which is strictly bound up with all the other moments of time. This does not, of course, imply that this great network of loci and moments, or, as an English philosopher like Lord Russell would say, of point-instants, forms in itself an exhaustive whole, forms, for instance, our complete universe of rational discourse; that, to my mind, is a meaningless hypothesis. No, what we have to acknowledge is merely that the privilege which, from the point of view of my immediate experience, attaches itself to the 'here' and to the 'now' cannot be justified from the point of view of pure thought.

But as soon as we bring into the argument my body, in so far as it is *my* body, or the feeling which is not separable from my body as mine, our perspective changes, and we have to recognize the need to postulate the existence of what I will call a *non-mediatizable immediate,* which is the very root of our existence. This is a very difficult notion; and intelligence must simply bombard this non-mediatizable immediate with its rays if we are to have more than a dark and groping awareness of its whereabouts. Yet this notion is the only means available to us of overcoming, at least in principle, all the difficulties we have come up against in our previous lectures.

Let us note that we are now in a better position to give a content to what we formerly said about my certitude, 'I exist', being a sort of touchstone, for me, of existence in general. Our temptation, when this argument was first brought up, may have been to consider this 'I exist' as a sort of kernel of *subjective* certitude—and yet such a subjective certitude would not, after all, would it, have taken us beyond the limits of idealism? It would remain an open question whether a real existence did, in fact, correspond to this subjective consciousness of existence. But this temptation is no longer a possible temptation for us once we have passed beyond the interpretation of sensation as the transmission and reception of a message. For it should be very clear that solipsism remains at least a menace so long as we insist on interpreting sensation as the translation or transcription of a message sent out from an emission post whose nature, and indeed whose very existence, had to remain in doubt. On the ground on which we now stand the case is quite altered, and that is what I want to make as clear as possible.

Fundamentally, we are in the situation of a man who has just perceived that the key with which he hoped to open a certain door will not, after all, fit into the lock. He must therefore try another key, try, that is, to interpret feeling and sensation in another language, a non-instrumentalist language. Yet let us be wary and let us notice that the term 'interpretation' is itself a highly ambiguous one. I am awakened, let us say, in the middle of the night by an unaccustomed noise. My imagination, startled into activity, suggests the most frightening hypothesis that can be: is it not a burglar who has just broken his way into the house? But I suddenly remember that one of my fellow lodgers warned me he would be home very late. I feel immediately reassured, I have interpreted, and in a sense even liquidated, the disturbing unusual sensation. In so far as I am an active being, whose activity must get to work on well-defined objects such with its proper place and unmistakable label, this is the kind of interpretation that I have need of in my everyday life. I might have had to look for a pistol and to face the thief, or simply to phone the police; happily, these unpleasant possibilities remained mere possibilities; I need only go to sleep again.

But the kind of interpretation with which we are concerned is essentially not only different from but, in a way, even opposed to this practical, everyday kind of interpretation; it has to do, for instance, in such a case as this, with the fact that I was able to be awakened so abruptly—and all to no purpose, indeed! How was that possible? Of course, in so far as we remain at a purely descriptive level of discourse, a physical explanation might seem to hold good; I am an extremely sensitive physical apparatus and I was shaken up by the noise of a window opening; but on the other hand, when I talk of this physical apparatus, it is not really about *myself* that I am talking, and it is impossible to make it and me completely coincide. It is for this reason that we have to bring in the notion of what I have called elsewhere an existential immediate, that is to say, of something I *am*. Perhaps we might say, to clear up this difficulty at least negatively, that we are dealing here with something that cannot be treated as a thought-content; every thought-content gives rise to mediations and is a thought-content only through mediations. I will be coming back to the topic later, but it may be useful here to anticipate a point I shall make in my ninth chapter: namely, that everything becomes much clearer if one brings in the idea of what I have called one's exclamatory awareness of existence. For there is something in the exclamation—in the 'O!', the 'Oh!', the 'Ah!', the 'Ugh!', the 'Ah, me!', the 'Alas!' —that transcends any thought-content which can be inserted into it.

All this being so, it seems that the key for which I shall be looking to open my door will be, in the widest sense, the idea of participation—sharing, taking part in, partaking of. The importance of the idea of participation was clear to me even in the days of my earliest philosophical gropings, before the first World War; and the idea plays a leading part, also, in the work of a French philosopher who is a contemporary of mine, Louis Lavelle. All the same, at the very outset we run up against a difficulty here, for we have got to take care that participation itself should not—like our former inadequate analogies of the instrument and the message—be conceived in objective terms. Here, as elsewhere, we have to deal with a sort of graduated scale. At one end of the scale we have what is objective, what can be possessed. A cake is brought in, I claim my share of it; it is only as something that is objectively in front of me, that can be weighed and measured, that the cake can be sliced or that the cake even exists. Let us add, that if I claim my own slice in a peremptory fashion, it is very probably to eat it, but that it may be not to consume it at once, but to store it away somewhere, and it may be even to give it to someone as a present. But there are cases in which the meaning of the verb 'to consume' is by no means so precise. For instance, if I claim my share of a collection of pictures, consuming my pictures, in that case, can strictly mean looking at them. Possibly, if I have the soul of a gambler in stocks and shares, my chief desire is to hang on to the pictures until I can throw them into the market at some favourable moment, when their value will have sufficiently risen; possibly, also, it is not myself but my son who is to make this financial kill; in such a case my share in the pictures is an ideal share, and it is very strikingly so if, for instance, I allow the pictures to remain provisionally in somebody else's house. However, though we can work out all sorts of variations on this example, underlying all of them there remains the objective character of what has to be shared. My participation in the ownership of the pictures remains, in spite of everything, my share in a share-out. But participation need not always have this character. We have only to think of what it means to participate, not in the ownership of something, but in some ceremony. In general, to speak of participating in a ceremony means that one is one of a number of people present at it, but such participation can also have an ideal character. I can, for instance, though tied to a sick-bed, associate myself with this ceremony through prayer. Let us say, to make our image more precise, that it is a ceremony of thanksgiving to God for the end of some national calamity, an epidemic or a war.

What, in a case of this sort, is objectively given to me? Very little, perhaps merely an announcement in the papers or on the radio that the ceremony in question is going to take place, and at what time, and at which church. Yet the obstacle created by my illness does in such a case appear to me as quite contingent and even, in the last analysis, as non-existent. What can it matter to God whether I am physically present or not in such and such a church? What can the place where I happen to be matter to Him, since it is for reasons independent of my will that I have not been able to come to church? Naturally, of course, if I had been well enough to come to church with a rather painful effort, and if I had refused to make that effort, my refusal *would* on the contrary have a definite significance, a negative bearing.

But we can erase from our minds, in imagining such an example, the strictly objective element that is still represented by the announcement of the ceremony in queston in the press or on the radio. I do not really need to know that at a given time and a given place such and such an office of thanksgiving will be celebrated. This thanksgiving ceremony is, after all, only a particular expression of an act of adoration with which I can associate myself, through prayer, at any moment. Thus we arrive at the notion of an act of participation which no longer leaves any place for the objectivity of a datum or even of a notification. Let us notice also that the whole question of the number of people participating has ceased to be relevant. It is not only that in this last case I am no longer interested in knowing how many of us, at a given moment, are participating in the act of adoration, whereas in our former case we were concerned with a ceremony held at a particular church at which a determinate number of persons were present; but it is also that in this last case I cannot be sure that the question of how many people are joining in the act of adoration has any meaning—it has at least,

I am sure no *bearing* at all. The more all of us
who are praying at the same moment are genuinely
melted into a single love, the less significance, obviously, the question of how many of us there may
be really has. *Melted,* I say: for nevertheless it is
not as if I were alone any more, I do really feel
myself strangely strengthened by the fact that it
is a multitude who are turning at one moment
towards Him whom we adore.

I have lingered over this example because it does
seem to give us a real glimpse of what non-objective participation means. We ought to linger, also,
over this idea of non-objectivity itself; emphasizing
its value, emphasizing the fact that it is the condition of the reality of participation itself. All this,
no doubt, will become clearer in the sequel.

It will perhaps be observed, and justly observed,
that even this non-objective participation does presuppose an idea on which it depends (the idea of
God, in our last example); however indistinct and
unspecific from the point of view of its metaphysical
attributes that idea may be. This, as I say, is true,
and it is in fact only by virtue of the idea that
participation emerges; the idea, around which non-
objective participation becomes possible, is itself the
principle of the emergence of participation. But can
we not also conceive of a kind of participation
which is not emergent but, so to say, *submerged?*
And is it not within the power of reflection to turn
*back* towards that level of submerged participation
once it has reached the emergent level, the level
illuminated by thought? Our point here is whether
the very existence of feeling, as such, does not bear
witness to the reality of this level of submerged
participation; it is on this question that we must
now concentrate.

Here, as elsewhere, our thought seems to come
up against the obstacle of its own tendency to represent things to itself in physical terms, in images,

metaphors, models, analogies; but we should be
proving ourselves all the more certainly the slaves
of material comparisons, if we supposed that all
thought has to do is to blast such obstacles out of
its way, as one blasts a rock when building a road.
Our situation here is far more complicated. Our
picture of participation as submerged in a sort of
sea and then emerging from it into the light of
thought cannot be treated as a sort of intrusive
foreign body, a mote in thought's eye; thought has
given us the image, and therefore it is only by reshaping itself that thought can escape from the image. Secondary reflection, as we have already said,
*is* merely this sort of inner reshaping, and indeed
this inner reshaping is also what takes place when
we wish to attain to participation. At the outset
we are still obsessed, in spite of everything, by
the visible shape that participation takes, and we
fail to realize that this shape is not what really
matters. What matters is a sort of inner bias of
which we cannot, really, make a picture. To understand this bias, it is enough to imagine, as vividly
as one can, how it is with a person who desires
very strongly to take part in a certain task, a self-
testing task—and who does not particularly desire
to take his share of some objectivized good which
can be more or less properly compared to a cake
cut in slices. No doubt, from the point of view of
the psychologist, it is still quite possible to depreciate
and belittle this desire to take one's share in a task.
It will be said, for instance, that what I desire above
all is to be well thought of by others and that I
should not be well thought of if I sat back with
my arms folded while other people were working.
But really to say this is merely to push the problem
one stage back; we can then ask the psychologist
why I bother so much about being well thought of
by others? Only a very stupid person would reply
that I bother about it because being well thought of

entails material advantages, and that it is these I am really interested in.

For it may well be that, by insisting on taking part in some self-testing task, I expose myself not only to suffering but to death; and this, if I am not a believer, without my being sustained by any hope of being rewarded in heaven. Let us notice also that there are historical situations, of which the last war was one, in which this will to participate in some dangerous task can be exercised against, as it were, the very grain of the individual's given social background. Very generally indeed, we can say that these aspects of human experience which we can least easily set aside we can also least easily explain, unless we reserve a very important place, and perhaps even a central place, in human nature, for the will to participate. But—and this is what matters, at this point in our argument—this will to participate is itself metaphysically possible only on the basis of a kind of human consensus (and a consensus, of course, is literally merely a common *feeling* about something, and so by definition is something felt, rather than something thought); one might add that this consensus could only become *intellectually* articulate to itself at the cost of a tremendous effort.

Where it is a matter, of course, of some large human undertaking, a war or a revolution, the statement of group feeling in intellectual terms is possible; there are appeals, exhortations, statements of a case. But such rationalizations of a consensus are only a single aspect of a much vaster reality which undoubtedly transcends the order of mere relationships between persons. Think, for instance, of the incredibly strong link that binds the peasant to the soil. Nothing could be wider of the facts than to attribute to this link an exclusively utilitarian character—than to say that the peasant is attached to the soil only because of what he can get out of it, or because his holding assures him a certain independence which he values, and so on. The peasant's attachment to the soil is something that transcends utility, that transcends gain. To feel the truth of this, we have only to think of the peasant who has sold his holding and his stock and has settled down in the city, living with his children who work there. Let us allow, even, that his children are fond of him and show their fondness. Materially, no doubt, this man is better off than he was in the past; but he does not succeed in adapting himself to his new life, he suffers from a kind of incurable internal bleeding. This is a favourite subject with French novelists, and has been very well treated, for instance, by Charles Louis-Philippe in *Le Père Perdrix*.

It seems legitimate to suppose that in searching more deeply into the nature of this link between the peasant and the soil, or between the sailor and the sea, for that matter, we are placing ourselves at a more favourable point of vantage for grasping what participation means and for seeing, at the same time, in what the specific nature of feeling consists.

In this connection, indeed, I would like to make the point that for a philosophical approach like ours, which is essentially a concrete rather than an abstract approach, the use of examples is not merely an auxiliary process but, on the contrary, an essential part of our method of progressing. An example, for us, is not merely an illustration of an idea which was fully in being even before it was illustrated. I would rather compare the pre-existing idea to a seed; I have to plant it in the genial soil that is constituted by the example before I can really see what sort of a seed it is; I keep a watch on the soil to see what the seed grows up into.

We have thus progressed, and progressed is indeed the proper word, towards a concept of real participation which can no longer be translated into the

language of outer objects. It is perfectly clear that
the soil to which the peasant is so passionately
attached is not something about which he can really
speak. We can say that the peasant's soil transcends
everything that he sees around him, that it is linked
to his inner being, and by that we must understand
not only to his acts but to his sufferings. The contrast between the soil experienced in this way as a
sort of inner presence, and anything that a landscape may be to the amateur of beauty who appre-
ciates it and who selects a few epithets from his
stock to pin down its salient notes, is surely as deep
and as firmly rooted as could be. On the other hand,
we could properly speak of participation (though
it is quite another form of participation, of course)
in such a landscape, in connection with its appre-
ciation by a real artist, particularly by a painter,
of participation just to the degree in which the
painter is authentically creative; and no doubt we
shall later on have an opportunity to emphasize the
intimate relationship that exists between participation and the creative spirit.

In our remark about the presence of the soil
being linked, for the peasant, both to his acts and
his sufferings, we have already had occasion to note
that effective participation transcends the traditional
opposition between activity and passivity; participation can be considered now as active, now as passive, according to the point of view at which we
place ourselves. This is probably true in all cases
of participation, except for the limiting case where
to participate means merely to receive a share, a
fragment of a certain given whole—but it is impossible, on the other hand, to participate with all
one's being in an undertaking, a task, even in a
casual adventure, without having, to some degree
at least, the feeling that one is being carried along,
buoyed up by an outer current; and this no doubt
is the indispensable condition without which the

individual who is participating in some enterprise would not be able to endure its fatigues—fatigues under which he would certainly succumb if he were acting only on his own behalf.

But these remarks have their relevance also to what has been said above about feeling. In spite of what an empiricist materialism has said, and has said for such a long time, feeling is *not* passive. Feeling is not suffering; to feel is merely to *receive* but on the express condition that we restore to the notion of receptiveness a positive value of which philosophers have generally sought to deprive it. As I have often had occasion to remark in the past, it does seem as if Kant was guilty of a gross confusion when he admitted, without argument, that receptiveness was a kind of passivity. Receptiveness is not passive except in the limiting case, to which the empiricism of the eighteenth century recurred so eagerly, of a piece of hot wax receiving an impress from a seal. But the general notion of receiving, when one looks at it more closely, is very different from this. In a previous work of mine, *Du Refus à l'Invocation*, I have written 'I will postulate it as an axiom that one cannot speak of reception (nor, in consequence, of receptiveness) except having regard to a certain prior orientation of the feelings or ordering of the mind. One receives a guest in a room, in a house, or, in the strict limiting case, in a garden; but not in a wide undefined wasteland nor in the depths of a forest'. In the same passage, I emphasized the metaphysical value that attaches, or rather that should be attached, in the French language to the preposition *chez*, our equivalent of the Latin *apud*: there is no exact equivalent in English, you have to use *at* and the possessive case, '*at* So-and-so's'. 'There is no point in using *chez* except in relation to a self, which may, moreover, be some other self than one's own: and by a self I mean someone about whom we must at least suppose that he is able to say, *"Myself,"* to see himself or to be seen as a self in the first person. . . . And it is also necessary—it is even the essential point that this *self* should regard a certain domain as properly his.' I do not know whether this point comes over very strikingly in English: but when one says 'at Smith's', for instance, that does imply that Smith is at his own centre, and that I can be aware of him as being at his own centre, not at mine, and also that Smith, to be Smith adequately, does need his own proper place that he can be at. Here, anyway, we touch again on what I said in the last lecture about having—about ownership or possession in the widest sense—and about its deep roots in feeling.

In point of fact, we shall not be able to have a real concept of participation unless we first of all emphasize everything that *chez,* in such a phrase as *chez soi* (the equivalent of the German *Bei-sich-sein*) implies; and what it implies, we should notice, is not at this point anything at all like *pour soi.* (Again, it is difficult to express this in English idiom: it is so obvious that 'at Smith's' does not imply 'for Smith', 'for Smith alone', 'for Smith's sole sake', or anything of that sort, that the point seems hardly worth making.) But if to receive is, in the widest sense, to receive *chez soi*—to receive in one's own prepared place of reception—then to receive (and do not let us forget that feeling as a kind of receptiveness is what we are talking about) is also in a sense to welcome, and welcoming is not something passive, it is an act. The term 'responsiveness' is probably our least inadequate way of designating the activity we have in mind; we think of responsiveness as contrasting with that inner inertia which is insensibility or apathy.

But can we, it will be asked, trace this elementary responsiveness to its sources? I think we must say categorically that such a backward exploration is

the idea that every phenomenon is the product of a certain given set of *conditions*. In his laboratory he hopes to reconstitute the set of conditions, however complex they may be, which, once they are fully reconstituted, cannot fail to give rise to the phenomenon he is after, life. In other words, he seeks to start off a mechanically fated chain-reaction; and, of course, in enumerating the conditions that have made it possible for him to manufacture his phenomenon he systematically discounts the huge mental toils, the plodding, methodical research, of himself and others. It is material conditions only that he is interested in. Thus, by a singular contradiction, he succeeds in convincing himself and, of course, attempts to persuade others, that he has arrived at the real origin of his phenomenon; and he sets out to demonstrate that everything in the universe runs perfectly smoothly by itself, without any creative power at any time intruding. It is against belief in such intrusion, indeed, that the technician, strictly speaking, takes his stand; his *hybris* lies precisely in an intention which is like that of a religious propagandist, with the propaganda turned inside out.

In the artist's case, however, there is no such intention. In his mental world, such notions as condition, origin, original condition, and so on, have no proper place; this is to say, if we go into it more deeply, that for the artist, as such, the problem of how creatures and things have gradually developed into what we see them to be today is not a matter of any interest at all. It is in the present form of things that he is interested. But just, strangely enough, to the degree to which he is *not* interested in such fundamental problems, he is a citizen of that kingdom of participation from which one exiles oneself as soon as one seeks to rediscover life's source or to play the drama of Genesis over again in the laboratory.

I have emphasized, in another work, * the necessity of distinguishing between man as a spectator and man as a participator, but I must confess that this distinction has latterly, in my own thinking, begun to lose some of its point; at least it is clear now to me that it is an inadequate distinction, and that the notion of the spectator is an ambiguous notion. The spectator is present on the scene, his dominating motive is a curiosity which has no touch of anxiety, still less of anguish, about it, for he knows very well that he is not himself caught up in anything that is happening on the stage; however bloody the conclusion of the tragedy may be, he feels sure that he himself can leave the theatre peacefully, catch his bus or his tube, and arrive home in time for a cup of tea, having, on the way home, brushed away whatever emotions the play may have aroused in him, rather as one brushes dust off a coat. And this, of course, is an attitude of mind which does not belong exclusively to the spectator in the actual theatre. During the first World War, it was still pretty much the attitude of plenty of people in neutral countries, who watched that war, from their safe seats, as if it had been a boxing match or a bullfight. In distinguishing between *homo spectans* and *homo particeps*, I wanted to put my emphasis on the fact that in the latter case there is self-commitment, and in the former there is not. But I was wrong not to have taken into account the case of contemplation, for the contemplative is certainly somebody essentially different from the sort of spectator to whom a war, from a safe distance, is a stimulating spectacle, and at the point we have reached now it is important to see where the difference between the two lies.

It seems to me now that the spectator, in the ordinary sense of the word, makes as if to partici-

*Etre et Avoir*, p. 25.

pate without really participating; he has emotions which are superficially similar to those of people who really are committed to some course of action or other, but he knows very well that in his case such emotions have no practical outcome. In other words he is the playground for a game of make-believe or let's-pretend, a game, however, which, as children know, is not really enjoyable unless the beliefs and the pretences are taken, for the time being at least, fairly seriously. It is this game of at least half-serious voluntary self-deception that enemies of the theatre, like Tolstoy, no doubt intended to condemn. But mock-belief of this sort is, of course, something quite alien to contemplation properly so called; and it is perhaps because we have become infected by the stage and the screen in one way, and by the attitude of the technician in a quite other way, that contemplation today has become something so extremely foreign to us that we find it hard to get even a glimpse of its real nature. I would like, in passing, to add that it is impossible not to ask oneself whether this almost complete vanishing away of the contemplative activity in the modern world has not something, at least, to do with the terrible evils from which mankind is suffering; and it may be that the discovery of this connection between the presence of evil and the absence of contemplation will turn out to be one of the most important results of this volume and its successor.

Without attempting, at this point, to go really deeply into the matter, we cannot, even now, fail to see that the relation of the contemplative activity to time—not to time in general, so much as to duration, to the concrete time of human experience —is something quite different from the relationship to time implied by the attitude of the spectator, Contemplation utterly excludes curiosity: which is to say, in other words, that contemplation is not

oriented towards *the future*. It is just as if for
contemplation the temporal polarities of past and
future—which are always relative in any case, since
what has been the future is always becoming the
past—had lost their meaning or, at the very least,
lost all their practical relevance. Time, for contemplation, is nothing if it is not present time; the whole
topic requires a deeper analysis, but what we can
press home, even at this point, is that contemplation
is a possibility only for somebody who has made
sure of his grip on reality; for somebody who floats
on the surface of reality, or who, as it were, skims
over the thin ice of that surface on skates, for the
amateur or the dilettante, the contemplative act
is inconceivable. And we can already divine that
the ascesis, the discipline of the body, which in all
ages and for all religions has been held necessary
if the soul is to be made capable of contemplation,
amounts precisely to a set of steps which, to certain
spirits, appear simply as having to be taken, if the
soul is to strengthen its grip on the real.

We may conclude from all this, and it is a very
important conclusion, that contemplation, in so far
as it cannot be simply equated with the spectator's
attitude and in a deep sense is even at the opposite
pole from that attitude, must be considered as a
mode of participation, and even as one of participation's most intimate modes. But, on the other hand,
a true artist, a Vermeer, a Corot, a Hokusai, is
also a contemplative—he is anything but a superficial spectator and nothing if not a deep participant
—only in his case contemplation embodies itself in
visible works. We shall have, perhaps, to ask ourselves later whether in the saint's case, too, contemplation does not embody itself—but in those
invisible works, which are sanctity's very fruits!

But what at once complicates and darkens our
whole quest is that the technician, as such, cannot
be lined up, either with the spectator—that should

be obvious—nor, or at least so it seems to me, with the properly creative spirit. In other words, does not the traditional notion of *homo faber*, man the craftsman, man the tool-making animal, mask an ambiguity to which we must discover the clue? I think we shall hit, in this connection, on a way of handling our topic that is not without affiliations to Bergson's distinction between intelligence and instinct. But I shall take care, in my handling of the topic, not to extrapolate as Bergson did, and not to deliver myself of rash speculations about the nature of instinct in animals. It is exclusively at the level of thought, that is to say, of human knowledge, that it seems to me either necessary or possible to follow out this line of investigation.

# CHAPTER VII

BEING IN A SITUATION

THE argument of the last lecture led us to recognize that we can understand feeling only as a mode of participation, but that the domain of participation, on the other hand, is much more extensive than that of mere feeling as such. To feel is in some degree to participate, but to participate in a higher sense is much more than merely to feel. This point is worth emphasizing, in so far as it may help us to get a clearer notion of the kind of answer—let us be careful not to say, the kind of solution—that will be relevant to our question: 'Who am I?' or 'What am I?'

It will be helpful also to revert, at this point, to the notion of contemplation as such. We shall find contemplation an intelligible notion if we are willing to recognize the ambiguity of the simpler notion (which is, however, the root meaning of the word contemplation) of looking. We can look at or for things in a way that wholly subserves some practical activity. If I am going across a patch of ground covered with boulders, puddles, briars, muddy patches, and other obstacles, I keep my eyes open, I look where I am putting my feet; my attention is continuously directed towards a certain wholly definable kind of activity—that of picking my way from one given point to another—and towards the grip such an activity can get on the material datum, in this case an imperfect thoroughfare, through which it is exercising itself. But a less simple example, one that takes us a stage further, is that of the botanist or geologist who makes use of a country stroll to look for some particular plant or mineral. (To a French ear, the English phrasal verb 'looking for' corresponds with wonderful adequacy to the notion it expresses, the 'for' just exactly suggesting the purposeful look of the searcher). This, as I have said, is an intermediary example between purely practical looking and contemplation as such; the geologist or botanist is on the look-out for knowledge, his looking does not subserve a practical activity in the usual sense of the term, but on the other hand the knowledge he is seeking to extend may be of a wholly specialized or specializing character; it is significant, in fact, that what he is looking for he would probably call a *specimen*.

But might we not say that the very essence of contemplation as such consists, negatively at least, in the fact that it can never be brought to bear on a specimen as such; its object, if it has an object, is not considered as being a member of a class or as having a place in a series; it is considered in itself, in its uniqueness, while for the specialist—in spite of any appearance to the contrary—that uniqueness can never be taken into account, *Sie kann nicht*, as the Germans say, *in Betracht kommen*. All this, as I have hinted, is assuming that contemplation *has* an object in the ordinary sense, or rather that what contemplation is brought to bear on remains merely objective: for we may be allowed to ask ourselves —and the question is an extremely important one— whether, when looking becomes contemplation, it does not switch over its direction, turn, as it were, inwards? In so far as we are accustomed to use the word contemplation to indicate the act by which the self concentrates its attention on its own state, or even on its own being, might we not very properly say that contemplation is a turning inwards of our awareness of the outer world?

This idea becomes clearer, it seems to me, if one remembers that there can be no contemplation without a kind of inward regrouping of one's resources, or a kind of ingatheredness; to contemplate is to ingather oneself in the presence of whatever is being contemplated, and this in such a fashion that the reality, confronting which one ingathers oneself, itself becomes a factor in the ingathering.

It is obvious that in the case in which the reality confronting me is interpreted as mere spectacle, mere outer show with no inner meaning, what I have just been saying makes no sense. If it is possible to turn one's impression of a spectacle inwards, that is because, after all, one is not interpreting it as *mere* spectacle but as something else and something more. Let us see, however, if we can make this clearer. A mere spectator, confronted with a mere spectacle, could properly be compared with a sort of visual recording apparatus; there would be no inwardness either on his side or on that of what he was recording. It may be objected that the notion of a recording apparatus implies one sort of inwardness at least—that of cogs and springs *inside* the outward casing of the apparatus—but this is mere quibbling. The cogs and springs are simply parts of a mechanical whole, and we must assert peremptorily that to be part of such a whole is not to have inwardness in our sense. This example, however, does serve a purpose in showing what an equivocal notion inwardness is; we seek, mistakenly, for an imaginative embodiment of the notion; but inwardness is really one of the borderlands of the imagination, it lies just out of reach of imagination's evocative power, and is, one might say, *transliminal*.

Let us recall, however, at this point what we said in chapter five about instrumentality: to be instru-

mental is, by definition, to be at the service of
powers that are not themselves instrumental, and
which, for that very reason, can be said to be really
inner powers, really to have inwardness. We are
betraying the very nature of such powers when we
seek to embody them for the purposes of imagination, for as soon as we do so we tend inevitably to
reduce them to mere instruments. This is why the
spectator, also, betrays his own nature when he
chooses to regard himself as a mere recording apparatus; and it is enough, indeed, for him to reflect
for a second on the *emotion* which a spectacle is
capable of arousing in him, for the image of himself as a mere apparatus, with which he was satisfied
enough at first, to be at once shattered. But it is
precisely to the degree in which the spectator is
more than simply *spectans,* it is to the degree to
which he is also *particeps,* that the spectacle is
more for him than a mere spectacle, that it has
some inner meaning—and it is, I repeat, to the
degree to which it is more than a mere spectacle
that it can give rise to contemplation. And our
term 'participation', even though it is so far for us
not much more than a makeshift, a bridge hastily
thrown across certain gaps in our argument, indicates precisely this 'something more' that has to be
added to the simple recording of impressions before
contemplation can arise. This whole domain is very
difficult to explore; but the way through it, I think,
is not that of coining new *ad hoc* terms like 'appresentation' but rather that of meditating on the
use of prepositions—such as *in,* and *towards,* and
*in front of*—in common speech.

The spectacle as such, we would all agree, is in
front of me, facing me, before me; but in so far as
it is something more than a spectacle, it is not
merely in front of me; shall I say that it is in me,
within me, inside me? These prepositions have a
subtle idiomatic range; and if I say in this case that

the spectacle lies within me, or, as you would more
naturally say in English, that it is in my mind, or
that it is an inner spectacle as well as an outer
one, my emphasis is largely a negative one; it
indicates that there is some sense in which the
spectacle is not external to me, or not merely external. For in fact we are now at a stage where we
have to transcend the primary, and fundamentally
spatial, opposition between external and internal,
between outside and inside. In so far as I really
contemplate the landscape a certain togetherness
grows up between the landscape and me. But this is
the point where we can begin to get a better grasp
of that regathering, or regrouping, process of which
I spoke earlier; is this state of ingatheredness not,
in fact, the very means by which I am able to
transcend the opposition of my inner and outer
worlds? There are profound reflections, of which
we could make good use at this point, on a relevant topic in a recent book by the Swiss Catholic
thinker, Max Picard, *The World of Silence*.* There
is reason to suppose that ingatheredness is the means
by which I am able to impose an inner silence on
myself. Such a silence, of course, must not be
thought of as a mere absence of mental discourse,
but has its own positive value; one might call it a
fullness of being which can be reinstated only when
the speech impulse has been driven, or drawn,
downwards. Human speech, as Bergson perceived
with his usual depth of vision, is naturally adapted
to the statement of spatial relationships, which are
relationships, fundamentally, of mere juxtaposition.
And that very sentence, indeed, illustrates this in-
adequacy of language to the truths of the inner life.
*Exclusion, shutting out,* is itself, of course, fundamentally a relationship of mere juxtaposition; when
I say that true awkwardness *excludes* such relationships, the structure of language is forcing me to
*Die Welt des Schweigens,* Zurich, 1948.

imply the contrary of what I intend to assert.

Let us get back, however, to our notion of in-gatheredness. There is a preliminary observation to be made, round which any subsequent observations will tend to group themselves. Ingatheredness is not a state of abstraction from anything, and in fact the attitudes behind ingathering oneself, and abstracting oneself, are diverse and perhaps at opposite poles from each other. One abstracts one's attention from something, which is as much as to say, leaves it, leaves it aside, perhaps even leaves it in the lurch; ingatheredness on the other hand is essentially a state in which one is drawing nearer something, without abandoning anything. All this will be clearer in a moment. One is drawing nearer something, I have said, but nearer to what? The most natural answer is nearer to oneself; is ingathering not merely entering into one's own self again? But an ambiguity, noticed by us several times already, crops up again here: what self, or rather which self, are we here concerned with? Let us take a literary example. In Corneille's tragedy, *Cinna*,* the Emperor Augustus has just discovered that a man who is his creature, on whom he has showered favours, is heading a plot against his life. His first reaction is anger, indignation, a wish to take vengeance on ingratitude. But there is something within Augustus that refuses to yield utterly to these very natural impulses, and in a famous soliloquy, which is one of the high points of French classical tragedy, Augustus forces himself to enter into his own inner depths—into a self which is no longer that of anger and the wish to take vengeance, nor indeed, more generally speaking, of desire or appetite at all. This is a necessarily inadequate version of his soliloquy, in the nearest English equivalent to the form of the original, the heroic couplet:

*Act IV, Scene 2.

Cease to complain, but lay thy conscience bare:
One who spared none, how now should any spare?
What rivers of red blood have bathed thy
    swords—
Now crimsoning the Macedonian swards,
Now high in flood that Anthony should fall,
Then high again for Sextus! Oh, recall
Perusia drowned with all her chivalry
In blood—such slaughter was designed by thee,
The bloody image of thy paths and ends!
Thou, turned a murderer even to thy friends,
Was not thy very tutor stabbed by thee?
Durst then tax Fate with an unjust decree,
Now, if thy friends aspire to see *thee* bleed,
Breaking those ties to which *thou* paid'st no
    heed?
Just is such treason, and the Gods approve! . . .
As easy lost as won, thy state remove,
See traitors' swords in treacherous blood imbrued,
And die, thou ingrate, by ingratitude!

The case of Augustus, in Corneille's tragedy, is
the case of any one of us who does really manage
to enter into his own depths. In a dramatically
personified, a wonderfully concrete shape, this soliloquy does exemplify that inner need for transcendence to which I devoted an earlier chapter. Only, as
I have already hinted, we must be very careful
indeed at this point to avoid artificially separating
one level of the self from the other; we must avoid
assuming that the self of reflection and ingatheredness is not the *same* self as that of lust and vengeance. We are not in the physical world, and cannot
say, 'There is this self, there is that self', as we
might say, 'There is an apple, there is an orange'. I
would prefer to call our two selves, which are not
really two selves, or our two levels of the self—
which have not, however, the sharp measurable gap
between them that the notion of a level physically

implies—different modulations of existence; let us remember what we have already said about reflection and its power of fostering such modulations. But, of course, this term, modulation, or modality, or mood—any of these words might be suitable in English—itself needs to be made precise. We are not dealing with what one might call predicable modulations, that is to say of modes of being which are definitely different from each other, but which can be predicated, at different times or in different circumstances, of one and the same subject, or, in the vocabulary of an older philosophy, of one and the same *substance*. The whole direction of our quest will by and by give us a better understanding of the kind of thing we are dealing with when we talk about these strictly existential modulations, or, if you prefer the phrase, about these varied tones or tonalities, of existence.

But let us resume our study of our example from Corneille's *Cinna*. Augustus finds himself caught up in a certain situation; he is the intended victim of a plot devised by conspirators of whom two at least owe to him everything they possess, and indeed everything they are, but who claim that in killing him they will be suppressing a tyranny that has reduced Rome to servitude. It is obvious that Augustus cannot ignore this situation; on the contrary he must as it were revolve it in his mind, so that he can see it from every side; and the surprising thing is that we here once more come up against what I said earlier about contemplation as a turning inwards of one's awareness of the outer world. It is not a matter merely of turning inwards, of *introversion;* the word that naturally occurs to us is *conversion*, though not in any strictly religious sense. The Emperor appears to himself not as the mere victim of human ingratitude, but as responsible, in the last analysis, for the situation in which he finds himself caught up. For in the past has he

himself not acted just in the same manner as those
who have now decided on his death? So that for
Augustus, entering into his own deeper self essentially means, in this case, seeing his situation from
the other man's point of view and thus making it
impossible for himself simply to condemn the conspirators in the straightforward fashion which at
first seemed his only course. The man who returns
to his own depths is forced to ask himself the
gravest question that can be put to any man's conscience: 'Who am I to condemn others? Do I really
possess the inner qualification that would make such
a condemnation legitimate?'

The kind of internal contradiction which we have
so often come up against here displays itself in a
very striking fashion: to enter into the depths of
one's self means here fundamentally to get out of
oneself, and since there can be, as I have already
several times emphasized, no question of our having
two objectively separable selves—a Dr. Jekyll and
a Mr. Hyde, as in Stevenson's story—we must suppose that we are here in the presence of an act of
inner creativity or transmutation, but also that this
creative or transmuting act, through a paradox
which will by and by become less obscure, also has
the character of being a *return*—only a return in
which what is given *after* the return is not identical
with what was given *before*: for such an identity—
let us suppose, for instance, that Augustus emerges
from his painful self-examination just the same
man, in every respect, that he was before it took
place—would rob the ordeal of all significance and
would in fact imply that it had never really taken
place. The best analogy for this process of self-
discovery which, though it is genuinely discovery,
does also genuinely create something new, is the
development of a musical composition; even if such
a composition apparently ends with the very same
phrases that it started with, they are no longer felt

as being the same—they are, as it were, coloured by all the vicissitudes they have gone through and by which their final recapture, in their first form, has been accompanied.

But the problem of the feasibility of bringing about a state of ingatheredness, and, more profoundly, of the metaphysical conditions of the ingathered state, entails, from the moment in which we face it in its widest scope, an anxious self-questioning about the relationship that subsists between me and my life; or in other words, it forces us to reflect on this notion of 'being in a situation' which we have already considered in the case of Corneille's Augustus.

The very fact that the bringing about of an ingathered state *is* feasible forces us to abandon an assumption which has been at least implicit in most philosophical doctrines up to our own time: the assumption that we can treat the given determinant conditions, that constitute my *empirical* selfhood, as contingent in relation to a kind of *abstract* self, which, in the last analysis, is identical with pure reason. If my real self were this abstract self, obviously the ingathering process would be a process of abstraction, too: it would be an operation, rather against one's natural grain, by which one withdrew oneself from life, towards reason. But this is just what it is not; the highest spiritual experience bears conscious witness against any such interpretation.

To treat the self of given circumstance as contingent in relation to a kind of transcendental kernel is fundamentally to regard that empirical self as a husk of which the rational self can, and in a sense ought to be, stripped. But I can only carry out this stripping in so far as I arrogate to myself the right to abstract myself from a given circumstance and, as it were, to stand outside it. Let us ask ourselves whether the assumption that we can step outside of our skins in this spry and simple fashion is not

merely an illusion or even a lie. In abstracting myself from given circumstance, from the empirical
self, from the situation in which I find myself, I
run the risk of escaping into a real never-never or
no-man's-land—into what strictly must be called a
*nowhere,* though it is a nowhere that I illegitimately
transform into a privileged place, a high sanctuary,
a kind of Olympus of the spirit. However, it is
against the idea of such an Olympus that we are
drawing up our forces. What I said at the beginning
of this book about *inclusion,* in relation to the notion of an omnicomprehensive experience, is equally
true about *abstraction;* these are merely mental
operations that subserve certain determinate purposes, and it is at an equally determinate stage in
our journey—not always and everywhere on our
journey—that they have their proper place. To arrive at this or that determinate result, we properly
make use of abstract thought, but there is nothing
in the method of abstraction itself that has any
note of the absolute about it. One might assert
indeed, taking one's stand against that mirage of
abstract, absolute truth that has been thrown up by
a certain type of intellectualism, that from the
moment when we seek to transcend abstract
thought's proper limits and to arrive at a global
abstraction, we topple over into the gulf of nonsense—of nonsense in the strict philosophical sense,
that is, of words without assignable meaning. There
is not, and there cannot be, any global abstraction,
any final high terrace to which we can climb by
means of abstract thought, there to rest for ever;
for our condition in this world does remain, in the
last analysis, that of a wanderer, an itinerant being,
who cannot come to absolute rest except by a fiction, a fiction which it is the duty of philosophic
reflection to oppose with all its strength.

But let us notice also that our itinerant condition
is in no sense separable from the given circum-

stances, from which in the case of each of us that
condition borrows its special character; we have
thus reached a point where we can lay it down
that *to be in a situation* and *to be on the move* are
modes of being that cannot be dissociated from
each other; are, in fact, two complementary aspects
of our condition.

I have been pondering over our present topic for
a great many years. It was about two years before
the first World War, that is, in the days when I was
starting on the investigations that led to the writing
of my first *Metaphysical Diary,* that I was first led
to postulate what I then called the non-contingency
of the empirically given. I was chiefly interested in
raising a protesting voice against a then fashionable
type of transcendentalism, but I was also ready to
acknowledge, from that date onwards, that the
non-contingency of the empirical could be affirmed
only in a rather special sense . . . as it is affirmed,
in fact, by the subject itself, in the process of creating itself *qua* subject. But in the sequel, though my
thought did not exactly *evolve* in the ordinary current sense of that term, I found myself attaching a
much more positive and actual meaning to this
notion; in the first instance, it had been a kind of
anticipatory glimpse of the *shape* of a thought
whose full content was still to come. The notion of
an ordeal, or test, to which the self subjects itself in
the state of ingatheredness has played an essential
part in our argument; Corneille's Augustus under-
went such a test. That notion, however, should
now enable us to grasp also in what sense a man's
given circumstances, when he becomes inwardly
aware of them, can become, in the strict sense of the
term, *constitutive* of his new self. We shall be
tempted, of course, and we must resist the temptation, to think of a man's given circumstances, or of
the self's situation, as having a real, embodied, independent existence *outside* the self; and of course

when we think of a man's situation in this falsely
objective way it does become hard to see how it
could ever become his inner ordeal. But, in fact,
as Sartre, for instance, has very lucidly demonstrated, what we call our given circumstances come
into our lives only in connection with a free activity
of ours to which they constitute either an encourage-
ment or an obstacle. These remarks about circumstances should be linked up with my earlier remarks,
in chapter four, about facts. I spoke there about
the reverberatory power of facts, as I might speak
here about the reverberatory power of circumstances; but I insisted also that *in themselves* facts
have no authority, and I might even have said no
autonomous validity, and I might say the same thing
now about circumstances.

There does, however, seem to be a very strict
connection, if not even a kind of identity, between
what I called earlier an *inwardness* and the non-
contingency of given circumstances. In fact, we
might say that we can hardly talk about inwardness
except in the case where a given circumstance has
positively fostered inwardness, has helped on some
growth of the creative spirit. An artistic example
might clarify things here. An artist like Vermeer,
we might say, did not paint his *View of Delft* just
as he would have painted some other view, if he
had lived somewhere else; rather, if he had lived
somewhere else, though he might still have been an
artist, he would not have been Vermeer. He was
Vermeer in so far as the *View of Delft* was something he had to paint; do not let us say, however,
'He was Vermeer *because* he painted the *View of
Delft*', for the conjunction 'because', in its causal
sense, has no bearing at all on the matter. Nothing,
at our present level of discourse can allow itself
to be reduced to a mere relationship of cause and
effect. If for Vermeer the view of Delft had been
a mere spectacle, if he himself could have been

reduced to the condition of a mere spectator, he would never have been able to paint his picture; let us even assert that he would not have been an artist at all. . . . One might be tempted at this point to proceed to an examination of the contrast, the deep-rooted contrast, between the artist and the photographer. But even there we would have to be cautious. For in the last analysis the photographer cannot himself be strictly compared to his own camera, his own purely objective apparatus for recording views; even he, in so far as he is endowed with a certain inwardness, has in an indefinable sense something *more* about him than there is about his camera, however perfect an instrument it may be (it is not the camera after all that chooses what angle it is set at). And in my own case, I who am neither painter nor photographer am still something more than a mere spectator, in so far as I am capable of *admiring* the spectacle that I am contemplating. Do not let us ever forget, indeed, that to admire is already, in a certain degree, to create, since to admire is to be receptive in an active, alert manner.

Experience, indeed, proves to us in the most irrefutable fashion that beings incapable of admiration are always at bottom sterile beings, perhaps sterile because exhausted, because the springs of life are dried or choked in them. But in the case in which we do genuinely admire a landscape, or for that matter even a human face, we cannot really feel at all that the coming together of this landscape and this face, and of ourselves, is merely fortuitous. In the case of genuine admiration, I am somehow raised above the level of mere contingency; and yet at a first glance I seem to be without the categories that would enable me to designate or specify the level to which I am raised. For if I am not at the level of mere contingency, I am certainly not at that of mere necessity either. But in fact, from this point of view, nothing is more important than to acknowledge—in this following in the wake of all philosophers, Schelling for instance, who have thought deeply about art—that in this realm the opposition between contingency and necessity must be completely transcended.

By twisting and divergent paths, we have now perhaps reached a point where we can arrive at a deeper understanding of the nature of ingatheredness. In 1933, in *Positions et Approches Concrètes du Mystère Ontologique*,* I expressed myself as follows: 'It is within my ingatheredness that I take my stand or, more accurately,' equip myself to take my stand towards my own life; in some sense I do withdraw myself from my own life, but not as the pure knowing subject does in idealist theories of cognition; for in this retreat, I am still carrying with me what my life is and also perhaps what my life is not, what it lacks. For it is at this point that we become aware of a gap between our beings and our lives. I am not my life; and if I am in a position to judge my life, it is only on the express condition of first being able to make contact once more with my being, through an ingatheredness that transcends every possible judgment on my life and every representation of it'. I think that today I would somewhat modify these statements. For instance it is not exactly the truth if one says, bluntly and flatly, 'I am not my life'; for, as one of the characters in a recent play* of mine says, 'Yes *and* no, that is the only possible answer where it is we ourselves who are in question'. I ought to say both that I am my life and that I am not my life; the apparent contradiction tends to vanish away if we understand that I am weighing the actual life I have been leading in the balance of the po-

* Included in *The Philosophy of Existence*.
*L'Emissaire, in Vers un Autre Royaume.

tential life I carry within me, the life that I aspire
to lead, the life that I would have to lead if I
wanted to become fully myself; it is into this life
of potentialty and aspiration that I penetrate when
I turn inwards. But here again, as we did a short
time ago, we have come to a place where the opposition between contingency and necessity must be
transcended. It must be transcended as soon as
anything at all resembling a personal vocation crops
up; it is in the name of such a vocation—which imposes itself on me not as a fate, not as the mask
of dire necessity, but rather as an appeal to me—
that I may be led to condemn a life which is the
very life which, up to the present, I have actually
been leading.

It is from a similar point of view that we must
treat the notion of an *encounter,* a notion whose
importance has apparently not, at least until our
own time, been clearly recognized by philosophers.
As long as we keep our argument at the level of
the *thing,* of the physical object, the encounter or
collision of two objects can obviously be considered
only as the fortuitous intersection of two series, of
which one at least must be dynamic. A car bumps
into a bus or into the side of a house. Their paths,
as we say, crossed. But at this point we may be
tempted to forget that, though there can be a
collision between two objects, there cannot be an
encounter or a meeting in the fullest sense of the
word except between beings endowed with a certain inwardness: and the encounter between such
beings resists, of its very nature, the attempt to
express it in merely visual terms, where the collision
of billiard or croquet balls, for instance, obviously
does not. It is also clear that, at the level of the
strictly human encounter, there is a whole scale of
possible meetings that ranges from the quite trivial
to the extremely significant. The nearer I get to the
lower end of the scale, that is to say to a basic

triviality, the nearer I get to an encounter that can be treated as an objective intersection of paths; humanly speaking it is nothing but a kind of elbow-ing. Every day in the street or the tube I elbow my way through hundreds of other people, and this elbowing is not experienced in any real sense as an encounter. All these unknown people present themselves to us, in fact, as mere bodies occupying a certain share of space in the *lebensraum* in which we have to maintain our own share of space and through which we have to thrust our way. But it is enough for some small thing to happen, some-thing which is objectively speaking nothing at all, for us to transcend this subhuman level: for in-stance because of something about the tone of voice in which someone in the crush says, 'I beg your pardon', or perhaps because of something about the smile accompanying such a simple phrase, there is a sudden spurt of clarity, of a clarity that has noth-ing in common with that of the intellect, but that can somehow light up, as a flash of lightning would, the obscurity—which is to say, fundamentally, the solitude—through which we are groping our way. Let us suppose now that two or three days later we encounter again 'by chance', in the house of some third person, or in a hotel, the person whose smile lighted up our way for us; we find something very significant in this fresh meeting; and if some-body says to us contemptuously that it is a mere coincidence, we shall have a very distinct feeling, though not one that we can justify, that the person who expresses himself in this way has never reached the level of a human reality that cannot be re-duced to the elementary schema of statics and dynamics that applies certainly well enough to phys-ical objects in whose repeated collisions, (if they were to collide several times), there certainly could be nothing but coincidence. This does not mean that we are acknowledging my right to explain this

second meeting in, as it were, a mythological fashion, but only that the meeting takes place at the
level of inwardness, that is to say, of *creative development*.

At this point in our argument, indeed, it should be
obvious that as soon as there is life, there is also
creative development. Or rather, to express the notion as I have expressed it already, in a vocabulary
which is also that of Karl Jaspers, there is creative
development as soon as there is *being in a situation;*
and, of course, for our purposes, the term life does
need to be defined in this way, phenomenologically,
and without any reference to the data of biology.
The etymological link between 'life' and 'liveliness'
in English—there is a similar link between 'vie' and
'vivacité' in my own language—is very instructive
in this connection; we ought no doubt to be able
to demonstrate that what we call life, in a phenomenological context, is inseparable from the living
being's interest, which moreover is a contagious
interest, *in* life. A really alive person is not merely
someone who has a taste for life, but somebody
who spreads that taste, showering it, as it were,
around him; and a person who is really alive in
this way has, quite apart from any tangible achievements of his, something essentially creative about
him; it is from this perspective that we can most
easily grasp the nexus which, in principle at least,
links creativity to existence; even though existence
can always decay, can become sloth, glum repeti-
tion, killing routine. It may be that these rather
simple remarks have a real relevance to ethics, and
that they enable us to safeguard the idea of man's
personal dignity without having recourse to that
ethical formalism, which is so often sterilizing in
its actual effect on conduct, and which is too apt
to disregard the element of the irreducible in human situations and acts. It should be added that in
placing creativity at the basis of ethics, we at the

same time transcend that sort of ethical individual-
ism for which the individual tends to be thought of
as something self-contained, a monad; while on the
other hand the direction of growth of our ethics
would be towards that open community of which
what I have called the ideal city is only the anticipatory skeletal form, the abstract ground-plan.

What is more important than anything else, in
fact, is to *recognize* the nexus which links these
different aspects of spiritual reality. To recognize
—it should be clear by now that it is around a
series of acts of recognition that the body of
thought I am striving to present to you is gradually
building itself up; and perhaps it may not be un-
helpful if we reflect for a few moments on the
essential nature of recognition. There is, however,
a language problem here, but we shall have to try
to get over it. The French verb 'reconnaître' needs,
apparently, two separate English verbs to cover
the whole scope of its meaning, 'recognize' and
'acknowledge': (though there are certain senses, perhaps slightly archaic, in which 'recognize' can be
used for 'acknowledge' even in English—to recognize somebody as your King is, for instance, the
same thing as to acknowledge him as your King).
Moreover, there is a third sense of the French
verb, a sense which expresses the activity of scouts
who spy out the land in front of advancing troops,
and the English do not describe this activity as
recognition but, borrowing the actual French verb
in an obsolete spelling, as reconnoitring. In what I
have to say about recognition, this range of meanings of 'reconnaître' and 'reconnaisance' in French
must be borne in mind; it being my assumption of
course that these are not merely three disconnected
meanings, which one word through some accident
of language happens to have, but that they are
intimately connected with each other, and even
really aspects of the same basic meaning. For the

Englishman, with his three different words for what are likely to seem to him three wholly separate uses of 'reconnaître', this assumption may not seem so obvious as it seems to me. In our use of the word 'reconnaître', in fact, in the present context, we are closer to the English ranges of 'reconnoitre' than to the English ranges of 'recognize'; I am reconnoitring, at the philosophical level, rather as I would if I had just arrived in a strange town. I begin by feeling quite lost there; that means that, wishing to explore the town, I find myself back, after a few minutes, where I started; or perhaps I find myself confusing two different streets because they look rather like each other. But my reconnoitring begins to lead to actual *recognition* from the moment when I find that I am at least sure of the route I have to follow for my immediate practical purposes; take the first turning on the right and then, a little farther on, turn left into a small square . . . This route that I feel sure of becomes a sort of axis, and I make little explorations first to one side of it, then to the other. It is clear in this example that the set of operations by means of which I carry out my reconnaissance and gradually begin to recognize my whereabouts is related to a certain desired line of action, an essentially mobile line; the thing is to get from one particular point in the town to another particular point; not just from anywhere to anywhere. There are a certain number of places that interest me for one reason or another: the post office, the town hall, the cathedral, the theatre, and so on . . . It is between these points that I must create precise relations, all referred to my own body or to the ancillary means which my body has at its disposal—buses, trams, tubes, and so on—for transporting itself from one place to another. It is interesting also to note that if there is any centre out from which these connective lines radiate, it is the place where I am living, a place which has a quite special relationship with my body. But let us notice that what we have to do is to create con- nivances, a network of connivances between my body and these secondary centres of interest, each of which itself is linked with some precise kind of activity: buying stamps, getting hold of an identity card or a ration book, attending a religious cere- mony, and so on. . . .

Let us notice, now, that we can also reconnoitre on this sense at the psychological or the social level. Perhaps it is a matter of some human environment in which it is necessary that I should learn to find my way about. Possibly somebody has warned me, 'You will meet such and such a person, he will be very nice to you, but be cautious, he is not reliable; on the other hand, there is another of your new associates who will seem to you at first rather brusque in his manners, even disagreeable, rather, but that's only on the surface, he's a very decent chap indeed, behind his forbidding facade'. Bearing this information in mind, I will modify my way of behaving . . . which in such a case, of course, is above all my way of talking. Perhaps I am a naturally trustful person, and I would be inclined to make friends at once with the person who was very nice to me; now I know that I ought to be a little wary of him, just as if I had been warned that in some dark corner of my house or my hotel there was a hidden step that one had to be careful not to stumble over.

Such examples could be multiplied indefinitely. They all converge towards a central idea, which is at once very simple and very important, that the act of reconnoitring, of getting to recognize my surroundings in the widest sense, is hardly separable from the sense of familiarity that is gradually created between me and the background, whatever it may be, of my habitual activities. We shall, of course, try to find a metaphor for this activity of reconnoitring; in each case it is as if I had to make a little mental sketch map, to which I could refer as I went on. But it is important to see that what matters is not the map as such, the map as a mental object, but the use I make of the map. We all know people who literally do not know how to read a map, that is to say who are unable to establish a correspondence between the map itself and the concrete conditions under which they are called upon to make use of it. But this correspondence—this ability to compare the map with the countryside around one, to get it orientated correctly, and to find one's way by it—is, of course, what is required. And there are other cases where the map is not properly comparable to a mental object at all, where it consists of a set of motor impulses that fit in with each other; this seems to be the case with animals, who, to all appearances, are capable of reconnoitring, of finding their way about, but who would, needless to say, not be capable of reading any kind of map at all.

We must now continue with our process of turning our awareness of the outer world inwards, and ask ourselves what it is to reconnoitre, or to fail to reconnoitre, at the level of our own lives; what it is to find our way, or not to find our way, in ourselves. A character in one of my plays, *Le Chemin de Crète*,* a woman, makes this speech to her lover: 'It is strange that you who cannot find your way about in your own life, who are lost there as in a dark forest, should plan the lives of others, should cut broad roads through them, never suspecting for a moment that your roads break down on uneven ground or get lost in dense thickets'. It seems to me that at this point we should place our main emphasis on the idea of a man's interests or

*Broadcast from London in June, 1950, under the title *Ariadne*.

values, an idea which cropped up a short time ago
when we spoke of life and its centres being created
in relation to extremely determinate modes of activity, modes of activity determined, in fact, *by*
such interests. To make no reconnaissance in life,
and thus to fail to recognize one's surroundings and
to find one's way, is to be a prey to confusion.
Life in such a case is like a page of manuscript
all scribbled over with erasures and alterations.
That is only a simile, of course, but its concrete
meaning is that a life, let us say my life, has been
so cluttered up with various odd jobs I have had
to do, and perhaps, too, with amusements that met
only some secondary interest of mine, that now I
am no longer able to make out what is the relative
importance of any particular occupation of mine
as compared with any of my other occupations. I
say the relative, not the absolute, importance: I
am speaking solely of the importance of an occupation for me, not for others, nor from some ideal
standpoint—of its importance merely from my own
point of view. What is very strange indeed in this
case is that I can no longer ever get at my own
point of view. Thus I may, for instance, impose on
myself a set of very wearisome duties, without taking account of the fact that they are in some sense
fictitious duties, and that I would be far more true
to myself if I had the courage to set myself free of
them. But it is not quite clear what 'true to myself'
means in that sentence; we are up against the old
difficulty that crops up every time we talk of the
self. However, it should be clear enough in this
instance that if we have a distinct conception of
what 'myself' means in the phrase 'true to myself',
that conception is related solely to the idea of
creativity. This self to which I have to be true is
perhaps merely the cry that comes out to me from
my own depths—the appeal to me to become that
which, literally and apparently, I now am not.

But we are now in a position to grasp the nexus that links the act of reconnoitring, and the fact of recognition on the one hand, with creation and creativity on the other. To recognize one's own nature at any level whatsoever is possible only for a being who is effectively acting, and to the degree to which he is effectively acting; though his activity may be exercised within extremely narrow limits and not be perceptible to the outside observer. A paralytic, for instance, who is placed in a seat beside a high window in Montmartre, say, or the Pincio, may still have to reconnoitre, to find his way about, in the scene that he is contemplating. He remains an active being, though his activity has been reduced to an exploring glance; and in so far as he is a reflective being his reconnoitring may lead to a kind of self-recognition. But obviously, if he is suffering from a total paralysis, and to the degree to which he is nothing more than an inert object (though to be *nothing* more than that, in the case of a living being, is inconceivable), this possibility of reconnaissance and of recognition no longer exists.

All these remarks should help us to get a more exact grasp of the meaning of the idea of a *situation,* an idea, indeed, of which we have already made use in a former lecture.

It is very difficult indeed to define the notion of a situation, in the sense of the word that interests us here, for every attempt at a definition runs the risk of transforming the notion into that of a set of objective relations, that is, of relations cut off from the being that I actually am, and indeed from any other being to whom my fancy or my feelings might lead me to compare myself. Our best course here, therefore, is, as it has so often been in the past, to start off from concrete examples. One can start, for instance, as I have done in one of my own books (*Du Refus à L'Invocation,* p. 116), with the idea of a house or a hotel which has 'a bad situation'. Let us take in fact, of these two alternatives, the hotel. I say the hotel has a bad situation, and underlying my assertion there must be a grasp, by myself, of certain objective relationships between the hotel and its surroundings; let us say that the hotel is near a tannery which gives out disagreeable smells. If the hotel has a bad situation, that is because the hotel's very purpose is to harbour travellers, and travellers will certainly be put out by the smell of the tannery. If somebody says to me after a certain lapse of time, 'The hotel has been sold, people were no longer going to it', I shall explain the hotel's failure by its bad situation. But the notion of a situation need not necessarily have a merely spatial application. I can say that a man is in a good or a bad situation. Here again, underlying my assertion, there must be certain objective data; but these data have reference to a being capable of saying, '*My* situation', have reference, that is to say, to the man's existence as something which he does not passively suffer but actively lives.

It should be obvious at once that a being of this sort (a being *in* a situation, a being that can say, '*My* situation') is not an autonomous whole, is not, in your expressive English phrase, *self-contained;* on the contrary such a being is open and exposed, as unlike as can be to a compact impenetrable mass. One might even say that such a being is permeable. But here as always the objective image must be subject to correction based on the fact of my existence, of my awareness of myself *as* existing. What we are driving at is not a kind of porousness, like that, for instance, of a sponge. It would be better to think of that sort of aptness to be influenced, or that readiness to take impressions, which is called in English 'suggestibility' or 'impressionability', a notion which reflection finds it hard to get a grip on, partly because we have a tendency to represent the notion to ourselves in physical terms, and these are obviously inadequate. Suggestibility or impressionability is usually linked to a certain lack, in the human character, of inner cohesion. Somebody who is all of a piece with himself cannot really be very suggestible or impressionable; and therefore it is the nature of this lack of inner cohesion that we ought to try to throw more light on. We shall be inclined at first, no doubt, to treat it as a *mere* lack. But that is a superficial view, and to realize how superficial it is we have only to think of the sort of man who is all stubbornness and resistance, the sort of man for whom it is as impossible to be receptive to a new idea as to welcome a new acquaintance. Is not his case the real case of inner lack? Can we possibly consider hardness and obstinacy as positively valuable qualities? This is the moment to recall what we previously said about receptiveness, and about how receptiveness cannot be considered as something merely passive.

But at this point we must obviously make certain delicate and subtle distinctions; for if there does exist a certain relationship between suggestibility, impressionability, on the one hand, and the gift of welcoming new ideas and acquaintances on the other, nevertheless the relationship can certainly not be considered as that of mere identity; for a mind can be welcoming without being inconsistent; but inconsistency is just what threatens the excessively suggestible or impressionable person, the person, that is, who lacks defences against the solicitations exercised on him from outside by whatever it is given to him to encounter in life. No doubt the man who is capable of welcoming somebody else's ideas does feel a momentary propensity to make them his own, to take them under his wing; but this propensity, if it were yielded to in every case, would obviously be a symptom of a kind of intellectual deficiency. We ought to be capable of understanding a new idea without therefore necessarily adopting it; and in reality there is no possibility of tolerance except in a society where that distinction, between grasping a notion and accepting it, is maintained. It must be regretfully asserted, however, that this distinction, which was respected by all the best minds of the last century, is today in danger of being altogether obliterated from the popular consciousness; is, indeed, almost obliterated already.

There are many reasons for this regrettable state of affairs; one of them no doubt is the gasping, hurrying rhythm of our lives; I am not referring only to the relative absence of true leisure today, but also to the increasing incapacity even of genuinely philosophic minds to follow out a long continuous task, the sort of task that requires perseverance and a good wind, in the long-distance runner's sense. Every student today is forced to get his results as quickly as possible, no matter by how many improper short cuts, so that he can get his degree or his doctorate and land his job. The results of scholarship are measured by a temporal coefficient; the point is not merely to get one's result, but to get it in as little time as possible. Otherwise the whole value of one's researches may be called into question, even the possibility of earning a modest livelihood may be swept away. This is a very serious matter, for such conditions are at the opposite pole to those required for the real flowering of the intelligence, in the richest sense of that word. The rather vulgar comparison that occurs to me at the moment is that of a man who needs a few suits in a hurry, who cannot spare time for a fitting, and who therefore has to take one off the peg in the nearest shop. But one cannot insist too much on the point already put so forcibly by Bergson, that true intelligence is the enemy of the ready-made, that, if one may put it so, all its genuine creations are made to the customer's measure.

One might also bring in at this point a notion of cardinal importance, though one that has been sadly neglected, the notion that is expressed, and expressed very exactly, by the German word *distanz*. I do not think that the word 'distance', either in French or English, denotes quite the same notion, and it has certainly not the same range of associations. We might, however, use for *distanz* the English word aloofness, on condition that we took that word as denoting a positive and valuable quality and not, what it can also denote, a mere disinclination to participate. What we are concerned with is a kind of borderland which thought must keep in existence between itself and its object; or, to express this more dynamically, we are concerned with the act through which thought is stiffened to resist the temptation to engulf itself in its own object and become merged with that object. There are more and more people today who give the impression of flinging themselves blindly into an idea or an opinion; and a rather vulgar type of pragmatism has, of course, played an utterly sinister part in encouraging this tendency. Nothing could be more false, indeed, than the supposition that, by maintaining this borderland of aloofness in existence between thought and its object, one is tending towards a scepticism which will by and by paralyse all one's positive thinking. On the contrary the human mind can remain properly critical only on condition that it preserves this aloofness, and the almost complete vanishing away of the critical spirit in our contemporary world is, without any doubt at all, one of the worst of the several calamities that today threaten the human race.

# CHAPTER VIII

## 'MY LIFE'

IN OUR last chapter we wandered over a wide terrain and were tempted into several sidepaths; today we must get back to the question that has been, as it were, the half-hidden theme of all these variations, 'Who am I?', and we must tackle it directly. Who am I, indeed—I, who interrogate myself about my own being? I cannot do better than refer myself here to what I have already written on this topic on one of the most important, but also one of the most difficult pages of my book *Being and Having*. But I must try as it were to de-compress what on that page remains too compact, too little drawn out from its implicitness.

When I ask myself, 'Who am I, I who interrogate myself about my own being?' I have an ulterior motive, there is a more fundamental question that I want to ask myself: it is this, 'Am I qualified to answer this question?' Ought I not to be afraid, in fact, just because the answer to the question, 'Who am I'? will finally be my own answer, that it will not be a legitimate answer? But such a fear implies an assumption of the following sort: that if a legitimate answer can be finally given to the question, 'Who am I?', it cannot be given by myself, but only by somebody else. Let us notice that this is not just a stage, to be transcended by and by, in the dialectical development of an abstract argument; all of us have at times had the feeling of being lost in ourselves as in a maze; in such a case we do count on somebody else, the nearest friend, the truest comrade, to help us out of the maze, or in a word to do our reconnaissance for us and help us towards self-recognition. 'You, who really know me better than I know myself, tell me, is it true—am I really such a selfish, heartless person. . . . ?' But here we are immediately up against a difficulty: the person whom I have chosen may really be able to enlighten me about myself, but it is I who have chosen him, it is I, that is, who have decided that he has the qualities that are needed to give me self-enlightenment. And once I have become aware of this, is not my problem as acute as it ever was? It is I myself who make it legitimate for my friend (and yet it is on that legitimacy I am relying) to tell me who I really am. If I chose this particular friend, was it not because, in the depths of my being, I felt I could risk wagering my self-esteem on his friendship for me? Of course the opposite kind of case occurs, though more rarely; it may be that far from turning to a tried and trusted friend I look for someone who will torment and wound me by his pitiless estimate of my character; one could find, in fact, quite a number of examples, especially modern ones, of such a lust for self-torture. But in this case as in the preceding one it is I who confer the credentials, it is I who bestow upon my supposedly pitiless judge, the necessary authority to pronounce against me what, let me repeat it, I and I alone have chosen to regard as a sentence from which there can be no appeal. But I have only to become aware of this fact, that is, to recognize myself as the source of my judge's authority, to be tempted to call that condemnation into question before which, only a short time ago, I was ready to bow my head.

Such observations may seem, to some of my
hearers, a little over-subtle. But I regard them,
nevertheless, as of capital importance, for they enable us to understand why we must reject the idea
of there actually being a legitimate answer, an
objectively valid answer, to the question: 'Who am
I?' 'Who am I?'—which is as much as to say, 'What
am I worth?'—is a riddle that, at the human level,
simply cannot be solved: it is a question that does
not imply, and cannot imply, any plain answer. It
seems hardly necessary to remark that if, still un-
convinced, we go on looking for a plain answer,
we need not turn to society, or to any particular
social group, with any hope of a successful end to
our quest. But, after all, it may be worth while
insisting on the impossibility of society's giving us
our answer, especially having regard to the sort of
prestige (in my humble opinion, an entirely hollow
prestige) which the notion of *the social,* as such,
enjoys in our own time.

From the moment when an individual joins a
political party or a religious sect (which of the two,
for our present purposes, makes no matter), it becomes a possibility that he may yield to this party
or sect the right to regulate completely all his
concerns. But let us pause for a moment and walk
warily: perhaps after all it does make a difference
whether it is a party or a sect we are considering.
Let us admit that in the case of the sect the individual who joins it may, at least in some cases,
refer himself directly to God and not merely to
the tenets and prohibitions of the sect; and let us
consider solely the case of the political party—of
the political party which, in our days, has laid hold
of a tyrannic power such as has not been even
dreamt of for centuries. If I have chosen to join
a party, it seems, of course, quite logical that I
should acknowledge its right to decide whether I
am, or am not, toeing the party line. But what is

clear enough in theory runs the risk of becoming a very complex matter in practice. If we have to do with the rule of a dictator, if the party is merely the emanation of the will of a leader, everything is simple enough; in such a case the individual party member alienates all his rights in favour of some other individual, he becomes, in the strict sense of the word, a fanatic. Notice, however, that even in this case certain factors are bound to crop up and confuse the issue. The party leader always represents himself as having been swept into power by some kind of collective will of which he is the delegate, so that I can always say that it is not for his sake, but for the sake of that collective will, that I have deprived myself of my natural rights and civic privileges. However, we know how fallacious the notion of such an unconditional delegation of power is; and the notion ought to be dealt with, once and for all, as severely as it deserves.

Yet, on the other hand, if there is no single leader who claims to be the delegate of the party's collective will, we are really in the dark; for even if a fairly solid majority is tending to take shape within the party, it may very well be the minority, even a minority reduced to a single individual, that has a clear view of the situation as it is; it is very difficult, except by a sort of arbitrary act of faith, a leap in the dark, to claim that the majority, as such, is infallible. The possibility that the minority may be in the right of it can only be denied in the name of what one might jokingly call a kind of mental arithmetic—a theory that one arrives at truth by taking a poll of opinion—which will not stand up to even the most cursory examination. It is, we know perfectly well, not by counting heads that we discover the wisest course. We do, of course, tend to accept it as a rule that the decision of a majority should prevail, but for coarse pragmatic reasons; within the state, the rule even of a ma-

jority that makes serious mistakes seems in most
cases preferable to civil war or anarchy; within the
party, the acceptance by minorities of certain de-
cisions with which they disagree seems preferable,
again in most cases, not necessarily in every case,
to the gradual fragmentation of the party by the
successive splitting away of small dissident groups.
It is only by the kind of argument that runs against
the grain of logic itself that we can convert such
a merely pragmatic acceptance into a mystical assertion that majorities as such are infallible, an
assertion which experience manifestly contradicts.
And there may come a point when even the pragmatic sanctions for the acceptance of majority de-
cisions by the minority cease really to apply. It
would be interesting, at least, in the light of contemporary history, to look into the methods by
which, in the 'new democracies', the majorities have
managed to discredit and dishonour their minorities,
making them, in fact, merely *qua* minorities, seem
guilty of high treason. The majority, in such cases,
has in fact found a useful way of getting rid of
the minority and of the logically insurmountable difficulties which its existence within a totalitarian
party creates.

On the other hand, however, we ought to add
that, except in the case where the individual party
member has become utterly and completely fanat-
ical, there is a risk of a tension arising in his conscience between the party line which he ought to
follow blindly, in strict obedience to the orders of
the day, and certain values which, in spite of everything, he has not managed, at his deepest and most
sincere level of self-awareness, to dismiss as merely
negligible. Thus—and I am talking about cases with
which I have been in direct personal contact—there
have been men who have left the Communist Party
just at the very moment when they were asked to
brand as a falsehood some statement which they

knew to be a true statement of fact. Quite obviously,
the very principle of totalitarianism excludes the
possibility of there being any realm in which the
individual can retain the right to judge for himself; but we should also acknowledge that the men
whom I am thinking of, and no doubt many other
men of their sort, joined the Communist Party
without having come to a full and clear awareness
of the unconditional and unrestricted nature of the
commitment that was being exacted from them.

This long discussion on politics may have looked,
on the surface, like a mere digression. But it leads
us to the conclusion that I cannot delegate to the
political party of which I am a member the right
to decide what I am and what I am worth, without
becoming guilty of a total alienation of my rights
and my privileges which is really equivalent to
suicide. One might say that the riddle, 'Who am I?'
is in this case not solved but merely silenced. The
question, indeed, has no longer any meaning. It is
a question that can be asked only by a person; I
have surrendered to the party everything that makes
me a person, so, in the last analysis, there is no
longer anyone who can ask the question.

At this point we once more come up against
that inner need for transcendence which we talked
about in our third chapter; but it meets us now in
a much more definite shape. Let us try to grasp
how it is that, if the question, 'Who am I?' is not
merely thrust out of the way in the fashion I have
just been describing, it is transformed into an appeal
sent out *beyond* the circle of those associates of
mine in whom, before I reached the stage of reflecting about it, I thought I recognized the right to
judge me. Here, with a single leap we touch the
extreme edge of our leading topic in this first volume. This appeal is supra-empirical, it is sent out
*beyond* the limits of experience, towards one who
can only be described as an absolute Thou, a last

and supreme resource for the troubled human spirit.
This supra-empirical appeal is the theme of what
I regard as one of the most important of my plays,
*L'Homme de Dieu*. I have been thinking over this
play of mine during the last month or two, for it
has recently been put on the stage in France, more
than twenty-five years after it was written. I shall
try to describe its story in a few words, for I think
the story illustrates very clearly the difficult notion
with which we are now grappling as the outcome of
our previous reflections.

The hero of this play of mine is a Huguenot
pastor in a Paris slum; he had been called to the
ministry a quarter of a century before, in a mountain village, but in those early days of his pastorate
he had gone through a terrible moral crisis. He had
doubts about his own inner strength, and doubts,
too, about whether he was really called to the
ministry; moreover his wife had confessed to him
that she had committed adultery and that her
daughter was not his child. He was plunged into
thick night; it was as if the ground were crumbling
away under his feet. However, little by little, gleams
of light began to pierce his darkness. He felt that
he had to forgive his guilty wife and help her to
regain her soul. But at the same time the fact that
he was able to forgive her restored his confidence
in himself, gave him back, at least in some degree,
his sense of being genuinely called to the ministry
by God. His reconciliation with his wife, his forgiveness of her, has in some sense been the corner-
stone of his new life. Twenty years have passed.
And suddenly the wife's old lover, with whom she
has broken off all contacts, comes back into their
lives. The lover is ill, he is in fact bound to die in
the very near future; before he dies, he wants to
see the girl whom he knows to be his daughter.
The pastor does not feel that he has any right to
refuse the dying man this last and legitimate satisfac-

tion. The pastor's wife, on the other hand, reacts
strongly against what she regards as her husband's
excessive mildness, she feels that if her husband
had a real, human love for her he could not bear to
welcome into his house the man who had betrayed
him; she is thus led to reconsider the whole past
and to discount her husband's forgiveness of her,
which she now tends to regard as a professional
gesture, something that was only to be expected of
a pastor; as a gesture, moreover, from which the
pastor profited as a professional man. But she also
infects her husband with her doubts; he loses his
bearings in his own life, he no longer knows what
he thinks about his act of forgiveness, nor, consequently, what he thinks about himself. I will not go
into the detailed working out of the plot nor into the
destruction which the pastor's inner uncertainty—
to which, however, it is not within the power of any
of his fellow humans to put an end—brings in its
train. In the last analysis, the poor pastor's only resource is to turn himself towards the One who knows
him as he is, whereas he himself perhaps is condemned to know himself only as he is not. One
might say that during the four acts of this play of
mine, we see the question, 'What am I worth?' rise up
in the pastor's mind, recognize itself, at the human
level, as an insoluble riddle, and finally transform
itself into an appeal to the absolute Thou.

But I think it is necessary at this point to anticipate and to examine certain objections—not, properly speaking, metaphysical objections—to the
general line of this argument, that may have occurred to some of my listeners.

For instance, might not somebody bring up the
following difficulty? 'You have assumed all along',
it might be said, 'that to the question, "Who am I?"
one ought to be able to reply with an answer of the
type, "*X* is either *A* or *B*, but not both*", that is,
"I am *this*", or, "I am *that*". But after all this is a

quite gratuitous assumption, which shows that your mind is still caught up in the toils of a grammar-ridden scholasticism. Why not say that to the question, "Who am I?" the answer is given by my life, my whole life—and certainly without implying, when one says this, that the essence of my life can be brought down to a few elementary propositions, of the type found in handbooks of formal logic!"

This objection is a very important one, and deserves close examination. But in order to examine it we shall have to try to discover what exactly I mean when I talk about my life, and we shall be obliged to admit that though the problem of my exact meaning here cannot be evaded, it is also a problem that is very difficult to solve in an unambiguous fashion.

My life presents itself to reflection as something whose essential nature is that it can be related as a story ('If I told you the story of my life, then you really *would* be astonished!') and this is so very true that one may be permitted to wonder whether the words 'my life' retain any precise meaning at all, if we abstract from the meaning we attach to them any reference whatsoever to the act of narration. What we have in mind here is not necessarily a story told to somebody *else;* I can obviously attempt to tell the story of my life to myself, but only on condition, of course, that I take up for the time being towards my life the attitude of some other person—of some other person who is supposed not to know about my life and to wish to know what it's been like. But to tell a tale is, essentially, to unfold it. 'Let us start at the beginning. First this happened to me, then that. About my earliest years, I can only speak from hearsay, for I have no personal memories', and so on. Thus my story will start off as the abridged version of a story that somebody else has told me. But all this changes as soon as I begin to get into touch with

my own earliest memories . . . Conceived or imagined in this way, my life presents itself to me, quite
naturally, in the shape of a sequence of episodes
along the line of time. It is obvious, on the other
hand, that I shall not be setting out to report *everything* that has happened to me, with all the
monotonous and wearisome detail of every successive day, one day on top of another. To narrate
can only be to summarize and yet the *summarizing*
of the parts of a tale is in a certain sense obviously
an opposite kind of operation from the *unfolding*
of the tale as a whole. If I say, for instance, 'My
earliest years were sad years, I was so often ill', I
am giving a condensed interpretation of a series of
events which were not given to me, when I did
experience them, in this condensed form. During
these childhood years, did I even know that I was
sad and ill? Illness is really an idea as foreign to
the small child as health is. So it is doubtful whether
I really knew that I was ill or sad. . . . Thus it is
just as if, retrospectively, I was dipping the web
or tissue of my past in some kind of dye. I only
become aware of this particular hue that tinges
my childhood *now,* in the light of what I have
learned or what I have lived through in subsequent
years. Probably therefore it is impossible (the impossibility being implied in the very notion of narration) for me to tell the story of my life *just* as I
have lived it. We have a naive idea of the story as
reproducing life—we talk, for instance, of some
story as a 'slice of life' or praise its 'documentary'
exactness—but anything like a reproduction of life,
in the strict sense, is just what a story cannot
provide. However concrete my thinking may be,
we have to acknowledge that my life, as it has
really been lived, falls outside my thinking's present grasp. The past cannot be recaptured except in
fragments made luminous by a lightning flash, a
sudden glare, of memory, for which the fragments

are present rather than past; and here, of course, we touch on the central experience around which Proust's great novel was planned and built up. For, though we are given certain such luminous fragments out of the past, the mind, all the same, has to work hard to rebuild the rest of the past around them; and in fact this rebuilding of the past is really a new building, a fresh construction on an old site, modelled more or less on the former edifice there, but not identical with it. What I mean is that it would be an illusion to claim that my life, as I turn it into a story, corresponds at all completely with my life as I have actually lived it. Consider what happens when we tell our friends the very simplest story, the story, say, of some journey we have made. The story of a journey is told by someone who has made the journey, from beginning to end, and who inevitably sees his earlier experiences during the journey as coloured by his later experiences. For our final impression of what a journey turned out to be like cannot but react on our memories of our first impression of what the journey *was going to be like*. But when we were actually making the journey, or rather beginning to make it, these first impressions were, on the contrary, held quivering like a compass needle by our anxious expectations of everything that was still to come.

From all this one might be tempted to draw a very simple and very practical conclusion: that the only thing that can give me an exact idea of what my life has been like will be a diary kept regularly from day to day, like that, for instance, of Samuel Pepys. But here we are up against new difficulties. Suppose I *had* kept a diary regularly, from day to day, during the greater part of my life. The diary will take up a certain amount of physical space. One imagines it as a heap of fat notebooks. I will be tempted to say, rather naively, 'There, on that shelf, lies my life!' But what does this really mean?

Because of the desire that possesses us all to embody our ideas, something in us is always happy
when we can point to an object that is localized in
space and say, 'There it is!' But after all the object
is only a heap of scribbled paper; if my maid cannot read, for her it is *literally* nothing but this scribbled heap, and she will be tempted to use it to start
the fire up, if we are short some day of newspapers.
Suppose that one day she is just about to commit
this irreparable outrage and that I dash up to stop
her, shouting, 'Wretched creature, my whole life is
there!', I will bet what you like that she makes no
sense out of what I am saying: what connection
can there be, for her, between my life and these
exercise-books?

At this point in the argument we have replaced,
obviously, the story-teller's problem by the reader's.
During a period of enforced leisure, brought about,
let us say, by my retirement from work, I decide
to read over my old diary. A great many of the
entries, most of them perhaps, leave me absolutely
cold, for they tell me nothing, they awaken no
living memory. I read on, just as if I were reading
about somebody else, and suddenly come upon a
detail that awakes an echo, that sets certain strings
vibrating. Here we have, at another level, the
luminous fragment once more, and how thrilling it
is; and yet at the same time the entry in the diary
has for me merely the character of an *allusion* to
something which, of its very nature, will not let
itself be fully expressed in words, and which is
something I have lived through. This experience
forces me to acknowledge quite definitely that my
life is *not* in these notebooks. At the very most, I
can think of the keeping of my diary as a set of
rather laborious experiments at which I have
plodded away in the hope of obtaining some day or
other the magical result we have just been describing. Naturally, of course, if I am an artist in words,

my experimental methods will more frequently bear fruit. We may suppose that in such a case my entries, when I re-read them, will arouse in me much more often that kind of ecstasy of the vivid, particular, remembered situation—the past situation, felt as if present—which lies at the basis of the achievement of Proust. But on the other hand, and from another point of view, ought not the artistic graces of my diary to make me a little suspicious of it? As a professional writer, am I not likely to make the loose pattern of life conform to the stricter pattern of my literary style—touching things up, giving them a twist which did not really belong to them? Or look at the matter more closely. Is something of this sort not likely to happen, whether I am a professional writer or not? I do not record an experience in my diary *while* I am having it but only some time *afterwards*; and because of this interval of time, I can quite easily, without meaning to, and without being aware of what I am doing, give this experience a kind of shape, a completeness, say, or a significance, which to start with it did not possess.

But there is another point we should notice. As I re-read it, my diary, packed with disconnected detail, produces a chaotic impression; but has my life really *been* this chaos? If it has, there is nothing more to say; life and diary are both rubbish dumps. Or at least I am in danger of thinking so; but at the same time I feel a kind of inner certainty that I cannot really have lived such a shoddy, discrepant, purposeless life. Only, does this inner certainty not lead me to the very discouraging conclusion that my life, now it is no longer being lived, has been changed by magic into its own corpse— into a record which no more resembles the life I did lead than a corpse resembles a vigorous, handsome living body? Or, to use a different metaphor, have I really good grounds for thinking that there

remains no more of my life now than there remains
of a burnt-out firework—up like a rocket, and
down like a stick! How can I admit that this is so?
To admit it would be to stand out against one of
the deepest of my own convictions. Thus, surely I
am under an obligation to discover what it is in my
life that subsists in spite of everything; what it is
that cannot be carted away like rubbish, nor blown
away like smoke. Is not my life, (in so far as I
can really speak about my life), what I have tangibly
achieved? Is it not, in fact, my works? To the
question put, ought I perhaps to answer: 'I am my
works, I am what I have achieved'?

But along this road fresh difficulties and disappointments lie in wait for us. No doubt in a
certain kind of limiting case, the case of the artist
above all obviously, such an answer might seem,
at a first glance, to be quite acceptable. Is not the
life of Cèzanne, or the life of Van Gogh, reducible
in the last analysis to the set of completed paint-
ings, of sketches, of drawings, of works of art of
all sorts, which the dead great man has left behind
for us? But here we run up against the same set
of snags that confronted us just now in regard to
the diary. And it would be the same if we took
the example of a novelist, Balzac or Tolstoy, or a
philosopher, Kant or Hegel. We are exposed in
every case to the same temptation. We see a certain
number of canvasses in a gallery, a row of volumes
in a library: *there,* we say, is Van Gogh, *there* is
Balzac. But what do we really mean? Van Gogh
is only there for the man who can see, Balzac for
the man who can read. Seeing, reading: think of the
mysteries, of the unimaginable complexities, of the
operations that are denoted by these two simple
terms! We must not be taken in by the apparently
grossly material nature of the thing that is in front
of us, that we can touch and handle. The work of
art is there for us to contemplate and, in a certain

sense, for us to draw more life from; but if we do draw more life from it, that is only by virtue of the act by which, opening ourselves to it and interpreting it for ourselves, we make it our own. For one's interpretation of a work of art is related fairly strictly to the sort of person one is, and therefore, in the case of every significant work of art, there is a wide and varied range of possible interpretations. It would be quite an illusion to imagine that there is a kind of nucleus which subsists independently of, and which is unamenable to, all interpretation, and in which one might say that the life and work of Van Gogh, or of Balzac, are literally embodied. But we must carry our argument farther. The achievements of a great artist may very often be uneven in quality; some of his works may be almost without his special personal flavour; glancing along the whole range, we often have to pick out the few high peaks. But in trying to make such an objective choice we run into serious difficulties. The works that are, for instance, an artist's own favourites are often not those that posterity will cling to *—but once we have mentioned posterity, we have raised all sorts of new and formidable questions.

We talk of the judgment of posterity, but have we any reason to suppose that this will be a consistent judgment? Are we to think of posterity as a sort of hovering spirit, mysteriously infallible? We shall have to ask ourselves later whether there is any real content that we can attach to the notion of the 'judgment of history'. But in our present much narrower realm of discourse—we are concerned merely with the judgments that have been made in the past and may be made in the future

*Gide in his last diary sees *Corydon* as his main achievement; almost any critic will consider this opinion nonsensical.

about works of art—everything seems to indicate
that it would be risky to the last degree to seek,
in the judgments of men at some given time, for
the definitive and the irrevocable: for our apprecia-
tions of a work of art are always, say what we will
to the contrary, affected by the 'climate of the age',
they reflect the unconscious general assumptions
which we share with our contemporaries during
some given period in history; the historically con-
ditioned attitude is something which, for all of us,
is quite inescapable; and perhaps we cannot even
imagine, without tangling ourselves in contradictions, a *dehistoricized* attitude in the name of which
completely objective judgments, judgments quite un-
tainted by the local, the temporal, the personal,
and in a word quite free from relativity, could be
made about works of art, literature, and philosophy.

But what is true of the artist is necessarily even
more true of the man who leaves behind him, when
he dies, no such tangible achievement. Might one
say that such a man has at least during his life
done certain things, and that his life is really what
he has done, is his deeds or his acts? But about
what deeds or acts are we really speaking? Shall
we fix our attention on a man's habitual line of
conduct or, on the other hand, on those exceptional acts of his in which he seems to rise above
or sink below his average level? Or should we be
content to recognize this contradiction, this contrast between the average and the exceptional, and
to say that this contradiction, in the last analysis,
is the man himself? But even here we are to some
degree still thinking in metaphors; we are imagining the contradictions in human character as being
something like the contrast of colours that clash,
that, as artists say, swear at each other. But this
metaphor does not properly correspond to the
reality of a human life, even if that life *is* contradictory. What we really want to know is whether

a man's conscience recognizes the contradictions in his life, whether it accepts these contradictions or, on the contrary, suffers because of them, whether it struggles to resolve them, and whether or not that struggle is crowned with success. Here we are up against something which transcends the deeds and acts in a man's life that can be objectively recorded, that can become part of outer reality: and, for that matter, just how literally can we take this notion of the transformation of the deed, once it has been done, into a kind of thing, of the committed act into an external fact? Let us recall what we said in an earlier lecture about the ambiguity of the notion of a fact; the same ambiguity is even more thickly present in the notion of an act. Sartre, in particular, has demonstrated very clearly in his last play, *Les Mains Sales,* the impossibility of my recognizing *myself* in my act once it has been committed; the very fact that the act is now over and done with, that it is irrevocable, makes it something that I can no longer intimately know; can I even call up in myself the state of mind in which I committed the act? It is infinitely probable that I cannot, for this act (we are thinking, naturally, of the exceptional rather than the habitual act) may have been linked to a kind of inner vertigo which, of its very nature, cannot be deliberately reconstituted in the mind.

But in all that we have said so far, we have been talking about my *past* life, and we have come to understand that it is pretty difficult to make it clear just what I mean by my past. My past certainly cannot be reduced to the wearisome succession of my days and my nights; but on the other hand I am becoming arbitrary, and perhaps I am merely mocking myself with empty words, when I attempt to resolve my past into a sort of synthesis. In the last analysis such a synthesis can only be a sort of synopsis, a schematic summary. Its tone will depend entirely on my mood at the moment when I undertake it. My past will take on a different colour to me according to whether I am going through a period of discouragement or whether my work is going ahead as vigorously and successfully as possible. So we must resolutely set aside the idea of the past as a kind of storehouse of documents on which various historical synopses could be based; that is a metaphor for the custodian of old parchments. In the mysterious essence of life there is something which just cannot be equated with such a custodian's beloved wills, and bills, and charters; it is, in fact, just those flashing moments in which our past relives itself in luminous fragments that deliver us, and deliver us very abruptly, from such metaphors for librarians.

However, our problem is really far more complex than we have so far admitted. When I talk about my life, I am still caught up in my life, I am still committed to living; thus my life is not essentially my past; to consecrate one's life or to sacrifice one's life to a task or to a cause, that is an act whose essential nature it is not easy for us to define, but the notion to which we relate it seems palpably different from those which we have so far evoked.

It is easy to show by an analysis of experience that my 'sense of life', or my vivid awareness of being alive, is a very fluctuating thing; the fluctuation is implied in the very fact of duration, or of personal lived time. Let us put it in a quite general fashion and say that the more definitely I am aiming at some purpose or other, the more vividly I am aware of being alive; but we must carefully distinguish at this point between my state of anxious expectation, when I am waiting for the arrival of important news or of somebody whom I love, and the act by which I concentrate all my energies on the achievement of something which depends on me, or at least in which I am in some sense really participating. The state of anxious expectation, when we really live it through and do not try to distract our minds from it, is experienced less as life than as a kind of agony that eats us up: your English word 'suspense' implies all this very expressively. But in the other case, in which I am concentrating all my energies on something, I *am* living in the fullest fashion, and we must look into the nature of this fullness of life. It is worth noting here that in the directly opposite case—the case of anxious expectation is not directly opposite —in which I feel my imaginative and creative powers flagging, in which I can do nothing, I seem to myself as if I were a dead man; I drag myself along, I seem to have survived my living self. This is, in the strongest sense of the term, our *lapsed* state; we are always in danger of falling into it under the influence of weariness or grief. Many roads can lead to it; what began as a creative activity can become a mere professional routine, the interest that I take in things and events can become blunted, and flat, and stale; the happenings of real life may come to arouse in me nothing more that the utter indifference with which I watch one episode succeed another in a really bad second-feature film. Whatever happens, it's all to me, I couldn't, as you say, care less. Your English word 'tediousness'—with the Latin *taedium,* and we should remember, too, the phrase *taedium vitae,* underlying it—conveys this feeling perfectly. But when tedium becomes general, when it seems to spread itself over the whole field of existence, it becomes something more than tedium, it becomes despair.

It seems legitimate to conclude from all this that the notion of my life cannot really be separated from that of a kind of interest which I take in my life, but in saying this we are only pushing the difficulty one stage further back: on what is this inter-

est brought to bear? Is it brought to bear merely
on the continuation of my own existence? Certainly
this sort of curling up in one's shell is quite a
possible course of action. We all know people who
do not seem to care about anything but 'keeping
fit', people whose interest in life does not extend
beyond the proper functioning of their own bodies,
but the very narrowness of their field reflects the
privation of their lives; everything indicates that
the more a man is encumbered, is loaded down,
with his own selfish concerns, the less intensely he
lives, or, if you like, the more poverty-stricken his
life is. We come up against a notion here which
seems to me of capital importance but for which it
is difficult to find an idiomatic English equivalent
—at least neither I, nor the English translator of
my previous work, *Being and Having,* managed to
do so. The French terms I use are *disponibilité* and
*indisponibilité.* Literally, in English, one would render
these as *availability* and *unavailability,* but it might
sound more natural if one spoke of handiness and un-
handiness, the basic idea being that of having or
not having, in a given contingency, one's resources
to hand or at hand. The self-centred person, in
this sense, is unhandy; I mean that he remains
incapable of responding to calls made upon him
by life, and I am not thinking merely of the appeals
for help that may be made to him by the unfortunate. I mean rather that, over a much wider
field, he will be incapable of sympathizing with
other people, or even of imagining their situation.
He remains shut up in himself, in the petty circle
of his private experience, which forms a kind of
hard shell round him that he is incapable of breaking through. He is unhandy from his own point of
view and unavailable from the point of view of
others. It follows from this that it is essential to
human life not only (what is obvious enough) to
orientate itself towards something other than itself,

but also to be inwardly conjoined and adapted—
rather as the joints of the skeleton are conjoined
and adapted to the other bones—to that reality
transcending the individual life which gives the individual life its point and, in a certain sense, even
its justification.

Nevertheless, and here we catch our first glimpse
of the central theme of a philosophy of inner freedom, the structure of my life is such that it can
shrivel away till it is no longer interested in anything but itself; in other words, it does lie within
my power (and this, of course, is part of my inner
freedom) blankly to reject anything that might extend my experience. I have at this point, as you
will have noticed, substituted the term *experience*
for the term *life,* but I believe that the substitution can be justified. There is one point of view
from which life and experience can be regarded as
equivalent terms. *One* point of view, notice, only:
for if it is possible to give one's life, to sacrifice
one's life (and we should not talk, in the same sense,
of giving or sacrificing one's experience), it is obviously only so on condition that we interpret the
notion of one's life in a different sense, which we
must now set out to define. But in this case, as in
so many others, a preliminary analysis is necessary.

We might be tempted at first to think of life as
something which I have, as I have an account at
the bank: as something which it is for me to spend,
if I feel like spending it. It is just as if I were
comparing the years that would in the ordinary
course of things be left to me to the banknotes
which still remain in my notecase and with which
I can do what I like. But the comparison is a clumsy
one and can only lead us into error; I talk about
having a certain number of years of life left to me,
but of course I do not really *have* them, I merely
count on them. It would be much better to compare
them to a cheque about which I am in some doubt

whether it will be honoured or not; and yet I have some grounds, at least, for supposing that it will not be dishonoured; to sacrifice my life, therefore, would be like throwing away such a cheque, about which I cannot be quite certain, but which is more probably worth something than worth nothing. But, even when corrected after such a fashion, our metaphor remains inadequate. A cheque is something quite distinct from me, I can get rid of it without ceasing to be myself. But is it the same with my life? Can I give my life without giving myself? It may be pointed out, of course, that the cheque may represent a sum of money which I have been counting on to carry out some long-cherished project, to make a journey perhaps which, as common speech puts it in its vivid way, I have *set my heart on*. To give up the cheque is to renounce the journey; and it is even in a sense to maim or cripple myself, for perhaps it is the thought of this journey that has been mainly keeping me going. I will have to find a new reason for carrying on, a new foundation to build my life on, and this is something difficult to do, and often very painful to do. But surely at this point we have come back again to the notion of sacrifice in the true sense of the word, and we have left the realm of discourse in which we can properly talk of my owning my life, as I own my money. The cheque, *qua* piece of paper, is now nothing but a sign, a symbol. What really matters is the act by which I set about reshaping my life.

The truth is, sacrifice—and I have in mind naturally the most complete sacrifice, that of a man who lays down his life—is essentially creative. So much so, in fact, that it is in danger of falsifying its own nature if it reflects on itself in an incomplete fashion; attempts, that is, to interpret itself in merely rational terms. One might say that it is of the very essence of self-sacrifice that it is not able to give a rational account of itself, or rather that all its attempts at self-rationalization are fatally inadequate. One does not, strictly speaking, lay down one's life *for some determinate purpose*. Otherwise, we would have to conceive of sacrifice as a mere exchange of goods—this life for this purpose—on the open market. But at this level the notion of any such trafficking is inconceivable. The man who gives his life, if he is aware, in the act of giving it, of giving himself entirely—without any hope of continuing to exist after death, for instance—cannot, in the very nature of his case as he states it to himself, receive anything. And this, in fact, is the point that anybody will make who is trying to dissuade somebody, in the name of common sense, from making such a sacrifice: why give everything for nothing?

As common sense, this is irrefutable. Only, may it not be that at this level it is common sense that is out of place? There is no shared ground on which common sense and the hero or martyr could meet; they are like two axes that can never intersect. In itself, sacrifice seems madness; but a deeper reflection, the secondary and recuperative reflection of which we spoke earlier on, enables us, as it were, to recognize and to approve it as a worthy madness. We understand that if a man were to shirk from such madness, he would be falling below himself. The truth seems to be that in this special case there is no middle ground between the subhuman and the superhuman.

But these observations can help us to throw at least some light on the mysterious relationship between myself and my life. I have said that giving my life seems the same as giving myself; does this mean that I am merging myself and my life together into a single confused concept? By no means. Let us notice that I said giving my life seemed the same as giving myself, not as doing away with myself. Self-sacrifice can be confused with self-slaughter only by the man who is looking on the hero's or the martyr's act from the outside, from its material aspect merely, and who is therefore incapable of associating himself sympathetically with the inner essence of the act. On the other hand, the person who is carrying the act out has, without any doubt at all, the feeling that through self-sacrifice he is reaching self-fulfilment; given his own situation and that of everything dear to him, he realizes his own nature most completely, he most completely *is,* in the act of giving his life away. But is not this a strange paradox we have run into, and ought we not to walk delicately here? Would it not be absurd to say that I fulfil myself by the very act with which I do away with myself? Indeed, it would be, and very absurd indeed. Only, this is not the formula that really applies to our case. We have to distinguish carefully between the physical effect of the act of self-sacrifice and the act's inner significance. The *doing away* has to do only with the act's obvious physical effect: one dead body more on a field of battle. It would be insane to say that I fulfil myself in becoming a corpse; my self-fulfilment takes place at another, an invisible level. I am thinking for instance of such a case as that of a French soldier who may have sacrificed his life in the dark days of May and June, 1940, without having any hope that his sacrifice would make the least difference to the outcome of the Battle of France. However hard it may be to express this without falling into the kind of rhetoric which every philosopher worthy of the name ought to detest, we do feel confident that such a man's sacrifice (and there were many such sacrifices) did save something; what we think of it as saving is probably honour, but, again, what we mean by honour is not very clear. This is another opportunity for the cynical spokesman of common sense to amuse himself by saying that all this talk of honour is so much wind; that I am using hollow words that canting politicians and lying journalists use when they want to sound noble. But would it not be truer to say that those men who sacrificed themselves in 1940 died at peace with themselves, and this in spite of all the horror that surrounded them? They answered a kind of call that came from their very depths, and it would certainly be arbitrary to assume that this call was articulately aware of itself, that it was formulated in words that could really be adequate to its meaning. It is only from this point of view, that is to say, in a way that we can only express in a rather negative fashion, that it is possible to conceive how it could be that what we call the death of these men might also have been the summit, the culminating peak, of what we call their lives. But at this point it seems as if a strange interflow is taking place between these two words and as if death might be really, and in a supreme sense, life. However, this can only be asserted on condition that we completely transcend the categories of biology.

Here we touch again on that extremely important truth of which we previously became aware when we were examining the nature of self-recognition —the truth that in the last analysis I do not know what I live by nor why I live; and that moreover, as a character says in one of my plays, perhaps I can only go on living on condition that I do not ask myself why I do. My life infinitely transcends my possible conscious grasp of my life at any given moment; fundamentally and essentially it refuses to tally with itself; as another character in my plays says, 'My life is the realm of yes and no, the place where I have to say at the same time that I *am* and that I am *not*'. However, what complicates and embroils this fundamental situation, inextricable as it is even to start with, still further, is that the practical conditions in which my life unfolds itself force me, in spite of everything, to attempt to make my accounts tally; but my sort of moral bookkeeping is of its very nature concerned with factors that evade any attempt to define their essence or even to demonstrate their existence. Perhaps there is a certain sense in which I might describe myself as condemned to make my calculations with cooked figures, and there, no doubt, is the source of the stupidest blunders into which I am led. The task of the profoundest philosophic speculation is perhaps that of discovering the conditions (almost always disconcerting conditions) under which the real balance-sheet may occasionally emerge in a partial and temporary fashion from underneath the cooked figures that mask it.

Here again I shall take an example from one of my plays, *Le Monde Cassé*, to which I referred also in an earlier chapter. This is its story. Christiane Chesnay, before her marriage, loved a young man who, just as she was going to confess her love to him, announced that he was going to become a Benedictine monk. From that moment, nothing seemed to matter for her; her life had lost its meaning, and she did not feel she was doing anything wrong in consenting to become the wife of Laurent, whom she did not care for particularly, but who was deeply in love with her. To distract herself, Christiane flings herself madly into a gay and brittle social round; she has beauty and wit, she fascinates everybody who comes near her; her husband, who is a dim, dull sort of person, suffers from wounded vanity because nobody ever takes any notice of him, except as his wife's husband. Christiane discovers after a time that Laurent is meanly jealous of her social success and that what would cheer him up would be to see her humiliated and rejected. Through a sort of ill-directed charity she hastens to give Laurent this satisfaction, pretending that she is deeply in love with the musician Antonov, who ignores her. But she feels a sort of horror when she becomes fully aware of the effect this lie has had on her husband. Suddenly she feels herself alone and lost and, obeying a kind of irresistible impulse, she gives herself to a young man who is in love with her and whom she had never taken seriously. It looks as if she is likely to elope with her lover and thus sink for ever into the world of emptiness and illusion. I should add that she has by this time had news of the death of the Benedictine monk, who is the only man she ever really loved. But just at this critical moment, the monk's sister comes to see Christiane, and tells her a very strange story. The young monk alone in his cell had learned in some way, perhaps through a dream, of Christiane's love for him. At the same time there had been abruptly awakened in him a mysterious sense of responsibility for her, of paternity according to the spirit. 'At a given moment in his life', says the sister, 'he became aware that the same act which for him was one of self-surrender to God for you signified despair and—who knows?— ultimate perdition. And from that moment he prayed with all possible ardour that to you, too, it should be given to see the light'. Christiane's reaction to this story is a feeling of repulsion, of instinctive reaction against this sanctified love, so different from the purely human love she had wished for. But little by little the light breaks through and it is the light of secondary reflection. She becomes aware at last of the truth within her own deepest nature, the truth against which, not wishing to recognize it, she had struggled. She perceives that it is not her real soul that has been animating her life, but a caricature of that soul, a false charity, all of whose commands were lies. And in the light of this inner revelation, even her relations with her

husband are given a new foundation, she acknowl-
edges how guilty she has been; but there is a
communion of sinners, as well as a communion of
saints, and without doubt it would be impossible to
separate the one communion from the other.

Obviously, this is an oddly special case. But it is
more or less true of all of us that the circumstances
in which our lives unfold themselves tend to make
those lives of ours strangers to their own underlying depths; and it is just from this point of view
that we can see how secondary reflection may
exercise a recuperative power. But it should be
added that this power, though it is intrinsic to
reflection, can only be exercised in one's own
case thanks to the mediation of somebody else.
This mediation, however, is essentially of the spirit;
it is offered or proferred to us, but it is always up
to us to acknowledge it and welcome it, and it always remains possible for us to reject it; we shall
see, by and by, that this possibility of welcome
or rejection constitutes the very essence of our
inner freedom.

# CHAPTER IX

## TOGETHERNESS: IDENTITY AND DEPTH

DURING the last two chapters, but particularly during the very last one, we have gradually come to acknowledge how impossible it is not only to give, on one's own account, an objective answer to the question, 'Who am I?' but also even to imagine the valid giving of such an answer by anybody else who was considering one's life from the outside. Little by little, we have been forced to insist that my life is essentially ungraspable; that it eludes me and indeed eludes, in all directions, itself. Nevertheless, I can be called upon to sacrifice my life or, at the very least, to consecrate it. We should pause for a moment over this notion of consecration; self-sacrifice can be considered, of course, as merely the consummation of an act that consists of living for something, of dedicating oneself to what Josiah Royce called a cause, meaning an idea or a quest. But we should pause here again to ask ourselves what the secret link can be that binds my life to such an act of self-dedication. Can we consider the act as a sort of seal set, as it were, on my life from the outside? It is obvious that we cannot: the words 'from the outside' are grossly inadequate, and in fact where exactly, when we talk of this act of dedication coming from the outside, do we imagine it as coming from? No, it is only from the very depths of my own life that this inner need for self-dedication can spring.

Moreover, we are here rediscovering, at a level of higher potency, the truth which we acknowledged in our third chapter when we recognized, as the phenomenology of Husserl recognizes, that every kind of awareness is essentially awareness of something other than itself; so human living, driven in this way to dedicate itself, seems also essentially the living of something other than itself. What can make our path difficult and uncertain at this moment is, however, that we are inclined to take it as an axiom that awareness and life are concepts different in kind. But the arguments of our last chapter in particular should enable us to grasp the fact that such a difference in kind can no longer be postulated when I am speaking, not of life as a mere phenomenon to be investigated, but of my own life. I cannot speak of my own life without asking myself what point it has, or even whether it points in any direction at all. . . . The pun there, by the way, may appear frivolous but it is necessary to convey the ambiguity of the French word 'sens', which refers here not only to the *meaning*—in one of the multifarious senses of that slippery English word—but also to the *bearing*, or *direction*, or *relevance*, or *orientation*, of my life. The verb 'to mean', in English, has, of course, these two among its many other senses: 'I don't see what you mean' can be the equivalent of, 'I don't follow the sense of what you are saying,' but also of, 'I follow the sense of what you are saying, but I don't see its bearing on our general argument'. 'Meaning', however, has far too many other senses, and is too vague and confused a word altogether in its popular usage to be suitable here. The Germans convey the two uses of 'sens' neatly by the words 'Bedeutung' and 'Richtung' and they have an intermediate word 'Sinn', though it does not strictly imply the notion of orientation.

After that little linguistic digression, let us repeat the proposition from which it arose. I cannot speak of my life without asking myself what point it has, or even whether it points in any direction at all; and even if I decide that it is in fact a pointless business, that it points nowhere, still the very fact that I have raised the question presupposes the assumption that life, in some cases at least, might have a point. If I could really uproot this assumption from my mind, at the same stroke my life would cease to be my own life. I mean that I would cease to apprehend it as my own; this would be that final estrangement from oneself that, in the ideal limiting case, can be reached only by a slave, and by a slave who has ceased to be aware of his own state of servitude. And in fact there is every reason to suppose that except in this abstract sense, as an ideal limiting case, such final self-estrangement is inconceivable. For I think that there can be no doubt that there does remain in every slave, fairly deep down, an obscure awareness of having been outraged, and with this awareness at least an indistinct, incipient protest, a feeling that one's life ought not to be a slave's life, that its proper growth has been thwarted.

When I ask whether my life has a point, it does seem that I am imagining a kind of significance, or relevance, which my life would go on having whether or not I wanted it to; I am, or so it seems to me, more or less explicitly relating my question to the idea of a play in which I have to take a part; I am asking myself about the possible theme of the performance in which I have been induced to participate. From this point of view I might compare my situation with that of an actor who has been given his own cues and lines, but who has not had the play as a whole read to him and has not even been told briefly what it is about. He has merely been told: at such and such a cue, you will make your entrance, you will speak the following lines, accompanying your lines by this piece of business, then you will make your exit. The actor has to suppose that his lines and his business, which in themselves seem to him almost pointless have their point in relation to the total pattern of the play. Thus if life as a whole has a point—or as we would say here, not to break the metaphor, a plot or a theme—then in some sense my own life has a plot or a theme, too.

However, if we stick to our actual situation, it is obvious that the life I have to live is not quite on all fours with the sort of episode I have just been describing. Keeping to the theatrical comparisons, which seem almost to be imposed on us at this point, we might say that in fact I am not told in advance what my lines and business are to be; I have to go right out there and improvise. But where the actor in the old *commedia dell' arte* had to improvise on the rough outline of a story given to him in advance, I am given no such rough outline. It is just as if—or so it seems at a first glance—the producer of the play had carelessly omitted to provide me with just the information I needed to carry out the task that had been entrusted to me in a proper fashion. Given all this, might I not be led into calling the very existence of the producer into question? Or, to put the point more precisely, would I not have solid grounds for asserting that, whether or not there really is a producer, everything is run just as if there wasn't one? This comes down once more to saying that there is no rough outline, no plot, or, to go back to the phrase we started with, that my life has no point. From this perspective, I will naturally be led to ask whether I myself, against the grain as it were of this general pointlessness, can by my own efforts give my life a point; can I myself confer a kind of significance on it? This is, in its atheistic form, the position of contemporary ex-

istentialism. Of course, we have already seen quite
a number of reasons for considering it to be an
untenable position.

Did I not affirm at the beginning of this lecture
that it seems impossible that the act by which I
consecrate my life to some idea or quest could be
regarded as external to my life, but that, on the
contrary, the act rather resembles the bursting of
my life into flower? But according to the hypothesis
of atheistic existentialism, which I have just formulated, this act of consecration would be something
external to my life. The hypothesis implies, apparently, something more or less of the following sort:
that my life has come into my hands by accident,
through the merest unforseeable chance, like a notecase that one happens to find dropped on the pavement. If I am an honest person, I have no doubt
tried to return the notecase to its owner; all my
attempts to find him have proved vain, and here
I am in possession of a considerable sum of money.
What shall I do with it, to what use shall I put it?
In this case, we should notice that our question has
a definite scope and implies a range of possible
definite answers; finding this money may give me a
chance to satisfy some old wish—or to pay some old
debt—or to help somebody who is not merely in a
state of poverty but in a state of wretchedness. I
must make a choice between such concrete possibilities. But such possibilities, it should be noted,
have their roots in my own life, such as it was
*before* I found the notecase. My life, itself, on the
other hand, cannot really be compared to this lucky
find. I do not *find myself alive*, in the sense in which
I might find the owner of these stray coins or notes.
My existence as a living being precedes this discovery
of myself as a living being. One might even say that,
by a fatal necessity, I pre-exist myself. But this
forces us to take up a position diametrically opposed to that, for instance, of Sartre, in that sen-

tence of his that has been so often quoted: 'Man's motto is to be a maker and, as a maker, to make himself and to be nothing but the self he has made for himself'. Everything that we have been saying up to this very moment forces us to take our stand against any such affirmation. 'It would be impossible,' I wrote, commenting on this sentence in my essay, *Techniques of Degradation,** 'to deny in a more aggressive fashion the existence of any sort of natural world, of anything that is inherited by us, or, more profoundly, of reality itself, that reality which is conferred upon us or in which we participate, and which gives us a greater impetus, the deeper we penetrate into it.'

The time has come when we should attempt to draw out all the implications of the notions of a situation, and of participation as we have attempted to elucidate them in our three previous chapters. It may be, however, that to reach our goal we may find it convenient to go back, in the first instance, to the problem of the relationships between myself and others, as that problem now stands, in the light of our previous observations, and particularly in the light of that criticism of the notion of a *state of consciousness* which I roughed out in chapter three. I think my best course will be to present you with a condensed version of my analysis in my essay, *Homo Viat*or, an analysis which is a kind of nucleus of the possible phenomenology of the relationships between myself and others.

We should notice, to start with, that the ego, as such, shows up in an extraordinarily vivid and aggressive fashion in the mental world of the child; and one might add that this vividness and aggressiveness persist, in later years, to the degree to which that mental world survives in the adult. The child,

*Included in a collection of essays on Evil, by various authors, Plon, Paris, 1948.

let us say, runs up to his mother and offers her a flower. 'Look,' he says, 'that was me, *I* picked it.' His tone and his gestures are very significant; he is pointing himself out as somebody who deserves the admiration and gratitude of grown-ups. Look, it is I, I in person, I, all present and correct here, who have plucked this flower! Above all, don't believe for a moment that it was Jim or Lucy who picked it. The child's, '*I* did it', in fact, excludes in the most definite fashion the deplorable misunderstanding by which *my* exploit could be attributed to others. But we find adults standing up in the same way for the ego's rights. Let us take the example of the amateur composer who has just been singing, in a throaty voice, a song for which he has written the tune. Some artless listener asks, was that by Debussy? 'Oh, no,' says the composer, bridling and smirking, 'that was a little thing of my own.' Here again the ego is trying to attract to itself the praise, the surprised and admiring comments, of a something *other* than itself, that it uses as a sounding-board. In every case of this sort one may say that the ego is present in the flesh, appealing or protesting, in various tones of voice, that nobody should infringe on its rights, or, if you like, tread on its toes. Notice, too, that in all such cases one essential factor is what I shall call, a little pedantically, *ecceity*: that is, a hereness and a nowness, or rather a here-and-now-ness; we can think of the ego in this sense, in fact, as a sort of personified here-and-now that has to defend itself actively against other personified heres-and-nows, the latter appearing to it essentially as just so many threats to what I have called its rights. These rights, however, have essentially a pre-juridical character, they are from the beginning inseparably linked to the very fact of existing and thus are exposed continually to all sorts of more or less mortifying infringements. In so far as I feel myself in danger of being passively overlooked or actively slighted in a hundred different ways that all cut me to the quick, one might say, in fact, that I have no protective skin at all, that the quick is exposed already.

The obvious example to take at this point is, of course, that of the shy young man who is making his first appearance at some fashionable dance or cocktail party. Such a young man is, as you so admirably express it in English, to the highest degree *self-conscious*. He feels himself the cynosure, and the extremely vulnerable cynosure, of neighbouring eyes. It seems to him that all the other people at the party, none of whom he knows, are looking at him, and looking at him, too, with what meaning glances! Obviously they are making fun of him, perhaps of his new dinner jacket which does not fit him as well as it should, perhaps of his black bow tie, which was all right when he last looked in the mirror, but now, he feels quite sure, has gone lopsided. And then, of course, he cut himself when he was shaving. And everybody must have noticed how clumsily he held his glass just a moment ago, so that some of the sherry slopped over. And so on, and so on . . . To such a young man it seems that he has been literally thrown (as Christians were thrown to the lions) to the malevolent lucidity of other people's glances. Thus he is at once preoccupied with himself to the highest possible degree and hypnotized at the same time to a quite supreme degree by others, by what he imagines other people may think of him. It is this paradoxical tension which your excellent word *self-consciousness* so compactly expresses.

But on the other hand this tension is quite at the opposite pole from what I have at various times called, and shall here call again, intersubjectivity. And the opposite nature of the two things cannot be too heavily underlined. Let us suppose that some unknown person comes up at our party to say a

word or two to the shy young man and put him
at his ease. The latter, to begin with, does not find
himself entering into the direct relation with his new
acquaintance that is expressed by the pronoun *you*
but instead thinks of him as *him*. Why is *he* talking
to me? What is *he* after? Is he trying to satisfy some
sinister and mocking curiosity? Let us be on our
guard anyway. Let us be extremely non-committal
in our answers to his question. Thus, because he is
on the defensive with this other guest, our young
man has to the least possible degree what can be
described as a genuine encounter or conversation
*with* him. He is not really *with* the other any more
than he can help being. But in a very general fashion,
indeed, one might say that it is the relationship expressed by the preposition *with* that is eminently
intersubjective. The relationship that *with* expresses,
here, does not for instance really apply to the world
of objects, which, taken as a whole, is a world merely
of juxtaposition. A chair is *alongside* a table, or
*beside* it, or we put the chair *by* the table, but the
chair is never really *with* the table in this sense.

But let us get back to our example and let us
suppose that the ice is after all broken, and that
the conversation takes on a more intimate character.
'I am glad to meet you,' says the stranger, 'I once
knew your parents', and all at once a bond is created
and, what specially matters, there is a relaxation of
tension. The attention of the young man ceases to be
concentrated on himself, it is as if something gripped
tight together inside him were able to loosen up.
He is lifted out of that stifling here-and-nowness in
which, if I may be allowed a homely comparison,
his ego was sticking to him as an adhesive plaster
sticks to a small cut. He is lifted right out of the
here and now, and, what is very strange surely, this
unknown person whom he has just met accompanies
him on this sort of magic voyage. They are together
in what we must call an elsewhere, an elsewhere,

however, which has a mysteriously intimate character. Let us say, if you like, that they are linked to each other by a shared secret. I shall have to come back, no doubt, to the notion of the secret as a mainspring of intersubjectivity, but let us notice, before we leave our example, that ties of quite a different nature might have grown up between the stranger and the shy young man. A man whom I run into quite casually learns that I am very fond of coffee, coffee is desperately scarce in France at the time, so he gives me a hint about how to get some on the black market. One cannot say that this incident is enough in itself to create a bond between me and him; all we have in common is a *taste,* and that is not enough to draw us together at the ontological level, that is *qua* beings. And neither, on the other hand, is a taste for coffee, even combined with a certain broadmindedness about means of getting hold of coffee, enough in itself to create the sense of complicity and freemasonry in vice that might arise from the avowal, to somebody who shared it, of some much more dubious inclination. But such a sense of complicity is not really what we have in mind, either; rather it is in the sort of case where I discover that a stranger has recognized the deep, individual quality of somebody whom I myself have tenderly loved and who retains a place in my heart, that true intersubjectivity arises.

We could also take examples of intersubjectivity from artistic and religious experience. But it is clear that there would be no absolute discontinuity between the examples taken from ordinary life and those from the higher reaches of the spirit; on the contrary there would be a kind of graduated scale, with something like the mystical communion of souls in worship at the top end, and with something like an *ad hoc* association for some strictly practical and rigidly defined purpose at the bottom. But it would be possible to show that a single human relationship can work its way all the way up and down this scale; this, for instance, is quite obviously true of marriage. There may be moments of drought in marriage when the wife becomes for her husband merely that 'silly creature who should have been busy darning socks, but there she was clucking round the tea table with a lot of old hens,' and there may be almost mystical moments when the wife is acknowledged and loved as the bearer of a unique value to which eternal bliss has been promised. One might therefore say that there is an hierarchy of choices, or rather of invocations, ranging from the call upon another which is like ringing a bell for a servant to the quite other sort of call which is really like a kind of prayer. But, as I tried to show in my first *Metaphysical Journal,* in invocations of the first sort—where we press a bell or make some other sort of signal to show that we want service—the Thou we are invoking is really a He or a She or even an It treated pragmatically as a Thou. When I stop somebody in the street to ask my way, I do say to him, it is true, 'Can *you* tell me how to get to such-and-such a Square?', but all the same I am making a convenience of him, I am treating him as if he were a signpost. No doubt, even in this limiting case, a touch of genuine intersubjectivity can break through, thanks to the magical powers of the tone of voice and the glance. If I have really lost my bearings, if it is late, if I fear that I may have to grope my way for hours through some labyrinthine and perhaps even dangerous warren of streets, I may have a fleeting but irresistible impression that the stranger I am appealing to is a brother eager to come to my aid. What happens is, in a word, that the stranger has started off by putting himself, as it were, ideally in my shoes. He has come within my reach as a person. It is no longer a mere matter of his showing me the way as a guide-book or a map might, but of his really giving a helping hand to somebody who is alone and in a bewildered state. This is nothing more than a sort of spark of spirituality, out as soon as it is in; the stranger and I part almost certainly never to see each other again, yet for a few minutes, as I trudge homewards, this man's unexpected cordiality makes me feel as if I had stepped out of a wintry day into a warm room.

On an occasion of such a sort, we have lingered for a moment on the threshold of intersubjectivity, that is, of the realm of existence to which the preposition *with* properly applies, as it does not properly apply, let me repeat, to the purely objective world. Within the realm of intersubjectivity, naturally, a whole throng of different sorts of relationship must be distinguised from each other. Words like 'ensemble' in French, 'together' in English, 'zusammen' in German, can be entirely deceptive, particularly in the cases where they refer to travelling or even to working together, to the togetherness of the bus or the factory. There are certainly cases in which what is called collective labour can be considered, at least from the point of view of how it looks on the surface, as the arithmetical sum of the various special tasks performed by each separate individual. And yet even in such cases as this there is certainly also something that arithmetic cannot account for. There is at least in the background a sense of a common fate, there is certainly an indistinct awareness of the conditions to which all the workers in such a factory as we have in mind must without distinction subject themselves, finding, perhaps in every case, that such self-subjection goes against the grain. This feeling of community in effort and struggle that such factory workers have is quite enough in itself to deprive us of any right to treat them as simple units of force that can be added to each other. But we should recognize all the same that the level of reality represented by the preposition *with* can be a rather low and barren level—and this is naturally even more true in the case of the togetherness of passengers in a public vehicle. The content of this sort of reality, the reality for so many people of work and the journey to work, enriches itself only in the degree they learn to know themselves and to know their companions of bus or bench both in the uniqueness of their diverse beings and in the single colour of their common fate. It is only on this condition that a true companionship can be created such as that, for example, which existed in the army during the late war between fighting soldiers, and perhaps in a greater degree still between prisoners-of-war and civilian deportees in various German camps. An ordeal endured in common is the cement of such companionships, it is what permits them to arise.

But when we talk of common sufferings cementing human *relationships*, let us notice that this word is likely to lead us into error, unless we take it in a much deeper sense than its usual one, for instance, in treatises on logic: we must think of the relationship between two terms as something that really does bind them, as something that causes them to negate themselves as simple, detached terms. We might make this point clearer if we said that relationships between things are external, relationships between people are internal. When I put the table *beside* the chair I do not make any difference to the table or the chair, and I can take one or the other away without making any difference; but my relationship *with* you makes a difference to both of us, and so does any interruption of the relationship make a difference. Between two people, in fact, who have an intimate relationship, a kind of unity tends to be created which makes a third person, who has not been initiated into the relationship, who does not participate in it, feel an intruder. Many women must have had this feeling—and it is a very painful feeling—when their husbands or their sons had re-unions with old comrades of the army or of the prisoner-of-war or detention camps in their pres-ence. We come up here, once more, against the notion of the shared secret (the secret, in our pres-ent example, *not* shared by the intrusive third party) which I mentioned at the beginning of this analysis; and we can see how important and also how am-biguous the notion is. What appears to the non-initiated person as a secret may be merely a few jokes, a few allusions, to which she has no clue, and which therefore inevitably irritate her. But the secret may also, and in a deeper sense, be a really in-communicable experience—generally a painful one —about which the initiated feel that others, who did not share it in the flesh, have no right to speak. It is just at this point that what we call in France pure sociology, and what you call anthropology, the study of customs and ceremonies, strikes on some-thing deeper than itself, something that constitutes us in our very selfhood. I have only, for that matter, given very simple examples here; from my own dramatic works I could take more complicated ones, particularly from my *Quartet in F Sharp*, of which the first version dates back to the first World War, but which anticipates in the most concrete fashion this whole philosophy of intersubjectivity.

In this play of mine, I present the extremely rich and in the end indefinable network of relationships that interweaves itself between a woman, her first husband (a musician whom she divorces) and the musician's brother, whom she marries after the di-vorce. The climax of the play is the woman's sudden awareness of a suprapersonal unity which in some sense subsumes under itself the two men she has successively loved; she is no longer able to dis-tinguish whether what she has loved in the second husband is, or is not, a mere reflection of the first. But on the other hand the fondness of the brothers for each other resists this new test, and the movement of the play is towards the discovery, as it were, of a kind of musical order of relationships in comparison with which the individual's usual hasty judgments about himself, and about others, seem precarious and destructive.

The notion of intersubjectivity is obviously capable of multifarious developments. In the first place, it is not in any hesitant fashion that I suggest it is only this notion that can throw light on the more obscure and more important aspects of what is improperly called psychical but should, I think, be called metapsychical research. As Carrington has made perfectly clear, telepathy is an inconceivable process unless we are willing to acknowledge that there is a region where the words *I* and *You* cease to denote two nuclei quite distinct from each other between which objective relations can be established by the emission of signals. And if one thinks it over, one will also perceive that all human intercourse worthy of the name takes place in an atmosphere of real intimacy that cannot be compared to an exchange of signals between an emission post and a reception post; this, of course, is the same sort of point as was made in a previous chapter when we talked about sensation and the impossibility of considering it as the equivalent of the emission and reception of a message.

But there is no doubt at all that we ought to go further, and to acknowledge that intersubjectivity plays its part also within the life of the subject, even at moments when the latter's only intercourse is with itself. In its own intrinsic structure subjectivity is already, and in the most profound sense, genuinely intersubjective; and it is at this point that the whole development of our argument becomes organically connected with the earlier part of this lecture.

We have already had occasion to notice that it is

impossible to reduce the notion of the subject either to that of a mere formal principle of unity or to that of an aggregation of states of consciousness. Our last chapter, however, should have prepared us for the path we must follow if this opposition is to be transcended; or, in more exact language, for the fashion in which original unity and plurality are yoked together within the borders of the unique being that I am.

It seems to me that we can never apply ourselves too strictly to the following problem: to what degree, and within what limits, can my relationship with my own past be brought before my mind? When, for instance, I see strange faces around me on a bus or in the tube, I am often haunted by the notion that each of them is carrying around with him his own past. But what does it mean to carry around something intangible, of this sort? There, as it seems to me, our whole problem lies. Of course, we might stop in our enquiry where the police stop. Each of my fellow passengers could be arrested, taken to a police-station, asked to state his identity, place of residence, and so on. . . . This means merely that each of them, unless suffering from loss of memory, has the data to hand that are required for the compilation of his or her dossier. There is a whole range of headings that might be relevant: illnesses, successive changes of residence, of job, religious affiliations, party membership, and so on. One might say perhaps that our imaginary detainee has a gramophone record inside that can reel off the answers to such questions. But just what we mean by that is still obscure. It will not do to say that he or she *is* a gramophone record; but only that he or she *can* become so if subjected, as so often happens in our contemporary world, to persistent questioning, and *will* become so only to the degree to which de-humanizing treatment brings about a state of self-estrangement. All we can say is that from the very

start there was something that could become, or
rather could be degraded into, a gramophone record. This means that we must take it as a basic
assumption that each of us has it in his power to
submit his own experience considered as a whole
to the kind of treatment that inevitably distorts its
nature. However, this *experience as a whole*, which
can be distorted in this fashion, is just what we have
in mind when we talk about somebody or other's
*past*.

It is obvious, of course, that the more a man
is detached from his experience, the more easily it
will lend itself to this distorting treatment; the more
his total experience is something which he is still
actively living, the less easy it will be for him to
extract from it the depersonalized data required
as answers to the police questionnaire. This is the
very reason why we assume that a child, the least
detached kind of human being we can conceive of,
will be incapable of filling in such questionnaires.
All this forces us to recognize that we cling to our
past in a very uneven way, that we *are* our past in a
very uneven way, and it must be added that this
unevenness is related to a similar unevenness in
our *present* situation. Here, as several times before,
it is Marcel Proust who can set us on our way. In
other words, we must not believe that we can at
some given moment make a distinction that will be
valid for all the rest of our lives between what I am
now, on the one hand, and what, on the other hand,
I am now so detached from that I can speak of
it in an abstract fashion, that I can reduce it merely
to the state of some external object to which I can
*refer*. On the contrary the moods according to which
such distinctions are made, or are not made, vary
with the fluctuation of our present experience itself.
This is enough to show how unreal it is to represent
the past to oneself as in some sense preserved or
pickled, as if it were last year's blackberries or

walnuts. At any moment in my life, a magic shutter may snap back and I am once more the small boy of eight who is in a state of deadly anxiety because his mother is so late in coming home and who is running over in his fancy all the accidents that may have befallen her. Ought I to conclude from this that I have never really ceased to be that small boy?

Here again we are up against the apparently self-contradictory answer, the yes *and* no, which seems to be inseparable from the fact of existing as a human being. It would be false to claim that the little boy has been continuing to exist all these years, just as a table or a chair continues to exist even when I am not looking at it. The little boy of eight years old—who, in some sense, nevertheless, I still am—cannot by any means be conceived to have persisted after the fashion of a physical object. But on the other hand my assertion that I have never ceased to be this small boy is correct if we are ready to admit, like the fairy stories, which are the perfect symbolical expressions of this kind of truth, that there are modes of existence that are not objectifiable, but that have infinite possibilities of resurrection. Yet, strange as the symbol may be, it is only the extremely simplified expression of a much stranger reality. Between this latent mode of existence and the active, waking state in which I go out to post a letter and have to pause a moment at the pavement's edge to let the traffic pass, and so on, there lies an innumerable multiplicity of mental presences, that get in each other's way, and that enter into relations with me of such various sorts that it would be extremely useful to classify them even in the roughest and most approximate fashion. We might express this state of affairs by the simple formula that I am not merely myself: more strictly, is there any point in saying I am myself, since I am also somebody else? I am, for instance, the man I have been until quite recently, the man I was yesterday: there is a point of view, and a deep one, for which 'have been' and 'was' in such sentences lose all precise significance. There can be a real struggle for existence between the man I was yesterday, the man I have been until recently, and the man I have a tendency to be, a yearning to be, today.

It may, however, be objected at this point that we are here on a very dangerous road that may lead in the end to a mere flat denial of continuing personal identity. And we certainly ought to pause and look into that notion of personal identity, and into how we ought to understand it.

There is, however, a preliminary remark to be made, and it has to do with the conditions under which a judgment of identity can be properly made; for there is obviously no point in talking about identity, apart from judgments of identity. Now, we have to acknowledge that it is in the world of tangible *things*, in the objective world as such, that judgments of identity seem to be necessarily and strictly applicable. I lose my watch, say, somebody finds it and takes it to a lost-property office, let us say to the very office to which I myself have previously put in an enquiry about it. The watch that I claim and that is restored to me, because it corresponds to my description of it, *is* strictly identical with the watch that I lost. I am able to assert this not only because I recognize it but because the man who took it to the lost-property office found it on the exact spot where I had been sitting and where I supposed I must have dropped it. Apart, however, from this whole question of valid *identification*, we can the more properly speak of identity in this case because there has been no perceptible change in the nature of the watch itself between the moment when it fell from my pocket and the moment when I got it back from the lost-property office . . . It is a matter of common knowledge that an incident of this sort can be the point of departure for the dialectical development of what I shall risk calling an aporetic argument. A few superficial modifications (my watch, say, got its case slightly dinted by its fall from my pocket) do not prevent us from affirming that the thing which has suffered these modifications remains the same thing; but when the modifications extend their scope (for instance, I get rid of the old battered case of my watch, and have a new one made, and then some time later something goes wrong with the machinery and I have new cogs and springs put in, leaving of the original watch only its face and the face's glass covering), we may well hesitate to maintain our judgment of identity, to go on saying that it is the *same watch*, and it is obvious that there is no means of determining in an objective and universal fashion the precise margin of alteration beyond which the identity of what has been modified with what it has been modified from, can no longer be maintained.

Should we say, therefore, with the nominalists, that the only thing that persists as an element of identity and a principle of identification is the name? (This is still properly called *my watch, the watch that I first bought in such and such a year*, however often all the parts of it are successively replaced by new parts.) But this solution is obviously a fictitious one; the real question is what is it that induces us to maintain the identity of the name, of the appellation, even in the case where the identity of the thing as a thing seems to have disappeared. To explain what it is that induces us, we are obliged to evoke some such notion as that of a *felt quality of identity*; but such a quality is in its very nature not objectifiable. A better example than the one we have used already, that of the watch of which all the old parts are gradually replaced by new parts, would be a parallel example taken from the world of the child. It is not certain that we do really regard the watch of which all the parts are new, as in some sense the same old watch after all. But for the child the doll, of which head and arms and legs have been successively broken and replaced, does remain in a very vivid and real sense the same old doll; because the variable elements of the object have been caught up into the unity of the subjective sense of possession, and almost of adoration, that the child feels for this specially beloved object.

But what considerably complicates the problem is that quite apart from this permanence of a felt quality in the object, or a feeling about the object— a permanence which we ought not to call identity in the strict sense of the word—there is in the object itself the continuity of an historical becoming, and this even in the case where the felt quality of identity is absent. Let us take an example. Two or three years ago, I ran into an old schoolfellow whom I had not seen for a good forty years; I remembered him as a boy with red cheeks and bright eyes; I rediscovered him as an old gentleman with a flaccid face, whose eyes were quite expressionless. There was nothing in the quality of these two appearances, nor in my feelings about them, that could confirm that they were two appearances of the same person. All I could say is that I had an abstract, theoretical certitude that I should have been able to establish the existence of a continuity between these two contrasting states of the same bodily organism. But, indeed, that is not quite all: I should be able to assure myself that this man had memories which corresponded with my own memories of the period when we attended the same school.

This example is rather an instructive one, for it enables us to emphasize the contrast, where identity is concerned, between the realm of the He, She, or It on the one hand and that of the Thou on the other. There was nothing within me that, when I saw my old comrade, cried out joyously: 'So it is you, so it is really you again. . . .' Life, in such a case as this, has eroded something away; yet on the other hand I have an indefeasible certitude—some would say a mystical certitude—that if beyond the gulf of death I were to re-encounter those whom I have really loved (those, that is, who have been linked in the most intimate possible intersubjective fashion to what I am) I should recognize them instantaneously and as if by a flash of lightning, and it would be just as if no separation had ever taken place. This, however, is an act of faith, and it is not until my second volume that we shall be examining its possible foundations.

What emerges, finally, from this long analysis is the extreme complexity of the problem, as we call it, of personal identity.

Between the objective identity that we can affirm in the world of tangible things and what I have called the felt quality of identity there is obviously a gap; we can have the objective identity without the felt quality, and also, of course, the felt quality without the objective identity. Given such conditions, and given the general background of our argument, it is impossible not to acknowledge the usefulness of the notion of a kind of manifoldness within the self. But before attempting to define the nature of the manifoldness, we should make the following observation. At the level of feeling as such, quality (and most philosophers of the past have acknowledged this fact without, however, recognizing its implications) infringes upon, or one might even say usurps, the place of subjectivity as such. A felt quality, or a quality of feeling, that is, is not a mental object; one can make a distinction, for instance, between seeing a colour and the colour one sees, but not between feeling a pain and the pain one feels. The felt pain is an indissoluble unity. If it is true, as we have seen already that it is, that sensation cannot be understood on the analogy of transmission or passive reception, this is *a fortiori* true of feeling. This is a very important fact in relation to personal identity, properly so called; it enables us to get a better grasp of what I tried to express earlier when I spoke of my past which, in a sense, I still am, and on which my present situation is at every moment forcing me to make petty raids. These are rather like withdrawals from a small current account at the bank, where the greater part of my capital is not so easily available, being on deposit. But even this deposit account, though blocked for my everyday purposes, remains, however unhandy a one, an asset; and this is where the metaphor breaks down, for my past really cannot be considered as an asset, even a blocked asset, of this kind.

These remarks presuppose, and I hope that to some extent they clarify, a notion of the nature of time that is not that of common sense nor of commonsense philosophers. I shall not, at this point, raise the question whether it completely coincides with Proust's notion, but it is certainly akin to his.*

It is invariably the case at this level of discourse that, when we begin to expound any important notion, we have first of all to express ourselves in negative terms. Thus I must first of all explain just how duration, or personal time, ought *not* to be represented. We ought vigorously to reject any attempt to represent my life, or any human life at all for that matter, as a sequence of cinematic images. It is not strictly speaking the spatial representation of time that is the snag here, but rather the supposed relationship between a sequence of images and the life which the sequence claims to represent. It is part of the notion of cinematic images as such that they succeed each other; they follow on each

---

*As expounded by George Poulet in his wonderful *Etudes sur le Temps Humain,* Edinburgh House Press, 1949.

other's heels and one takes the place of another. As a mere spectator, supposing myself to be in a state of extreme fatigue or perhaps merely of perfect relaxation, I let them flow past me, as on the edge of a stream one lets the current flow past. But in so far as there is a real substance in my life, or in anybody's life, it is impossible that my life should reduce itself to a mere flow of images, and impossible therefore that its structure should be merely that of a succession. Why, it may be asked *is* it impossible? It is not that we have run into something that is absurd at a merely logical level: it is simply that we have to acknowledge that our inner experience, as we live that experience, would be an impossibility for a being who was merely a succession of images. And for that matter the old idealist argument still does retain, in this case, all its force. A succession is only a succession for an awareness that in some sense transcends it.

Yet this idealist argument is still more or less merely an argument at the level of formal logic. We must go deeper. In spite of what the Herbartian psychologists thought, a feeling, as such, cannot be reduced to a mere play of images. What is intrinsic to a human life, as it is experienced from the inside, is that it can no more be translated into terms of film than it can be adequately translated—as we have seen already that it cannot—into terms of story. But can we transform these negative statements into some kind of positive assertion? This is just where we have to be careful, for, having set the idea of succession aside, we are obviously in danger of coming back to a representation of the inner reality of my life as something static and invariable, something that cannot be budged. But such a view of things would be a complete illusion. Everything budges; there is every reason to believe that even the things that seem to us to not be moving, the static tables and chairs, are in a state of continuous imperceptible change; and this, indeed, is what every positive scientific approach presupposes. The only thing that does not move, that cannot move, is the concept, the abstraction, which is treated as if it were a real thing, that is, hypostatized. It is part of the intrinsic nature of the abstract as such that it resists any attempt to introduce into it the flow of succession.

But let us not be misled by sheer fiction. If we are expressing our meaning with strict accuracy, all we ought to say is that from the moment I postulate some abstract notion or other—let us say, the notion of the truths of geometry—I in some sense withdraw that notion from the stream of time. Nevertheless, considered as a discovery of the human mind, the notion has its roots in history. It was in certain given historical conditions, to a conscious being dependent in some sense on these conditions, that the notion was first revealed. It would not have been possible for just anybody at all, living under any set of conditions whatsoever, to have hit upon the truths of geometry. Of course, as soon as they have been discovered, the theorems of geometry can, at least in theory, be taught to anybody, at any time, and at any place. I say *in theory,* for it is permissible to conceive that there might be certain kinds of given psychic or even social conditions under which it would be impossible for any child or even for any adult to concentrate on the theorems of geometry the kind of close, continuous attention that is needed to grasp them; though of course this purely contingent impossibility would not in any sense affect the validity of the theorems themselves. More generally, I should say that any truth of this sort, though eternal *qua* truth, can conceivably lie covered up, for an indeterminate length of time, and from an indeterminate number of individuals.

What conclusion can we draw from all this about the very complicated, very difficult problems that have exercised us since the beginning of this lecture? In the first place, it seems to be only the concept, the mental abstraction, that is intrinsically irreducible to succession; in the second place, however, we have seen that human life also will not really let itself be represented as a purely successive phenomenon, there being something in its structure that is not properly comparable to a succession of images. It would seem, then, that we are forced to conceive of the principle of life as being itself something at least akin in its nature to the concept arrived at by abstraction. On the other hand, we have acknowledged that if we want to remain loyal to the data of experience, we cannot cut the abstract truth itself quite away from its roots in history. We are thus impelled almost irresistibly to envisage the necessity of transcending the opposition between the successive and the abstract, between the endless changing flow of sensation and the static eternity of the concept, and to bring a new category, which we cannot yet properly locate; only everything leads us to suppose that this new category will have some relation not only to the spiritual in general, but to whatever the specific notes of the spirit, as such, may be. But at this point we ought to try to keep our thinking as concrete as possible; we should be alert for any messages from our most intimate inner experience. For in the last analysis our task is nothing less than that of perceiving in what fashion life can be organically linked with truth.

One might, indeed, say that all our investigations, from chapter four onwards, have been directed towards the discovery of this co-articulation of life with truth; we have, as it were, delicately stripped the surrounding tissue so as to lay the joint as bare as it can be laid. As it can be laid, I say: for when I talk about 'laying it bare', of course, I am still the prisoner of metaphors taken from sight. All the verbs I have been using refer to the

possibility of exposing to view something that has
been lying hidden away from view. Yet, in a fundamental sense, the point of juncture of life and
truth is not something that can be exposed to
view: for the simple reason that it lies in a dimension beyond life's probing, that of depth itself. Here
we discover the ultimate significance of the notion
of *the secret* with which we have had several en-
counters already. What we have to grasp is that
there is present in history this kind of depth, that
can uncover itself at many levels, but especially at
the level of one's own life, and especially when
one ceases to conceive of that life as something
that could be adequately expressed in terms of
story or film; for story and film are merely flimsy,
makeshift bridges flung by us across a gulf that
is always there.

In a fragment of my *Metaphysical Journal* that
dates from January, 1938, and that has not yet
been collected into a published volume, I have made
a real effort to disengage what it is that we really
mean by depth, or profundity, when we talk for
instance about a deep thought or a profound notion. A profound notion is not merely an unaccustomed notion, especially not so if we mean by
'unaccustomed' simply 'odd'. There are a thousand
paradoxes that have this unaccustomed quality, and
that lack any kind of depth; they spring up from
a shallow soil and soon wither away. I would
say that a thought is felt to be deep, or a notion
to be profound, if it debouches into a region beyond
itself, whose whole vastness is more than the eye
can grasp; the image I had in mind, in 1938, was
that of narrow tongues of water, like those which
crisscross among clusters of Dalmatian islands, at
the mouths of which one catches a sudden be-
wildering glimpse of the whole broad dazzle of the
sea. Our experience of depth does seem to be linked,
in this way, to the feeling that a promise is being

made, but that of the fulfilment of the promise
we can catch no more than such a glimpse. But
what we should notice at this point is that this
distant glimpsed prospect, this dazzling *yonder*, as
one might call it, is not felt as being elsewhere;
though we should have to describe it as a distance,
yet we also feel it as intimately near to us—'Near,
and hard to catch hold of', says Hölderlin, 'is God'
—and we have to transcend the spatial and merely
pragmatic distinction between what is here and
what is somewhere else. This distance presents itself
to us as an inner distance, as a land of which we
should have to say that it is the land we are
homesick for—as being, in fact, just what the lost
homeland is to the exile. A man's homeland may
be distant but it has a tie with him that cannot
be broken; his nostalgia is quite different from his
youthful dream of a strange, foreign country, for
it is that foreign country (however vividly he may
imagine it and even if he goes there and lives
there) that remains essentially a region of fancy,
a somewhere else. But a man's own country is not
something fanciful, it is something in the blood.

We must therefore, I said in 1938, concentrate
our attention on the condition of a being who is
not at one with his actual surroundings. Mere
chance has landed the exile where he is, his place
is only by chance his own place; he has a sense
of being an exile because he is aware, in contrast,
of somewhere that really would be his own place.
In the given, contingent conditions, to which he
must submit, however, this real place can only be
evoked as a beyond, as the home of homesickness.
All this could be related to those childhood experiences, that are at the basis of all the later imagin-
ings that really arouse our emotions, and that centre
round images of secret hiding places, of islands
and caves. We know, of course, that psychoanalysis
seeks to explain away the child's myth of the 'real

place' in terms of subconscious sexual symbolism; but in the last analysis we must recognize that this discipline, seeking to destroy all the old myths, offers us a new one in their place, that of the pre-natal Eden of the embryo in the womb.

Let us notice, however, that what we have been expressing in terms of space could also be expressed in terms of time. And this change of key is of the liveliest interest to us here, in relation to our own argument. In terms of time, the deep thought, or the profound notion, is the one that pushes well ahead; it opens, that is, a long path that can be followed up only in time; it is like an intuitive dive into an investigation which can be developed only over a long period of lived, personal, human time. Nevertheless, it would certainly be wrong to interpret the notion of depth in terms of mere futurity. What is important is that, from our present point of view, the future cannot be thought of, or represented as, mere novelty, as something new and unforeseeable which simply *takes the place* of the used, stale present. The novelty of the future may be as attractive a notion as you like, but we certainly do not feel we are moving into depth, as we thrust on to the future, merely because we are moving towards novelty. The notion of depth crops up, or so it would seem, only in the case in which we think of the future as somehow mysteriously in harmony with the most distant past. One might even say, however obscure such a notion may at first appear, that in the dimension of depth the past and future firmly clasp hands; and that they do so in a region which, from the relative points of view of all my heres-and-nows, and all your heres-and-nows, would have to be described as the absolute Here-and-Now; and this region where the *now* and *then* tend to merge, as the *near* and the *far* did in our previous illustration, would and could be nothing other than Eternity; this word that we

cannot do without, but which expresses a notion
that we cannot body forth in any tangible fashion,
in our present context takes on its full force. *Die
tiefe, tiefe Ewigkeit*—these are the words of
Nietzsche, to whom, in my second volume, I shall
need perhaps to refer explicitly. Let us acknowledge
in passing that his hypothesis of the Eternal Return
represents an attempt, justifiable at least in principle,
to express in the language of causality this mysterious linking of the future with the past which can
in reality take place only in some region transcending the world of cause and effect. These very
difficult notions that I have just been expounding
will, I believe, become easier to grasp in the second
series of these lectures, when I deal with the nature of hope. For the moment, it is sufficient if
my evocation of them permits us at least to get
a glimpse of the sense in which the opposition of
the successive, as such, and the abstract, as such,
can be transcended at a supratemporal level which
is also, as it were, the very depth or inwardness
of time.

We ought, in fact, to go over all that has been
said in this chapter, bearing our new notion, the
notion of depth, in mind for it is a notion useful
for throwing light, even if in itself a difficult notion
to throw light on. This paradox—a paradox which,
as we shall be forced to recognize in the final
lecture of this series, should rather be described
as a mystery—is undoubtedly at the basis of the
only valid way in which we can conceive the notion
of *essence*, in the sense in which that notion is
contrasted with that of *existence;* and in the sense,
also, in which to talk of something's essence or
essential nature, is not a mere abstract fiction—
the essence of something being in this case merely
the aspect that we cannot disregard, as, for instance,
in geometrical reasonings, we can disregard the size
and colour of represented figures—of use merely

for promoting enquiries of limited scope. The essence of a straight line is to be shortest distance between two points, but what is the essence of my being or my life?

To draw these remarks to a close, I should like to ask you whether you think that, in relation to my childhood and to everybody who was mixed up in one way or another in my childhood, my situation could, fundamentally, be anything other than that of an exile: unless I were to give myself over quite completely to abstract reasonings on a certain limited number of objective data, data which I should be substituting for the rounded and palpable whole of my childhood, my past, my life. And yet it is strange but true that this feeling of exiled homesickness does not necessarily imply that my childhood was an unusually happy one; except in extreme cases, which constitute abnormal exceptions, this nostalgia for childhood is connected merely with our sense that childhood is an irrevocable state of wonderful irresponsibility, of being still the object of protective care and tender guidance. I find all this splendidly expressed in Proust's great novel and in Sir Osbert Sitwell's autobiographies. But what is really strange is the fact that, in spite of everything that is implied by the current belief that time's arrow flies only one way, a man, as he grows older, has nearly always the feeling that he is growing nearer to his childhood; though the gap of years between him and his childhood is growing, at the same time, wider and wider. There could be no more striking demonstration that this arithmetical or linear representation of the temporal process is basically inadequate in relation to a life that has been really lived. It cannot be by mere chance that our contemporary interest in the civilizations of the remotest past has reached such a pitch of intensity. This fact would be absolutely inexplicable if it were true, as certain contemporary philosophers claim, that man is essentially a *project*, or if he defined his nature above all by the degree, at any given time, of technical progress and by the advances beyond old boundaries that such progress had made possible. These are both very superficial interpretations of the human situation, especially the latter one; nevertheless in our own day, man is more and more strongly tempted to accept such oversimplified interpretations, and to reject every view of life which they exclude.

At the beginning of the next lecture, which is also the last in our present series, I shall try to illustrate and make actual what I have just been saying, by stripping away some of the peculiarities that hide from us the true nature of the family bond. What it is to belong to a family, and to be attached to it, is something which it seems to me that neither biology nor sociology is capable of probing right to the core; and on the other hand, speaking rather generally, one might say that the family relationship is not one which up to the present has sufficiently engaged the attention of metaphysics.

# CHAPTER X

## PRESENCE AS A MYSTERY

IN THE latter part of the last chapter we saw that in some sense or other, certainly so far in a rather obscure sense, it does seem possible to transcend the opposition between the flux of successive images and the timelessness of the abstract concept; and if that opposition can be transcended at a supratemporal level, that is, at the level of time's other dimension of depth or inwardness, it follows that I must think of myself not merely as somebody thrust into the world at a moment of time that can be historically located, but also as bound to those who have gone before me in some fashion that cannot be brought down to a mere linkage of cause and effect. It is from this point of view that we ought to consider what I have elsewhere called the mystery of the family bond; which is itself, for that matter, only a particular expression of that general mystery of being to which we shall be devoting our attention in my second volume. No doubt, of course, it does seem rather odd to deal with a particular expression of the mystery of being before treating the whole subject generally. But we must not forget that our task is that of a quest or an investigation, following up successive clues, and not that of the didactic exposition of the consequences and corollaries that would follow from

242

the acceptance of certain initial axioms or the proof
of certain initial theorems.

It ought to be noticed, before we go on any
further, that the point of view from which we are
considering the reality of the family bond is what
might be called a metasociological one. I mean,
simply, that we are going deeper than sociology does.
Sociology, so long as it remains at its own proper
level, cannot begin to state our kind of problem:
which is, in fact, our old problem, 'What am I?
And how is it that I am able to ask myself what
I am?', with a new face.

We are living today, to be sure, or at least so
it seems, in a world in which the notion of sonship,
and the notion of fatherhood too, are tending to
be emptied of that richness of meaning which they
possessed for other societies. The philosophy that is
tending to triumph today is the old philosophy of
the eighteenth century, of the *Aufklärung*, in a
new dress. For that philosophy, the metaphysical
reality of sonship is one superstition among many
others and ripe for the rubbish-heap. It is important therefore for us to get a firm grasp of the
almost completely negative conception of sonship
which is tending to define itself and to assert its
authority before our eyes. It seems to define itself,
in fact, basically in terms of a refusal—a refusal
to acknowledge the existence in life, in the fact of
being alive, of a value that allows us to think of
life as a gift. The old French expression 'devoir le
jour à'—to owe the light of day to—would never
be used by anybody today. It is not enough to say
that it has become rather trite to talk of owing
the light of day to one's parents. The notion, or
rather the feeling, that these words express is no
longer experienced except in a residual fashion.
There are certain basic reasons for this state of
affairs; the most obvious of them, on the face of
it, is that to be alive in such a tragic and such

a threatened world as ours seems to many people not a gift but a penalty—but, a penalty, after all, pronounced by whom? And a penalty for what crime? Can one be justly punished for an offence that one is not aware of having committed? But this is not the whole story. Let us look at it from the side of fatherhood, as well as from that of sonship. In very many cases, is not the act of begetting a child something unpremeditated, the act of somebody who is not behaving in a responsible fashion, and who is very far from taking upon himself everything that his act will entail for somebody who never asked to be born? It is precisely this affirmation, reinforced by a question and by an exclamation, 'I never asked to be born, by what right—by what right!—has life been inflicted on me?' that lies at the roots of that contemporary nihilism, to which I shall have to come back much later. You will not have failed to notice, however, that we here touch again upon a state of affairs which took up our attention in chapter two. What we should notice particularly, however, is that from this negative perspective, this perspective of refusal, the bond between father and son gradually tends to lose every spiritual quality; it is conceived of now merely, in a rather vague fashion, as a somewhat obscure objective relationship, which can be of interest, from a strictly technical point of view, to the biologist alone. We might say that we are witnessing a more and more general disavowal of fatherhood, but a disavowal, paradoxically, mainly pronounced by sons. But naturally the process becomes to some extent reciprocal; when sons deny the rights of fathers, fathers are likely to refuse to acknowledge that they have any responsibility towards sons.

I know that I probably seem to be painting a rather gloomy picture here. In the majority of cases this basic situation of estrangement between father and son is masked by customary tolerance and ordinary human decency; but it breaks through to the surface in a very striking way in contemporary literature. In a body of work like that of Sartre's, a body of work whose importance cannot be brushed aside, this situation of estrangement emerges in a most definite shape; one might even say that Sartre's world is one where fatherhood, whether as a fact or as a value, has actually ceased to exist; it would be no exaggeration, in fact, to call this a world in which a man claims, in Sartre's slightly technical phraseology, to *choose himself* as the son of X, and therefore equally to *reject himself* as the son of X. But in relation to the general body of human traditions of feeling and behaviour, this is an innovation of a completely revolutionary sort. It is, in the most exact sense of the word, an impious innovation; and it is not by mere chance that Orestes, in Sartre's very first play, has the *beau rôle* just in that (not in spite of the fact that) he is the murderer of his mother.

It is rather important to ask ourselves how, or rather where, we are going to take our stand when we are faced with such a refusal to recognize life as a gift and therefore to acknowledge the metaphysical reality of sonship. It is pretty clear, at least, that we cannot simply condemn such refusals as infringing certain rules of morality, which we assert to be self-evident and beyond discussion; if we are to protest against this kind of nihilism, it can only be in the name of a sort of depth of reality which the nihilism refuses to recognize and, as it were, blots from view; it was just this very depth, in fact, that I was trying to make manifest in my essay, *Homo Viator*. This deep reality, that nihilism ignores, has to do with this same act of recognition and acknowledgement whose central importance for our thesis I have so often underlined. It is essential to the very notion of being a father that one

should recognize one's son, and acknowledge him to
be one's son; and to that of being a son, that one
should recognize and acknowledge one's father's
fatherhood. But I am not talking at this point,
naturally, of recognition in the merely legal sense.
I am not envisaging the case of the man who may
be forced to recognize, and to contribute to the
support of, a casually begotten bastard; what we
are concerned with is a much deeper and more
intimate kind of recognition—and a kind of recognition that is bound up with an activity of a very
actual and very vital kind. If a man, in fact, fails
to show any real interest in his child, he is behaving as if he did not recognize the child as his
own; we are within our rights in saying that in
such a case the father does *not* recognize the child,
and even that real fatherhood is lacking, at least
in the human sense of the term; from a purely
biological point of view, in so far as heredity is
a scientific fact, it continues of course, to manifest
itself, whether or not the biological father behaves
like a human father. But really, of course, the
notion of fatherhood has its true and full meaning
only at the human level; dogs, for instance, those
casual and promiscuous creatures, are not really
fathers in the human sense, though there are certain
animal species—one thinks particularly of birds—in
whose behaviour there is something like an anticipatory sketch of human fatherhood. We ought to
be aware, however, that in such cases we are always
interpreting bird behaviour on the analogy of human
behaviour; human behaviour, as we intimately experience it, is our point of departure.

What has just been said of fatherhood might also
be said of sonship—though, while the father has
often in the past refused to acknowledge the son,
it is only in our own days that the son, except in
very exceptional circumstances, has refused to acknowledge the father. What is also misleading is the

notion of a moral imperative, a notion really springing in the last analysis from the Ten Command-
ments: 'Honour thy father and thy mother that thy
days may be long upon the land which the Lord
thy God giveth thee'. Reflection shows us, however,
that this commandment can have meaning only
against the background of certain given structural
social conditions; in a world that had become
entirely proletarianized, the given conditions would
tend to abolish this commandment or at least to
rob it of any concrete significance. This is not to
say that in such conditions one would be within
one's rights in not honouring one's father, but more
profoundly that an entirely proletarianized world
would produce an increasing number of beings who
in their very depths would feel themselves as being
fatherless—as being *nobody's sons, Fils de Personne*
to quote the title of a contemporary French play\*
—and who would feel this even though the individual who had physically begotten them were still
alive.

It seems clear, therefore, that the notion of human fatherhood is one that is applicable within
fairly strict limits; at one end of the scale it disappears to leave in its place a mere biological phenomenon; at the other end the biological phenomenon disappears without destroying the essentials of
human fatherhood; I am thinking of the case of
adoption—and here, too, we must look beyond
legal definitions, for there can be legal adoption
without the accomplishment of that spiritual act
of which I am always thinking, and on the other
hand the act can be accomplished in cases where
legal adoption, for one reason or another, is impossible. The words 'spiritual act' here should be
taken in their strongest possible sense; one does not
become the adoptive father of somebody merely

\*By Henry de Montherlant.

through having a sudden impulse of affection, but only through a self-commitment to which one will have to remain faithful in spite of almost certainly inevitable lapses of interest, disappointments, and setbacks. Ought we to conclude, however, from the possibility of becoming a father by adoption, that it is necessary to make a radical distinction between spiritual and biological fatherhood? That, I think, would be a very rash thing to do. On the contrary, we ought to maintain that in normal circumstances the separation of the two kinds of fatherhood is something that ought not to be brought about, and even ought not to be able to be brought about; where there is such a separation it is because of some flaw in the individual's physical framework or social situation. But let us be wary about what we intend to convey here by the word 'normal'; I am not thinking of a norm in an abstract sense, some formal rule of ethics whose basis would be hard to discover and which would subsist somehow or other beyond the world of everyday experience, but rather to a certain fullness of life which, when spiritual fatherhood is separated from biological fatherhood, becomes something for which the reflective consciousness feels a certain homesickness. Thus parents who have adopted a child, and who love the child with all their heart, cannot fail to feel a certain regret, except in very exceptional cases, that it is not the child of their own bodies. The exceptional cases I have in mind are those where, if the child was physically their own, they would risk transmitting to it certain hereditary weaknesses; but a satisfaction of that kind is, after all, an extremely relative satisfaction—taking its rise in something that is in itself a smart, a wound, a humiliation.

It is, in fact, very possible that in our actual world a dissociation between the spiritual and the biological is becoming quite generally operative; but this is only one more proof that our world is a broken world; it is only a broken world that could give rise to such practices, for instance, as artificial insemination.

Such topics, to some of my readers, may seem strangely alien to the kind of investigation to which this volume is devoted. Such readers, however, I believe, are the victims of a mere illusion, an illusion which consists in the last analysis of adhering to that conception of the spirit as something at the opposite extreme from the flesh, or as something completely transcending the flesh, against which I have never ceased to protest. In a very general fashion indeed, one might say that the difficulty we have had, in the course of these lectures, continually to confront lies in the very fact that the spiritual seems to wish to claim for itself the dignity of a separate existence, whereas in a deeper sense it only constitutes itself effectively *as* spirit on condition of becoming flesh. The example, that we have taken already, of adoption is very significant in this new regard; adoptive parents only really become parents on condition that they lavish on their adopted child the most actual, the most material, and the most humble cares and services, the same which they would have bestowed upon him if they had really engendered him. In this sense adoption is a kind of grafting of the flesh on to the spirit, and it cannot be anything else; it is wonderful that it should be possible at all, and in fact its possibility shows up better than anything else the limits of every philosophy of life that claims to base itself on purely biological considerations.

Yet, on the other hand, nothing can give us a more intense feeling of insecurity and strangeness than this human situation of ours; the situation of a being placed at the point of juncture, or of co-articulation, of the vital and the spiritual. It is not a matter of the sense of strangeness that would

be felt by an observer of the situation from the
outside—but of the strangeness that is felt from
within by somebody who recognizes the situation
as his own. Let us recall, for that matter—what
goes without saying to anybody who has grasped
the significance of these investigations of ours—that
the very notion of observing the situation from the
outside is, in this context, a meaningless one. It is of
the very nature of our situation that it can be grasped
only from within its own depths. But at the same
time—and here we touch again on a point made at
the very beginning of this volume—in a world like
our own, which is becoming more and more completely subjected to the dominion of objective knowledge and scientific technique, everything, by an almost fatal necessity, tends to fall out as if this observation of our situation from the outside were a
real possibility. From that falsely objective point of
view, the very phrase 'spiritual reality' is in danger
of becoming emptied of all meaning; or rather what
is still *called* 'spiritual reality' is offered for our consideration as a mere superstructure, an epiphenom-
enal garment that masks, and rather thinly masks, a
basic hurrying of matter: it might be demonstrated
that an assumption of this sort, shared by both par-
ties, is the mainspring of that strange convergence so
often noted by scientists, at least in France, of strictly
biological generalizations, on the one hand, with
Marxist speculations on the other. Both biologists and
Marxists are seeking to arrive at an interpretation
of life at the purely objective level; only, unfortunately, the kind of objectiveness they are aiming at
entails a preliminary, and complete, elimination of
the subject as such.

We know of course that we are not, from our
own point of view in these lectures, to understand
the notion of the subject as it has traditionally been
understood by idealist philosophers. Neither the
transcendental ego of Kant nor the monad of Leib-

niz has any place in our argument. It is precisely in order to underline that fact that I have been emphasizing the notion of the family bond and its mysterious character. At the point we have now reached, it is on this new and difficult notion of *mystery* that we must concentrate; it is the notion in which this whole first volume logically culminates, and it is around this notion, as a starting point, that the lectures in my second volume will be built up.

When I talk about the mystery of the family bond some of my readers, I fancy, are disconcerted. The family is an institution; it is a fact; it is something which can be studied, at least in some of its aspects, by the methods of positive science. In talking about its *mystery*, am I not bringing in a touch of vague literary floweriness at a level of discourse where such battered ornaments of speech have no proper place? However, as we have seen already, the situation with which we are concerned, in our special context, is one whose true nature can be grasped or acknowledged only from the inside; there are no objective statements that can be made about it from the outside, for by definition it is *our* situation, the situation we cannot get outside of. That is why the kind of writer who makes the mystery of the family palpable to us is always, for example, the novelist rather than the historian of social institutions. However, though these remarks help to clear the ground a little, we have not yet succeeded in giving the term 'mystery' that very precise and almost technical sense which alone can justify its introduction into the vocabulary of a philosopher.

Perhaps the shortest way towards our needed definition of the notion of mystery would be to begin by working out the distinction, at the spiritual level, between what we call an *object* and what we call a *presence*. Here, as always, we are taking as our starting point certain very simple and im-

mediate experiences, but experiences which philosophy, until our own day, has always tended to over-
look. We can, for instance, have a very strong
feeling that somebody who is sitting in the same
room as ourselves, sitting quite near us, someone
whom we can look at and listen to and whom we
could touch if we wanted to make a final test
of his reality, is nevertheless far further away from
us than some loved one who is perhaps thousands
of miles away or perhaps, even, no longer among
the living. We could say that the man sitting beside
us was in the same room as ourselves, but that he
was not really *present* there, that his *presence* did
not make itself felt. But what do I mean by
presence, here? It is not that we could not communicate with this man; we are supposing him
neither deaf, blind, nor idiotic. Between ourselves
and him a kind of physical, but merely physical,
communication is possible; the image of the passing
of messages between a reception point and an emission point, which we have rejected on several other
occasions, is in fact quite applicable here. Yet something essential is lacking. One might say that what
we have with this person, who is in the room,
but somehow not really present to us, is communication without communion: unreal communication,
in a word. He understands what I say to him, but he
does not understand *me*; I may even have the extremely disagreeable feeling that my own words, as
he repeats them to me, as he reflects them back
at me, have become unrecognizable. By a very
singular phenomenon indeed, this stranger interposes
himself between me and my own reality, he makes
me in some sense also a stranger to myself; I am
not really myself while I am with him.

The opposite phenomenon, however, can also take
place. When somebody's presence does really make
itself felt, it can refresh my inner being; it reveals
me to myself, it makes me more fully myself than

I should be if I were not exposed to its impact.
All this, of course, though nobody would attempt
to deny that we do have such experiences, is very
difficult to express in words; and we should ask ourselves why. The fact is that the notion of the
*object*, as such, is linked in our minds wtih a whole
set of possible practical operations ('*This* object is
a typewriter, and this, and this, and this, etc. are
what you do with it. . . .') that can be taught and
that can thus be regarded as generally communi-
cable. But these considerations do not apply, in
any sense at all, to the notion of the *presence*, as
such. It would be quite chimerical to hope to in-
struct somebody in the art of *making his presence
felt*: the most one could do would be to suggest
that he drew attention to himself by making funny
faces! The whole business would be rather like
teaching a woman how to have charm. It is as
clear as can be that the notion of a *lesson in
charm* is a self-contradictory one (one could have
lessons in deportment, etiquette, and so on, but one
can know about these things without having charm,
and one can have charm without knowing about
these things). In fact the whole notion of teaching
charm, as of teaching people to make their presence
felt, is the very height of absurdity.

In my *Metaphysical Journal*, under the date, 23
February, 1923, I had this to say about charm:
'It seems to me that the more constrained a person's behaviour is, the more his attention is taken
up with precise, specific purposes, the less charm
he has. Thus men, in general, have less charm than
women and children. J., speaking about the odd
case of the child who lacks charm, is apt to say
that such a child is too finicky, too *exact*: and such
phrases express very well the absence of a sort of
aura, of indecision, or of vagueness, round the
charmless person's words and acts. There is nothing
more impossible to acquire, by a deliberate exercise

of the will, than charm; and in fact there is a
kind of willing—the willing that implies constraint
—which basically excludes the very notion of charm.
The tensed-up person cannot be charming, ever.
Charm is a kind of margin to personality, it is
the presence of a person spreading out beyond
what he actually says and what he actually does
... It is an overplus, a beyond ... And since it
cannot be created by an effort of will, it has, of
course, no ethical equivalent. Someone has charm
if he sprawls out easily beyond his virtues, if these
seem to spring from some distant, unknown source.
And only the individual, in direct contact with
another individual, can feel his charm. It would
be absurd to investigate charm as a kind of quality
which we could consider in abstraction from whose
charm it was. For it is not a physical quality, like
red hair; nor a moral quality, like self-control; nor
an intellectual quality, like a gift for mathematics.
Thus the assertion, "X *has* charm", or "X *had*
charm" tends to undermine itself. There would be
something rather grotesque, for instance, in mentioning the deceased's charm in an obituary notice'.

Though we cannot, of course, regard charm and
presence as merely identical, charm does seem to
be one of the ways, nevertheless, in which a presence makes itself felt. Felt, of course, by this, that,
or the other specific person; felt in an atmosphere
of a certain intimacy; not necessarily felt, obviously,
by anybody at all who comes across our charming
person at a large public meeting. And this very
fact that charm, which is the expression of a presence, works in some conditions and not in others,
for some people and not for others, underlines the
non-objective character of the notion of presence.
*Non-objective* does not, however, in our present
context, really in the least mean *merely subjective*,
in the privative interpretation of that phrase; it
does not mean being more or less of the nature

of an intermittent hallucination. Instead of subjectivity, we should think of intersubjectivity. Charm
is non-objective but it is intersubjective. However,
even the term 'intersubjectivity' might give rise to
misunderstandings, for one might conceive of a
content—still an objective content—that could be,
as it were, transmitted from subject to subject.
But the very notion of transmission must be excluded at this level of discourse; the communion
in which presences become manifest to each other, and
the transmission of purely objective messages, do
not belong to the same realm of being; or rather,
as we shall see when we embark on the subject
of the ontological mystery, properly so called, all
transmission of objective messages takes place, if
we may so put it, before we have yet reached the
threshold of being.

As always in the higher reaches of thought, we
must be on our guard against the snares of language; when I distinguish the notion of a presence
from that of an object, I run the risk, of course,
of turning a presence for some of my listeners,
into a sort of vaporized object that contrasts rather
unfavourably with the tangible, solid, resistant objects that we are used to in what we call real life.
But, in fact, when we say that a presence must
not be thought of as an object, we mean that the
very act by which we incline ourselves towards a
presence is essentially different from that through
which we grasp at an object; in the case of a
presence, the very possibility of grasping at, of
seizing, is excluded in principle. These distinctions
still define the notion of a presence in a quite negative way. We shall see our way more clearly if
we say that a presence is something which can only
be gathered to oneself or shut out from oneself,
be welcomed or rebuffed; but it is obvious that,
between the two notions of gathering to oneself,
or welcoming and seizing, there is a fundamental

underlying difference, a difference of attitude. If one thinks carefully, one sees that I cannot gather to myself, or welcome, what is purely and simply an object; I can only, in some sense, take it, or else leave it. It goes without saying that the kind of taking or prehension I am thinking of, is apprehension by the intelligence, or in a word, comprehension. In so far as a presence, as such, lies beyond the grasp of any possible prehension, one might say that it also in some sense lies beyond the grasp of any possible *com*prehension. A presence can, in the last analysis, only be invoked or evoked, the evocation being fundamentally and essentially magical: now, we may of course think of magic as a discipline that is concerned with objects as well as with presences—that brings rabbits, for instance, unexpectedly out of hats—but in point of fact it is concerned only with what we may call the *presential* side of objects. What the magician attempts is to make the rabbits present in his hat, to transform them into a presence, in the sort of case in which, apart from his efforts, the rabbits in his hat would be merely notional or even absolutely elsewhere. To grasp the nature of the contrast I am underlining between the presential and the notional, or the schematic, side of objects, we have only to compare an inventory with a poem: an enumeration of objects may, indeed, become poetic, but only if somehow or other it has a magical effect, if the objects, as they are numerated, become present to us. A rose in a poem can be something that is present to us in this way, but not, in most cases, a rose in a seedsman's catalogue.

We should, of course, recognize that this contrast between the use of words in a poem and the use of them in any sort of practical list of objects may not, in actual fact, be so clear cut as we are making it here. Words perhaps are essentially magical, it is in the nature of the word, as such, to evoke a presence. But we have to use words for practical purposes; so little by little this magical, evocative power of words tends to disappear. The function of poetry is that of restoring this very power to language, but the conditions in which it can be restored, today, tend to become more and more hermetic.

The purpose of these very brief remarks is to give us a glimpse of the nature of a presence, as something which can, indeed, only be glimpsed at. Let us notice, moreover, that the actual presences that surround us are very rarely consciously experienced by us *as* presences; in so far as we get used to them, they become almost part of the furniture, though it only needs something that jolts us out of our ordinary habits, such as a serious illness, to destroy this everyday aspect; the break in habit that an illness brings with it enables us to grasp the precariousness of that everyday atmosphere of our lives which we thought of as something quite settled. Thus there grows up, or there can grow up, a bond between the precarious and the precious. But under what conditions is this possible? If we place ourselves at a purely objective viewpoint, we can hardly see anything more in illness than the breakdown of an apparatus, but we already know, long before we reach the stage of analysis, that this so-called objective account of the matter is not really true to the facts; for an illness impinges on the being of the person who is ill, and, in the presence of his illness, he has to define his attitude towards it; but this is a kind of fact that can have no equivalent at a purely objective level. We should recall, at this point, what we said in an earlier lecture about the body; the latter is not merely an instrument, it presents us with a kind of reality which is quite different from the reality of any sort of apparatus, in so far as it, my body, is also my way of being in the world.

But let us notice, on the other hand, that if the
doctor's account of my illness as a breakdown in
an apparatus is inadequate, the priest who comes
to visit me and tells me to regard the illness as a
trial or tribulation inflicted on me by God is not in
much better case; for he also places himself outside the troublesome and mysterious reality which
is that of my illness itself. Just like the man for
whom I am merely a machine, the priest shows
himself incapable of transcending the plane of
causality. But it is just that transcendence which is
necessary here, and it is only on condition that we
effect such a transcendence that we can acknowledge the mystery of our illness. But let me express
myself more strictly: to recognize my illness as a
mystery, is to apprehend it as being a presence, or
as being a modification of a presence. What we
are essentially concerned with is somebody other
than ourselves in so far as he is a sick man, or it
would be better to say with my neighbour and
the call he is making to me—the call to show myself
compassionate and helpful. In the case, however,
where it is I myself who am ill, my illness becomes
a presence to me in the sense that I have to live
with it, as with some room-mate whom I must
learn to get along with as best I can; or again the
illness becomes a presence in so far as those who
care for me, and play the part of a Thou to me in
my need, become intermediaries between me and
it. Of course, in the case in which my illness has
utterly prostrated me, in a state either of complete
collapse or acute pain, my illness, paradoxically,
ceases, as a separate presence, to exist for me; I
no longer keep up with it that strange acquaintance-
ship which can be a struggle, or a dangerous
flirtation, or the oddest blend of both.

One might develop these remarks at length in
order to show how suspicious we ought to be of
those lectures on illness which people seem so spe-

cially apt to deliver if they have never been seriously ill themselves: what rude health they always seem to enjoy, those bluff haranguers of the sick! Quite literally, they do not know what they are talking about, and their smug loquacity has something very insolent about it when we consider the terrible reality they are faced with, a reality which they ought at least to respect.

If I have lingered rather over this example, it is firstly because in the special case of illness the co-articulation of the vital and the spiritual is really palpable, and secondly because the example shows us how and why it is that the co-articulation cannot give rise to knowledge. We are still at the level of the test or the ordeal, with all its ambiguity. I may be tempted to see in my illness the prelude to my death, and therefore to let myself float down its current, without making any real attempt to turn upstream. But I can also think of the illness as of a battle in which I must take the initiative; and from this point of view my first attitude will seem to me a kind of treason of which I must never be guilty. But these are still superficial contrasts; it may fall out that, though in the first stage of an illness I have to show this will to resistance, later on, however, I am forced, if not exactly to 'give up', at least to recognize the inevitable, and by my recognition to change the meaning of the inevitable and thus to change at the same time the very nature of the climax which I am powerless to modify. We shall have to come back to this point in my second volume, when we deal with the topic of death; but even now we can see how all our previous arguments lead up to an interpretation of death that will make it seem a mystery and not a mere objective event. To judge otherwise would be to forget everything that has been previously said about the impossibility of severing the spiritual from the vital, and about the misunderstanding, which all such attempts to arrive at the spiritual in a 'pure' state imply, of the conditions of existence under which we belong to the world.

So far, however, we have merely been approximating, through concrete examples, to the definition we are looking for: but we must now try to determine, with as much precision as possible, just where the opposition between the two notions of *the problem* and *the mystery* lies. I shall confine myself here to reproducing the most important passage on this topic from my book *Being and Having*. I am quoting from the English translation of the book.

A problem is something which I meet, which I find complete before me, but which I can therefore lay siege to and reduce. But a mystery is something in which I myself am involved, and it can therefore only be thought of as "a sphere where the distinction between what is in me and what is before me loses its meaning and its initial validity". A genuine problem is subject to an appropriate technique by the exercise of which it is defined; whereas a mystery, by definition, transcends every conceivable technique. It is, no doubt, always possible (logically and psychologically) to degrade a mystery so as to turn it into a problem. But this is a fundamentally vicious proceeding, whose springs might perhaps be discovered in a kind of corruption of the intelligence. The *problem of evil*, as the philosophers have called it, supplies us with a particularly instructive example of this degradation.

Just because it is the essence of mystery to be recognized or capable of recognition, it may also be ignored and actively denied. It then becomes reduced to something I have "heard talked about" but which I refuse as only "being for other people"; and that in virtue of an illusion which these "others" are deceived by, but which I myself claim to have detected.

We must carefully avoid all confusion between the mysterious and the unknowable. The unknowable is in fact only the limiting case of the problematic, which cannot be actualized without contradiction. The recognition of mystery, on the contrary, is an essentially positive act of the mind, the supremely positive act in virtue of which all positivity may perhaps be strictly defined. In this sphere everything seems to go on as if I found myself acting on an intuition which I possess without immediately knowing myself to possess it— an intuition which cannot be, strictly speaking, self-conscious and which can grasp itself only through the modes of experience in which its image is reflected, and which it lights up by being thus reflected in them.

For those who have read so far, it does not seem to me that the actual meaning of this passage will be very difficult to grasp. One ought, however, to underline the following points. The opposition between the problem and the mystery is always in danger of being exploited in a tiresomely 'literary' way by writers without a proper philosophic grounding, who lose sight of the technical relevance of the distinction. The sort of philosophy that I have been trying to present to you in this volume makes a very special appeal to the eloquent amateur, and that, in fact, is one of its most disquieting features; we have only to compare it, in this respect, to the exact sciences, to see just where the danger lies.

The man who states a mathematical formula, even if he does not judge it necessary to go over the proof that has established the formula, is always in a position to do so if he wants to. I have expressed that elsewhere, in a metaphor which perhaps sounds rather frigid in English, by saying that round the cogs and springs of mathematics the golden watchcase of demonstration, a sort of handsome protective covering, is never lacking. And it is the same with all the laws of nature. It is always at least theoretically possible to repeat the experiments from which such laws have been inductively arrived at. But this cannot be the case for us. Existential philosophy is at all times exposed to a very serious danger; that of continuing to speak in the name of various kinds of deep inner experience, which are certainly the points of departure for everything that it affirms, but which cannot be renewed at will. Thus the affirmations of existential philosophy are perpetually in danger of losing their inner substance, of ringing hollow.

And perhaps it is at this point, as we draw, for the time being, towards the close of these difficult investigations, that we at last get a precise notion of one of the essential notes of the type of philosophy that is being put forward here. It should by now be very clear that a philosophy of this sort is essentially of the nature of a kind of appeal to the listener or the reader, of a kind of call upon his inner resources. In other words, such a philosophy could never be completely embodied into a kind of dogmatic exposition of which the listener or reader would merely have to grasp the content. It is, in fact, from this very point of view that the question of the opposition between problem and mystery ought to be approached. When I am dealing with a problem, I am trying to discover a solution that can become common property, that consequently can, at least in theory, be rediscovered by anybody at all. But, from the very commencement of these lectures, we have seen that this idea of a validity for 'anybody at all' or of a thinking in general has less and less application the more deeply one penetrates into the inner courts of philosophy; into, that is to say, that spiritual reality with which, in fact, our investigations have been concerned. In the last analysis, the idea of an *acquisition* (as it is an acquisition to know how to speak French, or how to play the piano, or how to work out quadratic equations) is inadequate in such a context as this. The greatness of philosophy, though it will seem to most people the disappointing side of philosophy, is just this impossibility of regarding it as a discipline which can be acquired; where we are concerned with the highest matters, with if you like, presences, we cannot hope to come across anything at all comparable to the permanent acquisitions of the elementary sciences. I underline, there, the word *elementary*: for I think it is true that when we leave the teachable elements of, say, mathematics and climb up towards the principles, the enabling acts, of the science, our perspectives begin to blur, just as they do in philosophy. We cannot be sure, after all, that in a hundred years from now men may not have a notion of the principles of mathematics that will be different in very many ways indeed from the notion that prevails today.

At the very highest level, in fact, the line of demarcation between philosophy and the sciences tends to fade away; and I am convinced that there are many mathematicians who would not refuse to acknowledge that mathematics, too, has its mystery. But below the very highest level, the word 'mystery', in such a context, has no meaning; given some system of signs or other, whose structural validity one deliberately refrains from questioning, it is clear that arithmetic, algebra and geometry can push on ahead with no fear of running into any obstacles; and the person who sets out to prove a group of theorems, one after the other, will feel that the same calm light of truth is shed evenly over all of them. What shows very clearly that this is the case is the greater and greater perfection and efficiency, in our own time, of calculating machines. It would be very interesting—and it would be a task for which I would be quite incompetent—to investigate the general conditions within which the functioning of a machine is feasible. It is clear that these conditions, whatever they might be, would be quite incompatible with whatever it is that we indicate by the term *mystery*, (in passing, let us notice that 'indicate' is improperly used in this connection, since strictly speaking we can only use a term to *indicate*, or *point at*, an object,) since it is inconceivable that the most complicated machine which we can imagine would be able to undertake the speculative and reflective task of working back to its own sources, and of determining the conditions that make its achievements feasible. For in speculation and reflection we soar above every possible kind of mechanical operation; we are, in the strict sense of the phrase, in the realm of the spirit—though here again, alas, language undermines itself, for when we speak of the *realm* of the spirit we are still thinking vaguely of some place or other, and yet at this level the very act of providing any kind of spatial background for the operations of the mind is inconceivable, unless, indeed, we bring in the notion of a space of inner experience—comparable to the time of inner experience —to which we referred at the beginning of this volume. We cannot, in fact, dispense with some remnants of spatial imagery, and yet it will be difficult to justify their use.

But what can be at the basis of this kind of secondary reflection, (which seeks, as it were, to establish the conditions of primary reflection and of the more mechanical operations of the understanding,) except a sort of fundamental dissatisfaction? It is probable, indeed, that the philosophical activity has no other boundaries than those of its own dissatisfaction with any results it can achieve.

Where that dissatisfaction disappears, and instead we have a sense of somehow being snugly settled, the philosophical activity has disappeared, too. It might be objected that the scientist, too, has to be on his guard against the danger of snugly settling down. But we must distinguish: this is true of the scientist who aspires towards philosophy, but not, it seems to me, of the scientist *qua* scientist—for the simple reason that the scientist, in his conception of the external world, is and must be completely a realist; he is concerned with an order of truths which he must consider as wholly outside of, and completely distinct from, his own self. The strange greatness of his task and his mission consists in the fact that he really is lifted out of himself in this way, and the word *ecstasy,* in its literal root meaning, would apply exactly to his state, if, by a regrettable perversion of language, we did not usually reserve it for the sort of lyrical orgasm which is still the activity of the self. With the scientist, the self has, in so far as it possibly can, vanished away. His task is to bring order into a world which is as little as possible *his own* particular world, which is as much as possible *the* world in general; and from his own point of view, it is certainly not up to him to ask whether this notion of '*the* world in general' is a fiction. Thus when order has been established among things, the scientist must declare himself satisfied; only, this order can never be anything more than a partial order; if his activity has a theoretical side, that consists still merely in the stating of the kind of hypothesis that will temporarily hold together his partial and verifiable results. And these results themselves have been obtained either by experiments or, in the most refined case, by primary reflection relating solely to our experience of things, of objective data, strictly so called.

But the philosopher finds himself in a completely

different situation, and it is essential to *his* activity
that he should reflect deeply on this situation, in
order to get a gradually more and more ample
insight into it. Now, one thing that we may feel
we have really established in this first volume is
that this process of getting an insight has essentially
nothing to do with the objective as such; we do
not get an insight into something whose reality,
by definition, lies completely outside our own. We
have been forced to insist more and more emphati-
cally on the presence of one's self *to* itself, or on
the presence to it of the other that is not really
separable from it. And we have, in fact, real
grounds for stating that we discern an organic connection between presence and mystery. For, in the
first place, every presence *is* mysterious and, in
the second place, it is very doubtful whether the
word 'mystery' can really be properly used in the
case where a presence is not, at the very least,
making itself somehow felt. In the course of a recent conversation on this topic, I brought up the example of the mysterious character that attaches to
the presence near one of a sleeping person, especially of a sleeping child. From the point of view
of physical activity, or at least in so far as the
notion of physical activity is defined in relation
to the possible grasping of things, the sleeping child
is completely unprotected and appears to be utterly
*in our power*; from that point of view, it is permissible for us to do what we like with the child.
But from the point of view of mystery, we might say
that it is just because this being is completely unprotected, that it is utterly at our mercy, that it is
also invulnerable or sacred. And there can be no
doubt at all that the strongest and most irrefutable
mark of sheer barbarism that we could imagine
would consist in the refusal to recognize this
mysterious invulnerability. This sacredness of the
unprotected lies also at the roots of what we might

call a metaphysics of hospitality. In all civilizations of a certain type (not, of course, by any means merely in Christian civilizations), the guest has been regarded as all the more sacred, the more feeble and defenceless he is. In civilizations of a certain type, I say: not, I might have added, of the type dominated by the ideas of efficiency and output. We are touching here, once again, on certain social topics to which we referred at the beginning of this volume. The more, it might be said, the ideas of efficiency and output assert their supreme authority, the more this attitude of reverence towards the guest, towards the wounded, towards the sick, will appear at first incomprehensible, and later absurd: and in fact, in the world around us, we know that this assertion of the absurdity of forbearance and generosity is taking very practical shapes.

The above remarks may appear to have a merely cursory and superficial value. But that would be a mistaken judgment. The example we have just presented does throw into very bold relief that co-articulation of reflection and mystery around which the whole of this final chapter has been built up. When we talk about the sacredness of the defenceless, because it is defenceless, we are not dealing merely with a pragmatic and in a sense ceremonial attitude of which the sociologist, or perhaps the psychoanalyst, might claim to discover the origins. It is precisely against all such claims that philosophy, if it is to be true to its own nature, must take its strictest stand. It is something really *essential* that is here at stake.

And it is with an attempt to define this new term, *essential*, that I would like to draw this first series of Gifford Lectures to a close. Probably, in seeking to discover what we mean by *essential*, it is best to start by seeking to discover what we mean by *important*. At a first glance, it seems that when I decide that something or other is important I am relating it to a certain purpose of mine or perhaps, more generally, to a way in which I organize my life. If I centre my life upon some predominant interest, say, for instance, the search for pleasure, power, or money, everything that seems likely to subserve this interest will strike me as having positive importance, and everything that does not as having negative importance. Experience, however, shows us, and its lessons cannot be rejected or ignored, that our special ways of organizing our lives are always liable to collapse like houses of cards under our very eyes; leaving something else in their place, something which the original structures of lust, ambition or greed had merely masked from us. This *something else*, which we are not yet in a position to define, and of which we have not perhaps even a direct apprehension, is not *the important*, but *the essential*, the 'one thing needful'. It is obvious that the believer, at least, has a name for this 'something else': he will say that the one thing needful is salvation, but the latter is a term of which philosophy ought not to make a premature use. The first question, rather, that can be asked at a strictly philosophical level is whether one can, or cannot, affirm that in the life of the individual something of absolute, not merely of relative, importance is at stake. It is round this theme, in fact, that my second series of Gifford Lectures will be building themselves up. But we can acknowledge even at this moment that by our labours up to this point we have cleared away some of the obstacles from the path that leads to an answer to this question.

These obstacles, there can be no doubt at all, have all to do with a tendency within us to transfer the definitions and the categories that are valid only in the purely objective world into a realm of discourse where they do not properly apply. Following in the steps of Bergson, we have seen that this temptation to make a falsely objective representation of the inner world is at work not only when I am thinking of such a general concept as time, but when I am thinking of what I call my own particular life and history. We have thus been brought to recognize what one might call the transhistoric depth of history; which is, no doubt, the best short cut we can take towards the idea of Eternity. Moreover, as we shall see by and by even more clearly, the nexus between the ideas of Eternity and mystery is as strict a one as can be. In the first place, Eternity cannot be anything other than a mystery; we cannot, as it were, figure it to ourselves in terms of a map, even an endless map, that could be rolled out on a table. The spatial images, through which we get our first insight, no doubt always a rough and inadequate insight, and one needing much correction, into so many other concepts, are here, even in the very first instance, totally out of place. In the second place, every mystery is itself like a river, which flows into the Eternal, as into a sea. All this, of course, must be taken in a very vague and general sense; but it is true for each of us, and true especially in relation to our roots in the family, true, that is, in relation to the conditions under which we have been able to make our appearance in the world.

But to what degree, and within what limits, is it possible for us to raise ourselves above that condition of *being in the world* which is our specific mode of existence? To what degree are we within our rights in turning our glances up towards a higher sphere than this? What are—at the point where we are supposed not yet to have received the enlightenment of any special revelation—these floating, glittering, these unfixed lights, that can to some degree throw light into the obscurest depths of our being? These are the formidable problems that will be facing us in my second volume. I am under no illusion that we are moving forward on a plain and beaten path; may we be granted, during this arduous journey, that help that is rarely refused to those who are animated by the love of truth alone. Of truth alone. That is indeed the first and the last word, alpha and omega; and lest we seem to be drawing these lectures to a close with too hopeful a flourish, let us say, as our very final word, that every society pronounces sentence of doom or acquittal on itself according to the throne of state which it reserves, both within itself and high above itself, for that Truth which is not a thing, but a spirit.